FOREWORD
by Jimmy Santiago Baca

Antonio, We Know You, is the title of Antonio Salazar-Hobson's new memoir. It is by any measure a great read but no light journey, and yet, on many levels it reflects how a man can endure a difficult situation, one after the other, as a helpless child, as he does in this memoir. I can't think of many who could have survived what he did, and then even less who might have gone on to flourish in life, becoming all the stronger for the tragic and sorrowful circumstances that ensnared him. His illimitable love for his lost family and his search to find them and reunite with them again, propelled him through some of the fiercest and most horrendous situations in this book. This is a book about a journey of a child into manhood and arriving in the present time to tell his story—abducted by pedophiles and trafficked to older men, tortured by the alcohol-fueled couple who kept him hostage in a motel room. This memoir answers the questions in any reader's mind—How? How did he make it out alive? The story is told with a certain empathy for who the child was and what the child went through, it is told factually, leaving all hyperbole and fanciful flights of advocacy, and instead the writer's voice reaches into the furthest reaches of the heart and relays the story from there, from where the author loves and hopes and dreams and remembers. Read it and be prepared to change the way you see your own life.

Antonio,
We
Know
You

Antonio, We Know You

a memoir

Antonio Salazar-Hobson

Wyatt-MacKenzie Publishing
DEADWOOD, OREGON

Antonio, We Know You

Antonio Salazar-Hobson

Softcover ISBN: 978-1-954332-24-9
Hardcover ISBN: 978-1-954332-25-6
Library of Congress Control Number: 2022934240

I'LL BE AROUND Words and Music by Phillip Hurt and Thom Bell © 1973 Warner-Tamerlane Publishing Corp. (BMI) All Rights Reserved. Used by Permission of ALFRED MUSIC.

Cover photo of Antonio Salazar-Hobson, and other photos included in the book, are part of author's personal collection.

DISCLAIMER: This book is a memoir. It reflects the author's present recollections of experiences over time. Some names, places, and characteristics have been changed, and some events compressed, to protect the privacy of certain individuals.

Wyatt-MacKenzie Publishing
DEADWOOD, OREGON

www.WyattMacKenzie.com

DEDICATION

To my wife, Katherine Salazar-Poss, our children Beto and Adela and for my Salazar family.

TABLE OF CONTENTS

	Prologue	1
CHAPTER I	A Cherished Child	3
CHAPTER II	The Revelation	13
CHAPTER III	The Hobsons – The Six Months at Our Projects	22
CHAPTER IV	The Farmhouse	27
CHAPTER V	California Burial Grounds	37
CHAPTER VI	The Adobe House	47
CHAPTER VII	Little Lake Elementary School	54
CHAPTER VIII	The Ranch and a New Mexican Family	62
CHAPTER IX	Darkness in the Forest	75
CHAPTER X	The Third Summer	88
CHAPTER XI	The Hobsons' Decline Brings Moves and Separation	99
CHAPTER XII	Lodi, Stockton, and Room 204	114
CHAPTER XIII	Field Work, Cesar Chavez, and Trotsky	129
CHAPTER XIV	Friends and Girls and Chicanitas and Chicanitos	139
CHAPTER XV	Meeting Cesar	147
CHAPTER XVI	A Savior Emerges: Dr. Norman O'Brown	154
CHAPTER XVII	A Rough Start Turns Around, The 1973 Lettuce Strike and Cesar Chavez	161
CHAPTER XVIII	Latin America	170
CHAPTER XIX	Just One Look and a New Forty-Year Love Begins	176
CHAPTER XX	Coming Home to Petra and the Salazars	182
CHAPTER XXI	Marriage, Work, Family, and Faith	194
CHAPTER XXII	Familia	206
CHAPTER XXIII	Knowing	223
CHAPTER XXIV	Photo Collection	230
	Appendix	248

PROLOGUE
from the Author

I WAS BORN IN PHOENIX, ARIZONA in late August of 1955, as Antonio Salazar y Bailon, to Petra and Jesus Salazar. I am the eleventh of fourteen children. My earliest memories are being in the fields with the rest of my family. We were on the national crop-picking circuit until my father's accident, which resulted in the amputation of his arm and qualified us for the first public housing in Arizona.

Few would guess if you saw me in my capacity as an attorney working in federal court representing large international unions for decades and Native Americans from California to the Sioux Nation for twenty-five years, and a husband with a loving, forty-year marriage, what I overcame to be this person.

Through it all, I have taken heart in the statement I once heard when a group of workers were standing around Cesar Chavez talking about my character. At the time I was a 17 old college student, who had met Cesar Chavez at age 15 when I was in high school working as a farmworker. As they discussed whether they could trust me and depend on me to do the right thing, I overheard my mentor Cesar Chavez reassure them. He turned to me and said, "Antonio, we know you, we know you well." He affirmed that he knew I would always serve my people. That statement has served to lift me up in the darkest days and pushed me onward when I no longer felt an ounce of strength or hope to carry on—that statement is my guiding light and this memoir an extension through which the world could know my story. It illuminated the journey of faith that I was going to make it. It reminds me that I have had saviors along the way who knew me. They saw into my soul and intervened at crucial moments. This memoir is an attempt to tell my story so that you can know me and find hope in these words. See the sorrows I have endured, the abuse that almost broke me but never did, and the beauty I have found.

1

A Cherished Child

IN THE BEGINNING, I knew only happiness. I knew only the joy of being loved and welcomed by the world, contained in the furrows, plants, leaves, and roots as the voices of my parents and siblings called back and forth with laughter, as their sweat mingled with the scent of the earth, their backs bent to the crops they picked. When the harsh Phoenix sun rose into a white ball, all I knew was that it warmed me. I was in love with my mother Petra Salazar and my father Jesus Salazar. I basked in the attention of my siblings, who were kind to me and understood that I was a special child, the eleventh of what would be a total of fourteen. Up until the age of three I did not speak, just nodding my head to signal "si or no." I recall no ridicule or shame for this condition, just acceptance and inclusion. In my loving family, my parents and siblings simply took my condition in stride.

It was 1955 when I was born. The family was my world, creating a place of safety in our public housing unit. We qualified for the first public housing in Phoenix, the Duppa Villa projects on E. Villa Street, because my family could no longer travel the migrant farm-worker circuit as they had done for decades. My father, Jesus, had lost his right arm in a car accident in 1950 and his impairment, combined with the sheer size of our family, gained the Salazars their first permanent housing. It was the only family home I ever knew, and my family continued to live there for many years. As just a toddler, to me it seemed like a palace, so large and welcoming and bustling with my brothers' and sisters' energy. And to my older siblings this home was considered salvation, a miracle that somehow appeared in their lives, where they could finally "settle out."

Our home had been built in a development with about 100 similar project units. The homes were set in rows around large

U-shaped layouts, with a front yard that was shared by all tenants within each U-shaped quadrant. My house was at 607 North 19th Street, number 96. It was located at the bottom of the U and was the largest home design available, with four bedrooms and two bathrooms. The floors were left as raw concrete, without tile or linoleum to soften the surface. Our home, as was common in Phoenix construction, was made of cinder blocks, single story, with a decent size kitchen. We had a regular front door and a back door abutting an alley. Each door had screens in place. The sole way to cool our sweltering, cinder block home was to keep all the windows open. The screens had locks, so when we were home my parents left both doors open to try to catch any passing breeze. Nonetheless, our migrant family had never known such luxury prior to 1950. Before this time as the family traveled throughout the country each year, they scrambled for rare housing that was provided to skilled farm hands outside of the picking season. Only Jesus' additional skills as a farm hand allowed our family to remain on farms during the winter in migrant camps, as both my parents continued to work.

I shared our home with nine siblings. Roman, the eldest, was no longer living at home as he was already in his early twenties and married. Still at home, starting with the oldest, was Helen, followed by Alicia "Licha," Stella "Stellita," Ralph, Rudy, Robert "Spaceman," Virginia "Victoria," Jesus "Jesse," Armando "Mando" and myself. Three additional births quickly followed mine, with my three younger brothers, Daniel "Danny," Enrique "Henry" or "Cuckoo," and my youngest sibling, Rogelio "Roy."

In this home, I found joy in our family routine. Petra was in the kitchen by 3:00 AM making the ten dozen tortillas that were required to feed our family each day. My father arose every morning at 3:30 to begin his work preparation ritual. Jesus had a bathroom to himself and generally he just washed off his face and shaved. He was about 5 feet 11, appearing much larger and taller, with a thick build and powerful chest, and known for his strength. With his penetrating eyes and gorgeous smile, Jesus was considered strikingly handsome by all. Like several of my brothers, I share some of my father's facial characteristics such as his full, curvaceous lips.

My brothers, sisters and I were awakened by 4:00 AM, jostling each other in the other bathroom to be ready to leave for the fields at 4:45, when dawn broke and picking cotton soon began. The early morning's cool hours made it essential that we pick as quickly as possible. Work eventually slowed as the temperatures rose steadily to 110 degrees or more. Nonetheless, my family picked in these conditions, along with the other members of the large crew with whom we worked.

My earliest memory is a happy one. This recollection became the touchstone of my life, leading me back to Petra and the love she taught me. I was around two and a half, far too young to help my parents work in the fields. We were roused from the bed, usually shared by five of us, in the wee hours of the morning. I struggled to untangle myself from the reassuring warmth of my siblings' bodies. We had all bathed the night before, so the older siblings just threw on work clothes and then dressed their younger siblings and the babies.

We ate breakfast in what appeared to me with my two-and-a-half-year-old eyes to be an enormous and shiny kitchen. My father and brothers had covered the raw concrete with lustrous pink flowered linoleum, defying the coldness of the floors. The kitchen contained a real stove and a full size 1950s refrigerator. Then began my sustaining memory, the miracle of the breakfast burrito line, under the loving eyes of my hard-working mother Petra.

Petra normally dressed at home in house dresses. But for field work she dressed like all the other farmworker women, wearing khaki pants, long-sleeved shirts, and a large-brimmed straw hat upon her head. Except for the hat, these work clothes were the clothes that Petra wore while serving us our breakfast. To me my mother was at her most beautiful in these early morning hours. Petra was small, maybe five feet two inches tall, with a womanly body that by then had given birth to twelve children with two more soon to come. Petra had been married since she was thirteen years old, chosen by my father to raise his nearly six-year-old son, Roman. She had a broad face with high cheek bones, dark brown warm eyes, a ready smile, and an effortless embrace that reached my heart when she hugged me. Of course, she was a mother to us all. But to me as the family's mute child, she was tireless in her affection, and her embraces and kisses were like desperately needed oxygen for my soul to breathe. Kindness came naturally to Petra.

And it would be these four short years that I spent with her when she taught me to love. Although I have thousands of images of my childhood with the Salazars, it is this pre-dawn scene in the kitchen, the image I could return to as a touchstone, that is the reason I was never broken.

I lined up with about eight other siblings in no order as we waited in the kitchen to be fed. My mother, who had been up since 3:00 AM, served us breakfast only using one hand. There were fresh warm tortillas, which she placed in the palm of her hand, scooping from the fresh pot of beans as she effortlessly rolled the completed burritos for each of us. She bent down to me, as I was almost her youngest, and as she prepared my food, she often gave me a kiss on the head and urged me to eat. This small gesture sustained me from my youngest years and remained in my core, pristine, protected and filled with Chicano pride in my family that could not be destroyed.

All of us except for the babies were served coffee with lots of milk. I remember the deliciousness of that hot morning drink, which I looked forward to as my siblings' breakfast treat. It meant everything to me that I, too, was offered coffee and milk every morning. My brothers and sisters quickly gobbled down their first burritos, often heading for a second or third. There were always plenty of burritos for us to eat before we left the home for work.

After breakfast was finished, my parents and the older children joined another family and their two vehicles going into work at the same field. We brought an enormous plastic jug of water, a large thermos of coffee for my parents, diapers for the babies and a hard container packed with burritos, usually filled with beans and rice. There were also times that the burritos were mixed with scrambled eggs for lunch. Looking back, I can only assume now that well over fifty burritos were necessary for lunch each day to amply feed what was then a full family of twelve. I recall my older sisters helping my mother prepare the lunch box each morning in time for our prompt 4:45 AM departure. We had one main rule about the lunch box. Only my mother and father could open it. Sometimes we would be a little hungry and sorely tempted to pry open the top, but we knew they were somehow able to tell if even one burrito was missing. Lunch usually came early anyway due to the dawn starting time, and we never failed to stuff ourselves into contentment. Also, if we were especially lucky, we would be given a sack of cheap Mexican candy for us to share in the afternoon.

After our borrowed wagon had been loaded, we would jump into it knowing that we could never, ever risk being late for our parents. To me the station wagon was like riding God's chariot. It held both family and sustenance. It was filled with the laughter and the yawns of my siblings as they slowly woke into the day. Since my father could not drive due to his amputated arm, he sat in the front passenger seat, the wagon was driven by our family's farm contractor Juero Mula, who also became a close friend of our parents. My mother Petra was in the back seat with the older siblings. Spanish music flowed throughout the vehicle. The youngest babies were kept home, watched by my teenage sister Stella, who babysat them all day and supervised their naps. The rest of us were simply placed behind the back seat of the station wagon, as no one was aware of the dangers we would have faced in a collision. All families who worked with us took similar risks with the children riding in their station wagons, unable to take their children with them unless the vehicle was stuffed both front and back.

Placed in the back of the wagon with my younger siblings, I gazed out the back as we smoothly moved into the early dawn. I was content and happy to be included in the daily work schedule. I was not there to work, but I felt part of my family's work effort. As my parents emerged from the vehicle, the older siblings pulled themselves out and headed for the fields. There was always one girl, age eight or nine, who remained with the younger children all day to watch us, and to change our clothes if needed. The back of the station wagon remained open both for the fresh air and to escape the crushing heat that emerged during the day. We used the wagon as our playroom, crawling over the rear seats but never touching the fronts seats, which was forbidden. We knew we could never blow a horn, that we could not pretend to drive or sully the front seats used exclusively by adults.

We relied on the hot metal car roof to shade us as well as the infrequent cooling and dusty winds. I remember that we were not often bored, simply because we had each other and we knew eventually if we behaved, we would be able to leave the station wagon under the strictest of conditions. We were never allowed to enter the actual fields of crops, be they vegetable or cotton. Our station wagon was parked well off the isolated country farm roads, within ten feet of the fields. There often were dozens of cars all aligned off the country road creating a steel snake of metal glistening in the sun.

Each morning our wagon carried an enormous container of water that we used throughout the day, as well as a large thermos of coffee reserved for our parents. More than anything else, our relief came from our permitted and heavily guarded escapes from the wagon itself. The station wagon to my recollection never moved from where it was first parked in the dawn. The crop rows appeared miles long to me. As the first few rows were finished, we could emerge with the sister who was guarding us. We then immediately began to play, throwing clods of dry Arizona earth or playing with rocks. I remember my feet breaking the crisp dry earth and my fascination with following the cracks that filled every step of the parched soil. Although our clod throwing was promptly stopped, the older kids played marbles with each other. Our older sister was always next to us, carefully watching our conduct, never leaving a single child behind in our wagon.

All of this was a prelude to the highlight that we looked forward to each day, along with the *abrazos* from our mother and the lunch that awaited us. This highlight was a ride on the cotton sacks. We were never allowed to follow down the rows as our parents and older siblings picked. But each day our sister took us a few feet into the field to meet up with our mother. As we walked, we heard the Spanish songs coming from the many portable radios in the parked cars or in the fields blaring music for the workers and families.

The pale, sun-struck sky was broken by low-flying crop dusters spraying the very fields we worked in. The planes and the sounds of their engines were initially frightening to me. It was only the acceptance, the feigned indifference of my family to the crop dusters as normal, which allowed my fear to turn into an obsession with the crop-duster planes. I became thrilled at the sighting of each plane, no longer scared by their noise and eager to watch them as they dumped pesticides over the stooped brown bodies of my family.

We waited for our big moment, our daily rides on the gunny

sacks of cotton. My father did not participate. He was no longer able to be a regular farm worker despite having a prosthetic right arm. Instead, he worked out of a portable shack brought into the field where he punched a ticket for each bag of cotton picked for every individual worker on the large crew, including our family members. We were so proud of his station and felt that he was respected as a semi-foreman of the field.

Our big event was instead carried out by my mother and older brothers, who would grab a cotton bag, a coarse woven gunny sack soaked in pesticides made of muslin-like fabric that seemed to me to be a block long. They called for us, never more than two small children at a time, to jump on. I hopped in the middle with one other child as we were pulled down the row, likely a maximum of ten feet. The rides were always kept short so not to damage the gunny sacks needed for work. The dry cotton stalks waved around me, and the dusty parched Arizona earth rose up. I longed to play with the cotton blooms even though this was not allowed. I sensed from the blood on the hands of my older siblings that cotton could hurt, but I saw only the cloud-like beauty. No ride has ever given me such pleasure.

I returned to this memory many times as I grew into a man. I would call to mind the voices of my brothers and sisters as we played tag. I remember that in the heat of the day with all the windows open, we curled up like puppies to nap. But most of all it was the thrill of the bag rides and the moments when Petra rushed in from a distant field. The joy for me was her visit to the car, not the lunch. It was her chance to see her cherished mute boy and for me to maybe get a quick hug or a squeeze on my shoulder. These early memories would become my shield.

I recall the many times, after my family had returned from the fields, my sister Stella plunging me into the bathtub making soap crowns as she played with me, and I squirmed like a little eel. Then she wrapped me in a towel, and I was warm and safe. I was part of a pack, never left alone. I had my siblings as constant companions for games in the yard. Except for my eldest brother Roman, who by then was twenty-four, had been in the army and recently married to Cecilia, a marriage that would endure sixty-three years, we lived as one large crew, dominating our housing project.

My brothers and sisters chased each other in the large front yard that was shared by all the tenants around our large U-shaped apartment block. We wrestled and laughed, running in and out of our home, which we could do only when Jesus was not there. We collapsed into a pile in a tangle of dusty brown limbs so intertwined I couldn't tell my own brothers' or sisters' arms and legs from my own until we all rolled off each other. In my home, I was surrounded by the scents of tortillas, flour, and the beans from a constant pot on the stove, plainly made with only full cloves of garlic and salt. The other scent that was strong was the ivory soap used by the entire family and the cheap shampoo, or sometimes dishwashing soap, for cleaning our hair. I embraced every smell and for me the house was perfect. My world was made of laughter, life, loving care and the constant companionship and protection of my family.

My entire family accepted my lack of speech. They devised roles to include me as a full member of our family. I was never isolated. Instead, I was included in everything. This meant not only was I part of their daily work routine, but I was always called over to play in my siblings' games. I looked forward to our games of basketball that took place through the early spring, the sweltering summer and the cooling fall nights. In general, we were impervious to the Arizona heat. By evening it was cooling down, in the summers often from a high of one hundred and fourteen degrees. We waited a bit until the heat subsided, but we were ready to begin to play in nearly all conditions.

Every possible late afternoon and early evening, when our chores were done and the house left in perfect condition, we could escape with bellies full, and head out to our coveted basketball court. It was located five rows down and all the children attended, with the older babies carried to the game. My mother Petra tried to be present if she could. My father Jesus stayed at home. Although each evening we brought with us a plastic jug of water to drink, we were often lucky enough to get our favorite, delicious Kool Aid. We all drank from a collection of small, hard plastic cups of different colors brought by my sisters from home every evening.

This was the end of 1958, and the basketball court back then was in overall good condition as it was relatively new, having been built in 1950 with the rest of the project. The fact that there were no lights did not stop us from playing until darkness, giving us hours to enjoy the court by ourselves. We were such a large family that I do not recall anyone else outside our family playing. Both ends of the court had back boards faded by the harsh Arizona sun, but the two baskets still had their dirty gray nets. The asphalt court was smooth, vast in size to me, but a secure place as I was surrounded by my siblings. The white lines of the court gleamed, only interrupted by the many cracks in the paint.

What did frighten me was the enormous height of the basketball poles. I remember how difficult it was for me to make any sense of their height in comparison to my own frame. I was anxious to over-come this fear but even the early reassurances of my siblings were not initially enough for me to be comfortable under them. I could not understand the tallness of these poles. I knew that although I could get my hands around the pole, I could do nothing more. I finally settled on imagining climbing the pole with my siblings where we were able to sit on top as they held me up and I could look out over my world. It was this image that finally allowed my fears to slowly subside.

All the boys and the girls came out to the court. We were young, although some of the oldest were in their early teens. Helen, Licha, Stella and Virginia jumped in with my older brothers Ralph, Rudy, Robert, and Jesse, with the boys leading the way. Although at times they played the full court, usually they limited themselves to half-court play. The rest of us were the cheering audience for the Salazar team, with cat calls and friendly teasing of the players.

Being mute, I could not join into the verbal fun. But what made this the quintessential memory of love and pure happiness is the role my siblings gave me at each game. They placed me eight to ten feet directly behind the pole. The pole became my friend as well as protecting me from oncoming balls. They told me to stand up and clap at each successful basket. This I wildly did with an enormous sense of responsibility and unbridled accomplishment at having this unique role to perform.

My sense of hearing was acute. I could tell the footsteps of each of my siblings as they played. I could tell the dribbles of all the players, sometimes slowly executed and sometimes with the boys showing off a bit more of their skills. I relished their friendly cries of competition, watching breathlessly the speed of the game as well as the frequent time outs. At the basketball courts my muteness was meaningless. I had eyes to see, heightened hearing, and I fully understood my honored role and how to carry it out. I was seamlessly included and protected.

CHAPTER II

The Revelation

YOU SENSE IT IN THE MORNINGS mixed in with the bird songs: the chirps, quick little trumpet shards that fly through the air and make you turn. When you're three or four, you hear this. But you also notice something far away at the horizon, coming toward you. For a moment, you feel a tendril start to snake toward you and cause to coil in your stomach a fear you've never felt before. Me in my bedroom at 4:00 AM getting ready to go with my family to the fields and the voices and body smells of my siblings the same, like earth, my mother ready with her warmth and steadiness to hold us up sometimes when we can't hold ourselves up; but still, it is there, at the horizon, reaching, and makes me often turn to look, expecting to see some menacing beast coming at me. It was my loss of innocence. It was the gray scrim we pass through as humans when we become conscious of ourselves in the world. That's what was coming at me from the horizon, like the Arizona monsoons that gather and burst in fury over the drought-baked land.

Now the days start at this new stage, and events, some blessed, others shattering, tossing me like a seed in the sieve of life, rolling, catching, dropping from contentment to terror, and so starts my journey as a three- or four-year-old facing the storm.

I was learning great new things. I recall the excitement of learning to put on and tie my own shoes, something which I mastered quickly. I remember being able to dress myself after my clothes were set out for me by my sisters. I was proud to be such a big boy! I had a wild sense of freedom as I ran around on my own, fully dressed, beginning to play as hard as I could. I could do tasks that were important and exciting for me earlier and better. My new-found independence allowed me to be the first child in the kitchen with my mother and sisters, just for a few glorious moments alone with them before the other children finally shook themselves out of bed for our early morning departure. I was awakened at the same time as everyone else, but it seemed to me like seconds were all I needed to dress myself and tie my shoes to be the first boy to burst into the morning kitchen.

My core earliest memory from around age two-and-a-half is being in the breakfast tortilla line with my siblings; my new independence at age three gave me opportunities I had not had before. I now found a new way to have rare, stolen moments with Petra, something that my heart deeply needed. I knew to stay out of the way of the cooking, but Petra and my older sisters indulged me and let me stay with them. Our large kitchen, lovely to me with our rose-flowered linoleum floor, had a tile counter, taller than myself, holding the savory food and coffee.

There I was surrounded by the smells of my mother's tortillas. I gulped one down with a slice of fresh butter that melted into a glorious treat that leaked out of the bottom and onto my fingers, which I always licked. The smells of coffee dominated the kitchen, and after I entered and absorbed every hug and embrace by the women in our family, my sisters served me my all-important grown-up coffee. They poured a quarter cup of the amber liquid, filling the remaining cup with milk and plenty of precious sugar. Our mugs were thick and heavy for my little hand to hold, so I grasped it with both hands. In the Arizona predawn of the kitchen, I was in my heaven.

I began to lose my muteness at the age of three in 1958, and my ability to speak grew to just after the age of four in the fall of 1959. As for my muteness, I did not understand or have the need to understand why my ability to speak finally emerged. Perhaps the security I found in my mother and sisters gave me what I needed to begin to speak. But I simply did. The change was so rewarding to my little pride. I noticed that I was somehow more involved in my family's life. My sudden gift from the heavens brought me the start of my first voice, one that was unique to me. When my muteness began to recede, I seemed to quickly gain the ability to better follow my family's communications. I could not know why I suddenly became able to make small sentences of my own, something likely perceived as impossible by my family only months earlier. I was too young to grasp my extraordinary loss of muteness, but I did feel that my world seemed much larger than before. For the first time I could speak and answer to my own mother. I can only imagine her sense of relief that she had a non-mute child with an apparently intact mind. I learned Spanish quickly. She could now speak to me as before, but she began to patiently ask me simple questions with responses beyond a simple "si" or "no."

Petra was a smart woman, monolingual with a third-grade education gained in El Paso, Texas, during the teen years of the 20th century. Petra knew how to raise a family, and she certainly knew well how to teach her own children our Spanish language. With her treasured mute boy, she must have relied on her experience of raising her other children as she taught me to speak. She asked me basic questions and provided an appropriate response for me to mimic and learn. "Are you hungry?" and I slowly learned to say, "Yes, I am hungry." "Are you tired?" and I learned to say, "Yes, I am tired."

My world was equally changed with my siblings once I began learning to talk. I, of course, knew my own name, "Antonio" or "Tony." I knew the names of my siblings, but I could never make the sounds of their names emit from my mouth. I simply could not enunciate their names in any way. My new ability to speak meant that I was no longer just tagging along with them. Now for the first time, I could speak the names of my brothers and sisters, including the names of the new babies, Daniel, Enrique, and Rogelio. Their new births brought the total number of children in my family to fourteen.

The most important event of the day continued to be our family basketball games. Although I already had the coveted and important role of clapping after each point was made, I was now able to call out the names of my bigger brothers as they played. I could verbally cheer with my sisters and my other brothers who were too young to play. I could finally say and call out "pelota "for the basketball game. I learned to tease with the word "payaso," a taunt we used against those players making poor plays. I could now talk with my siblings sitting on the sidelines of the basketball court. My early conversations were not long, but I was learning to understand and respond. I could ask for candy or Kool Aid, and my mother or sisters provided it.

My child's voice was uncharted, but full of promise. I was instilled with a sense of mysterious achievement that made me feel like an equal member of the family. I had already endured a profound sense of unease that, while mute, I was not normal. The discovery of my voice changed my sense of belonging. But the loss of muteness, along with simply getting older, also had immediate implications for my emerging consciousness. Although I had been so overwhelmingly handicapped by my complete muteness, it had never fully locked me out from my family. My memories beginning at two and a half are a testament to that early survival. But when I slowly began to speak, reality now came in dangerous waves carrying doubt and anxiety. These waves were only navigable by me due to the unstoppable love of Petra as her special child and the uninterrupted acceptance and kindness of my siblings.

Despite Petra's love, however, my comprehension of my benign world was altered forever. A malevolent spirit had invaded my home and my soul, and I would never see my family with the same innocent eyes. My understanding of reality came in bits and pieces, breaking into unknown and painful patterns for which I had no name. I became a conscious witness to the harsh side of our family's life. I could see the crushing, nonstop ruthlessness of my father Jesus toward his children, including me. I now knew, but could not explain, the daily physical brutality he showed my mother Petra, and what she suffered at Jesus' hands and fists.

Jesus controlled our family with many constants that dictated how our family lived under his rigid and unassailable rules. Jesus refused to waver from our six-day weekly work schedule. Despite his limited ability to work in the fields after the loss of his right arm, his work standards for the family were not to be questioned. Our family continued to pick all available seasonal crops in the Phoenix area, including cotton, as well as vegetables such as onions and broccoli. The family daily endured the waves of unrelenting Arizona heat, visible to the naked eye. These heat waves covered the fields in the slightest of breezes, baking us like bricks in an oven. I could see the waves coming in toward our station wagon, implacable, inescapable. The waves were foreboding and all powerful, almost suffocating the air from my lungs. I remember the complaints of my family and the other farmworkers when the heat waves covered us, but no one had an alternative but to work under these conditions. Despite these obvious terrible working conditions, to my child's mind picking fruit was mostly a friendly daily game. Prior to age three, I did not have any understanding of the suffering my family endured, along with all the other *campesinos.*

In my family, the children as young as seven or eight, particularly if they were boys, were immediately placed in the fields to work with our mother and the older siblings. I had no concept of the missed schooling of my siblings during the picking season, only my comfort of being with the entire family. My siblings did attend school once the lengthy picking season was over, which began in the spring and ended in the early fall of each year. I recall my older siblings rushing to get prepared for school every morning once the picking season was over.

Jesus was mostly a loner. Although he was our father, at work I sensed an indifference to us as family. He seemed to regard us as merely members of the large *campesino* field crew. Instead, I saw the worry and weariness in my older siblings' eyes and some other unknown emotion that my mother Petra carried with her throughout the day that was about Jesus and not us. I do not ever recall interacting much with my father other than to follow his orders. I was generally in a large group of children and was rarely, if ever, taken aside by him as an individual son, much less for him to show affection toward me.

Except for going to our station wagon for drinks and lunch, Jesus stayed to himself during the day in his portable timekeeper's shed. His shack appeared like a little house to me, but it was probably about only five feet by five feet at the most. The shack's size was limited because it had to fit on a truck when moved to the next field. This shed was made of light, unfinished wood panels, turned brittle from the heat, with a small roof providing insignificant shade in the sweltering Arizona summers. Most important was the window built in the front of the shed where all the workers lined up to have their punched picking tickets totaled for the workday. My father sat on his stool directly behind the interior windowsill where the tickets were placed and counted. There my family also lined up before him to have their work tallied.

Jesus never altered his work routine for himself or the family from the entire period that I remember from ages two and a half until four. In the fields, all that matters is the sheer quantity of fruit or produce picked, bagged, weighed, and ticketed. His status of timekeeper allowed him to monitor the productivity of all the workers on the crew. For our family this meant he was always aware of our family's hourly picking production. Our status as his own family seemed barely of importance to Jesus, but I do recall the ending rituals of the day when, with all the other *campesinos,* we turned in our tickets to be totaled. I began to notice that our family waited in an eerie silence, unable to join in the chatter of the workers around us. Jesus made sure that the end of the day for his own family was not meant to be a moment of relaxation after our day of hard work, but a moment of public subservience. There was a tension that I did not understand other than to make sure I, too, remained quiet as we waited in line with all the other *campesinos.*

Something dark happened at the timekeeper's shack where my father sat behind his window in judgment of our workday. I could feel fear from an exhausted mother, shushing us as she submitted our tickets, a bowed head before an open window. I began to realize that work was not play, that my family's fear in the fields was a constant and that the cruel indifference of Jesus to us as his family in the fields would never change. This daily work violence was when I began to understand and to feel my first raw emotions against Jesus.

Jesus' nightly physical violence began in our home in the Phoenix projects. As you entered the four-bedroom, two-bath cinder block house, there was a kitchen on the right and a living room located directly ahead, with the back screen door facing the alley way. Immediately on the left side of the entrance there were three bedrooms next to each other. At the end of our hallway was the one bathroom that all the children shared. This bathroom included the tub where my youngest siblings and I were bathed every afternoon and early evening. Directly across the three bedrooms was the other bathroom reserved exclusively for my father.

At the back of the house was the fourth bedroom adjacent to the back alley that was used by my parents. Their bedroom also held the three newborns who followed in quick succession after my own birth. They were Daniel, Henry, and the youngest, Roy. As each of my youngest brothers reached the age of one, they were moved into my sisters' room to be cared for.

My brothers and sisters were divided up among the string of three bedrooms. Mine was the first bedroom shared with about four of the youngest siblings who were no longer babies, sleeping in the same double-size bed. I shared it with my younger siblings, Armando, Virginia, Rudy and Ralph. My older brothers still living at home were next to our bedroom, which accommodated Jesse and Robert. Our third bedroom along the same side was the girls' room used by my oldest sisters Alicia, followed by Helen and Stella.

During my mute period, I lived more within my own mind. I did not clearly observe the strictness and the oppression with which Jesus ruled our family. Now I began to realize something was deeply wrong, although I had no ability to place into words the loss of peace I felt. The physical violence, the drunken nightly rages of my father, Jesus, became the defining and remaining constant in my family's life. I was turning four in August of 1959. Time passed quickly as my newfound realizations came pouring in. Each passing month I rapidly became more lost in my terror because I, too, became a subject of Jesus' regular nightly beatings.

Jesus used his large bulky build to physically dominate our household despite the loss of his right arm. At the same time Jesus was considered handsome with his rakish hat that seldom left his head and that beautifully framed his carefully groomed hair and face. Petra was not allowed to leave the home other than to work, due to Jesus' extreme jealousy. Neither was Petra ever allowed to wear anything at home other than shabby housedresses. In contrast, Jesus approached every evening as an opportunity to show himself off as a vain, well-dressed Mexican man. After his shower and dinner, Jesus donned a sports coat over freshly washed clothes from our handwringer-style Maytag, clothes perfectly ironed by my sisters.

Jesus's nightly drinking was a ritual. He began by inspecting the house, ensuring spotless rooms, no mess left outside of our limited drawers, the mopping of the linoleum-covered kitchen and living room floors and a kitchen devoid of all dirty dishes, with only a pot of beans simmering on the stove. Jesus sat either on the living room sofa or on a chair placed on the small front porch. He would start to drink. He took out his Chesterfield Kings and chain smoked the filter-free cigarettes, sending their strong and familiar scent wafting over our home. Jesus settled down with his initial beers, mixed with sips of tequila. It seemed to me that it only took moments of his drinking before Jesus became a vicious and resentful drunk who took his disappointments and vengeance out on his family.

We almost always were present when our mother's initial evening beatings began. As the beatings usually took place in front of our eyes, we bore direct witness to Jesus beating her on her face and shoulders. We were witness to Petra's every scream, every cry, every pathetic attempt to beg him to stop, all to no avail. Petra's invariable second beating of the night took place in their bedroom as we overheard the accompanying noise of Jesus' fists upon flesh, ceasing only when Petra fell into a complete and frightening silence.

All that intervened between Petra's two sessions of nightly beatings was Jesus' beating of his own children, including me. We waited to hear the heaviness of his menacing footsteps as he barged into each of our bedrooms. As soon as we heard his approach at the door, we jumped under the blankets in a panic, desperate to cover ourselves, to take particular care to protect our heads, hands, and feet as best we could. We gripped our small hands in terror, sweaty wet child hands struggling for a grip on each other's bodies, with the oldest sibling doing his or her best to cover us.

We knew what was coming. Jesus would throw open our door, often with it smashing into the cinder block wall. He frequently had already taken off his belt before he entered our room. The only questions were for how long he would beat us and whether he chose to strike us with just the strap or his belt buckle, cutting into our flesh leaving harsh bruises on our young bodies. Once this nightly ritual was over, he left our room, foul breathed, gasping from exertion, his voice raspy from his screams of some unknown infraction. It left me both paralyzed in fear but also with an odd feeling for which I had no words, simply a vague sense that he was leaving the room satisfied, maybe having been calmed briefly by the sheer exhaustion of his drunken efforts to beat his own innocent children.

Jesus did not stay content or satisfied enough to stop with just the beatings in his younger children's bedroom. Instead, he always kept going on to my remaining siblings before he finished for the night. Jesus moved down the row to my older, stronger brothers' room, one which he often skipped in favor of my older, yet physically more vulnerable sisters. I would have already seen him throughout the day and evening disciplining my sisters with switches and his belt on their legs. In the evening I heard their adolescent cries, their high-pitched screams of terror as my father whaled away at them two doors down from my room. Both the screams of my siblings and our mother pierced through the thick cinder blocks as if the blocks were air, providing no barrier to the sounds we overheard from each room as he flailed in his fierce and uncontrolled rages.

By the time I reached four, I lived in fear of Jesus. I had an insurmountable foreboding, that there was some unknown terrible outcome that would exceed even the worst of our nightly beatings. Although I could not fully understand what was occurring in my family, I finally understood that my father's actions were not acceptable. I understood that the bruises on Petra's face were not normal. And even worse, I began to remember that the bruises had appeared on her face since my earliest memories of Petra. I began to question all of it. I began to feel for the first time a child's sense of injustice without any terms to describe it. Despite this obliteration of my innocence, I had already learned what love was from Petra, who had also given me a stark will to survive at all costs.

CHAPTER III

The Hobsons – The Six Months at Our Projects

OUR PROJECTS HAD BEEN UNIFORMLY SET OUT in a U-shaped format with a large lawn-filled quadrangle directly in front of our home. The Hobsons, a white couple, moved into the same quadrangle as my family for a period of six months. The story they presented is that they were the project's new managers, and that part of their compensation was their one bedroom apartment.

Most important to my family was that the Hobsons were both older, childless, and fully bilingual. Sara had lived in Bogota and Caracas for seven or eight years as the wealthy spouse of a Standard Oil executive, who subsequently died in 1950 after she returned to the States. John married Sara in the mid-1950s. He also spoke Spanish well due to his extensive experience as a general contractor hiring Mexican crews. When the Hobsons became our neighbors in early 1959, Sara was in her 40s and John was in his 50s.

We were told by both my mother and father how the Salazars met the Hobsons. The Hobsons lived in the same quad as ours at Apartment 92, 607 N. 19th Street. Our home was located about one hundred feet away from the Hobsons at Apartment 95. The colors within each of the quads varied depending on what side of the U-shaped layout your apartment was located. The Hobson's apartment side was a rust red, with a strong metal screen painted the identical color, one story of eight inch concrete bricks, a cheap tiny mail box affixed to the outside. Our home, located at the bottom of the U-shape, was the largest unit. It was gun metal grey with the same rust colored security door and mail box, with flower pots in

22

front. We used the full large quad's lawn directly in front of our unit as our playground.

They initially introduced themselves in Spanish to my parents. Their initial hook into my family was the Hobsons' promise to help with the Salazars' ongoing labor struggles with the working conditions affecting all *campesino* crew members, as well as my family. Yet, my father was at the heart of the system that deprived his fellow workers and his family of their wages. Jesus, in his role as timekeeper, was forced by the growers to carry out devastating losses of weekly income to every crew member he ticketed. The workers would approach the timekeeper's booth and be asked to sign a receipt for the week's wages. Once signed, each worker or family was given an envelope in cash. Inside the envelope was exactly fifty percent of what the workers were owed. I do not know what level of resentment or culpability these other *campesinos* may have attached to my father's full cooperation in denying everyone their full wages, but it may have served as another reason why Jesus kept almost exclusively to himself in his semi-foreman role. Jesus did not exclude his own family in the deprivation of income, assuring that we also were only paid fifty percent of our earnings.

John and Sara, in their fluent Spanish, promised the Salazars that they would intervene with the growers. My parents told us that this white couple, the first we had ever known, would take care of us and solve the problem of the lost wages with John's promised visit to the growers. Nothing happened. Nothing changed. But it nonetheless gave my parents the confidence to allow their young children to enter the Hobsons' adjacent home.

This next step in the insinuation of the Hobsons into our family's life was through their offer to hire my older sister Stella to do their dishes every afternoon. Soon my brothers and sisters, from two on up, could visit the magic of the Hobsons' home for hours at a time. Within the walls was the astonishing invention of a brand-new television, something to which we had never been exposed. As Stella worked to clean an already pristine kitchen with virtually no dishes to wash, we turned on the television to watch cartoons. For us, visiting the Hobsons was an invitation to a banquet filled with more delicious and strange food than we had ever tasted. Sara was an exceptional cook, and we waited eagerly as we drew in the delicious scent of the ample white food she prepared for us to eat. We came to expect Sara's fresh baked goods that she always served. But the top priority for almost everyone else was watching the astounding modern television. I was invited without fail to enter the Hobson's home with some of the other younger siblings. This generally included Stella, Armando, and Virginia, as well as my younger brother, Daniel, but all of the Salazar children were invited.

I enjoyed my siblings' company and relished the treats, but I had little interest in watching television. Instead, I discovered two rows of art books with full-page, color pictures by classical artists. I enjoyed every picture from every book, but my imagination was transformed when I opened a book on Francisco Goya, the Spanish painter. I have precise memories of his dreamlike images of God, the royal court, and his portraits. I did not know what I was seeing; I could not verbalize the beauty that it held for me, but my entire consciousness was swept and overrun by his images. I can remember that my dreams suddenly changed. Instead of the child-like images I once had, my dream figures became Goya's. I felt a deep release of tension having discovered his beauty, Goya's images immersing and captivating my mind. I returned to Goya's book on every visit, my own escape, my own source of reassurance that I had a new source to help calm my increasingly worried and desperate state of mind.

After a few months and before their departure from the projects, three major events occurred that further lured my parents into trusting the Hobsons. These were of such a magnitude of unexpected generosity that it for a time brought our family fully into the Hobsons' fold. It began with the Hobsons slowly building enough trust with my parents that they permitted weekend stay-overs in the Hobsons' home. It seemed to me that my father quickly gave his permission, but it likely took several weeks before these overnight visits began. I, as always, was among the preferred children expected to participate in these overnight visits. The weekend stays were generally just one night, and all of us looked forward to them. For my siblings it meant snacks, dinner, and breakfast with the accompanying treats. It also offered them much more time for coveted television watching on Saturday night as well as Sunday morning cartoons. Since television held no interest for me, I simply reveled in longer access to my art books and to my familiar Goya.

These overnight stays led to an ideal setup by the Hobsons to carry out their next two efforts to gain the Salazars' trust. This second step was Sara's inspiration to buy new shoes for all the Salazar children. Petra accompanied us to the shoe store while Jesus stayed at home. My family stayed, lived, and purchased only in Spanish-speaking little stores and secondhand shops within the barrio. We did not shop in white stores used by white people, places of such intimidation that we would have never felt comfortable entering them by ourselves in our heavily worn *campesino* clothing. The Salazars' garb, other than my father's clothing, was reduced to hand-me-downs from each older child down to the next sibling in size. This included all shirts, pants, underwear and of course the heavily worn shoes passed down to us, stuffed with paper in the toes to make them fit. New shoes were something for other people, for maybe smaller families. I don't recall any embarrassment over my clothing because I simply had no other context to compare our lives with that of others.

The fancy shoe store, with its chrome and glass displays, gave me the disorienting feeling that I was in a different world. I can still see the discomfort and nervousness of my mother as she struggled to keep us quiet while we tried on this unknown luxury of new shoes for each child. Each one of us was quickly measured, and there was no discussion of style. The store clerks seemed eager for us to leave, and we knew that we were not welcomed in this glittering establishment. Nevertheless, we were accompanied by a white woman who they understood would be paying. For Petra, I saw a tense mother trying to be brave, but there was no hiding that she felt lost in such a new, unwelcoming environment. I recall Petra's sense of relief as this innocent-appearing, benevolent female white Samaritan actually paid the bill.

We were finally able to leave the increasingly suffocating shoe store. As we left, we seemed to come to life, with each child able to do so proudly carrying their own box of new shoes. None of us wore the new shoes out of the store. Instead, we were told to wait until we reached home to put them on. I was among those big enough to carry my own shoes, an impressive pair of black tennis shoes with a fully rounded toe, and large whitewalls on the sides. My shoes were fresh and clean and free of the odor and dirtiness of multiple prior users. I recall that I was very proud of my new look, one that came from a magical source of newness and was just for me. All of us children were thrilled to have our first new shoes in our lives, without regard as to how they were acquired. For the children, the buying of the shoes was a saintly gift that required no further thought.

The Hobsons took a third step to overcome Jesus' and Petra's natural distrust of the attention this white couple was paying to their children. This struck at the heart of our poor yet utterly devout Catholic family. Sara and John arranged to pay for the baptism of many of Petra's children. I was not included for some still unknown reason, although younger siblings were included in this quintessential expression of profound faith. I do not recall my father Jesus being in attendance.

One of my most treasured memories is seeing my mother quietly enter the church to meet us as we children assembled at the altar and the first pews. For the first time in my recollection, my mother was allowed to purchase a nice dress rather than to appear in just her worn-out housecoats. My mother was transformed in her real church dress, white and flowered, with a light shawl on her shoulders. She looked beautiful to me but so much tinier than I had ever noticed, her round face framed by barely wavy graying hair, with an emerging small smile and hint of happiness and pride. I don't recall other examples of happiness in her except when she embraced her children and murmured the words that gave us the faith to survive.

The Hobsons were paying a church Petra deemed as sacred to her faith for a baptism carried out by a priest who for her was a representative of God. To our knowledge these were the first and only children baptized during the history of our family. The Hobsons had presented themselves as the kindest and most benign people in the world. They spoke our language with ease and effortlessly provided a cosseted environment where the Salazar family could feel safe and content. The Salazars could not have been more betrayed by any souls on earth as they were by the Hobsons.

CHAPTER IV

The Farmhouse

IT WAS THE LATE FALL OF 1959. Six months had passed, and the Hobsons finally left our projects. They moved several miles from the city center to their own ranch-style farmhouse in outer semi-rural Phoenix. It was a large, three-bedroom home, located directly across from an enormous wheat field that was still being farmed. To me their new house was enormous, with an elegant dining room, a wide living room with new furniture I had never seen before, and a large, private backyard for playing. The farmhouse itself had a spacious entrance, a breakfast nook to the immediate right from the entrance hallway, with a third bedroom adjacent to this area. The dining room was part of the living room, sharing one large space and located just feet from the kitchen with a pass-through wall between the kitchen and the dining room. John and Sara's bedroom was located to the left of the living room, with my preassigned bedroom near theirs. The only thing which separated us was the bathroom located between our two rooms.

The first two visits to the farmhouse included my younger siblings. These visits smoothly followed the pattern of good white food, delicious baked treats, and the all-important television. My continued lack of interest in television allowed me to return to my coveted art books without disturbance. My siblings were happy with their visits, and I recall nothing out of the ordinary taking place while my siblings were with me. I continued to chat freely with my siblings, as well as John and Sara as my comprehension and vocabulary continued to rapidly improve.

On the third weekend, Sara and John came over to our house as they now normally did on Saturday morning, ostensibly to invite my siblings and me to their home. We had already spent two great weekends, and we all looked forward to a known and well-rehearsed visit. But oddly, no one else was invited to visit them except me. I was excited to go visit the Hobsons, look at their books and to continue to use my new ability to speak. The fact that I was the only one invited made me feel special. I did not know why the others were not invited, but my focus was returning to the Hobsons' home, returning to my art books and spending a private night in my first ever unshared bed. All I had known before that time was that in the presence of my siblings, I could rely on the Hobsons' persistent kindness. My trust in them was complete, and my parents and I had no reason to doubt their intentions.

It was approximately mid-November of 1959 when my first solo visit to the Hobsons' farmhouse took place. My assigned bedroom held a single bed placed in the middle of the room with the top of the bed placed up against the middle back wall. It faced a window overlooking a large and protected backyard, one that was totally hidden from the prying eyes of neighbors.

When this third weekend began, Sara absolutely insisted that I drink an oddly sweet drink of chocolate milk, my favorite, handed to me along with her freshly baked cookies. I obeyed Sara, and within the first few minutes I felt sleepy. Sara told me I should nap and took me to my bedroom. My bed had been strangely stripped, and now had a large towel on it, likely a beach towel of some sort. Sara then, by herself, removed all my clothes as I began to lose consciousness. Only then did John enter the room. The sexual abuse began. Sara remained in the room, holding down my small arms and legs as I weakly flailed and struggled. I fell into an unknown world, coming in and out at times, panicked, attempting to cry out, but no words would come forth. At that moment my muteness returned.

My mind retreated into a shock so severe that all I knew was pain. Due to my drugged state, I had no idea as to the source of my pain, only the raw sensation of where it came from. I could not comprehend what digital penetration was, but I could feel the insertion of John's fingers in my anus. I could not tell or describe the acrid scents of his emissions on the front part of my body, as this substance was a complete unknown to me. After this initial assault and after each subsequent assault, John and Sara pushed me into the one bathroom for what seemed like hours of forced cold showers. I was never provided any soap or warm water. I could not clean myself of the lubricant used, and the needles of icy water hurt my small behind, which screamed in agony. But the worst was John and Sara's eternal observation from the bathroom doorway, with their two bodies barely fitting into that limited space. They both stonily stood as witness to my rapes, their sole utterances being yells at me to stop crying. The shower never stopped until it had beaten me into silence. When the shower ended to their satisfaction, I was thrown a towel to wipe myself off without their help, but always under their direct and condemning eyes.

John and Sara kept me to just the two of them for the first two weekends of abuse. Initially Sara was present the entire time. Her role was to secure my barely struggling skinny limbs. Her additional role was to help John decide which side of me he wanted at any given time, but he generally moved from my front to ending with me on my stomach. John and Sara next began sharing me at their home with a small group of ageing white men. These men who arrived at the farmhouse were first well fed by Sara, and the drinks seemed to be unlimited. After the men had sufficiently eaten and drunk, Sara always disappeared, never to be in the same room when more than John worked on raping my body. These older white men took turns, assisting each other with the important role of restraining my limbs, holding my feet and wrists with a harsh firmness. I could feel their crazed obsession for which I had no name. I could smell the repellant scent of their sweat oozing from their arm pits, foreheads, and eyebrows. I can remember the laughing and the jeering as they contented themselves with my helpless frame. I began woozily to notice even more the sensation of strange liquids falling from their bodies onto me, at once warm but also accompanied by a sickening heavy breathing I could not make sense of. I could barely make out body hair on these white men, but the worst for me was being exposed to their gray strands of pubic hair. This coloring deeply frightened me. I had never seen a grown man's genitals, much less that of a white man with an oddly colored, pinkish graying penis. I subsequently had both sides of my body roughly wiped off, with scant attention to cleaning my behind, leaving me to wait for the horrific cold shower after the men departed the Hobsons' home.

John started to take me to meet his close pedophile friends at a barber shop located in downtown central Phoenix. The Salazar home was located only three and a half miles from downtown Phoenix, but the barrio was a world away from the white business district. Our family did not use barbers of any kind. Instead, we relied on Jesus, a former barber by trade, to cut our hair with his remaining left hand. I remember John's barber shop with precision. It had a large front window with the classic barber's rolling round sign of red, white, and blue stripes that upon first viewing caught my imagination with its mysterious pattern. Inside were three or four barber chairs. The floor was a checkerboard of green, black, and white vinyl. The traditional barber chairs intrigued me with their classic shiny steel frames. I recall being allowed to sit in one of the barber chairs once or twice. Directly across the barber chairs was seating for at least five customers in green vinyl chairs, a row of picture magazines at the side.

When we arrived, most of the men were already waiting for us to show up. Then the sign on the door was turned around and the shade pulled down. All the men sat in their waiting chairs, drinking freely and patiently waiting for my drink to be made. It was some sweet concoction, generally made with a strawberry or vanilla fla-vored milkshake from the corner ice cream parlor. I was somehow drawn to gulping these thick shakes down as quickly as I could. I felt a desperation for the escape that was held in this milkshake, instinc-tively looking for my body and mind to collapse, to do anything to escape from the certainty that followed. I recall an obscure image of the crushing of pills into the drinks I was offered and the bitter taste. But I could tell that John and his friends were simply waiting to see how long it would take for the laced drink to take effect, for my body to slump and my eyes to droop.

Everyone, especially John, seemed thrilled at his prize that he offered his men friends: this little brown boy with the big brown eyes, thin frame, and mop of black hair. John simply waited until I became sleepy, and I could be transported listlessly to the back room. The back room held supplies, but also a large metal table illuminated by huge, bright lights. On the table was another large towel covering the cold steel of the table. The lights were always kept on, and I could feel the warmth they emitted. The only thing that broke up the relentless lights above were bright flashes of light coming from all angles. In their white hands I saw little boxes with light bulbs flashing, the magnified horror of child pornography casually added to my abuse.

John's role was to take my clothes off for the other men and to ensure that I was sufficiently immobilized by the drugs. I don't recall there ever being more than five men, crowding the small utility room. I recall the men's sweaty hands eagerly devouring me like wolves on a silent but still alive small body. As they abused me with their terrifying genitals and covered me with their foul emissions, I became numb, often unable to feel my legs.

All I had during this time were the crazed assurances, often made through absolute force by the Hobsons, that everything was normal. Of course, I knew it was not, and in my own way I tried to rebel. Within the first two weekends of the sexual abuse, I simply started to refuse to eat any of Sara's food, generally for the full time that I spent with them. I had learned to have a deep, instinctive suspicion of the sweet drinks I was served at the Hobsons', fearing the near total loss of consciousness that occurred once I consumed the drinks. I instinctively knew what to avoid at all costs, but I paid dearly for my absolute resistance. Sara devised a punishment for my new refusal to eat that began at the large kitchen sink. She bought a small step stool so she could place me on it directly in front of the sink. Sara would have filled the sink with unbearably hot water, deep enough to ensure that she could plunge my arms up to my elbows into the scalding water. She came from behind me, grabbed my wrists firmly and forced my tiny dark hands and forearms into the water. I invariably screamed, I struggled, I tried to jump off the step stool to escape, but with the full force of her body holding on to me from behind, I was overcome by her strength. Then Sara or John took me back to the table and tried again to force me to eat. This ritual of torture happened countless times, since I continued to refuse to eat their food.

I would sit at the dining room table where Sara placed the food in front of me. Often just Sara was present, but at times John was there. Sara was enraged because I refused to eat. She grabbed my head and tried to force food down my throat despite my firmly closed lips. She then held my wrists down on the table with the full force of her strength, causing me crushing pain that shot up my arms. I still refused to eat. When John arrived home, he was enlisted in my discipline. Sara beckoned him to my plate, and now it was the even stronger John facing me from the front, holding my wrists down so hard that I thought they would break. Once in this position, Sara again stood behind me, and began trying to shove food past my closed mouth. I decided then and there, after the initial torture, I would not break. I would not part my lips, and instead I allowed her to smear the food across my entire face. I was now voiceless, but I seethed in anger through every cell in my body. Although I was fully captured by them, my mind went to somewhere else in their home. Other than clinging to the hope I would be returned home, the one thing I could do was to refuse to eat the Hobsons' food.

During my six or seven weeks of visits to the Hobsons, my schedule of visits did not vary. They picked me up Friday evening and returned me on Sunday morning. Every morning, be it Saturday or Sunday, John and Sara woke up and pretended everything from the day or night before was completely normal. But Sara and John were particularly obsessed with how quiet I was on my Sunday morning return to the Salazars. Their nervousness was extreme, knowing I would be facing my parents as a fully traumatized child who had become mute again from the Hobsons' abuse. Sara would have made a Sunday morning breakfast of some sort, begging me with threats to eat. I always refused, somehow knowing that on a Sunday morning, moments before I was to be returned home, that they would not force me to eat. The Hobsons were clearly anxious that I not return home visibly crying. As we headed back, the Hobsons always put on mainstream music on the radio to distract from the tension in the car. As an exclusively Spanish-speaking child, the words and the melodies were foreign to me, providing little reassurance that I could survive the next visit.

I did not know how to ask for help. People my parents had trusted had turned into monsters. So, my four-year-old imagination created a fantasy, one so powerful that I started to convince myself that maybe escape was possible. I fantasized that if I just ran through the wheat fields directly across from the farmhouse that surely, I would find my Salazar family. I tried three brief escapes from the Hobsons' home. My first concern was the intimidating country road. I knew I could only get to the wheat field by crossing a road that to me looked as large as the horizon itself. I finally summoned the courage to do the impossible. On one of the very few times the Hobsons were absent, I walked out the front door and left the farmhouse to cross the road to freedom. My intent was to run through the wheat fields, certain I would show up at my family's doorstep. Once I had run across the road as quickly as my short legs could carry me, I was finally in the wheat field, prepared to head home. I entered the wheat field, but I became fearful of its size, the height of the wheat as well as the surprising harshness of both the stalks and stubble. I only walked maybe six or eight feet inside the field, before I felt so overcome with being lost that I had to rush out. I patiently waited until I could reassure myself again that the road was crossable.

My escape attempts occurred two more times under nearly identical circumstances before I was caught by the Hobsons. I had come home unaware that my socks had wheat burrs in them. John and Sara saw them, and the world seemed to grind to a halt. To me they appeared much more hysterical and fearful than I had ever seen them before. They first attempted in Spanish to cajole me about not leaving, about how important it was to stay at the house. But hysteria and visceral fear came raging out of their bodies and voices. The anger became uncontrolled between the two of them. I watched them battle about something unknown, which for a change terrorized them, not me. Both of them switched entirely to the unknown English. I could see their flush faces, a deeper worry between them that was one I could not understand.

I recall one essential last act the Hobsons did to try to keep my parents' trust before they stopped me from going to the Hobsons' house. It was Christmas of 1959, a holiday the Salazars did not really celebrate. Instead, we had a tiny artificial Christmas tree Jesus had purchased. We did not have Christmas gifts. Jesus handed a can of food to each child. He instructed us that this was all that we should rightly expect, and we should be grateful. For the Hobsons, their Christmas scheme would be "el colmo" (the "turning point") that made my parents halt outright further contact with the Hobsons.

The Hobsons' plan was that I alone would be invited to their home for Christmas. There, they had an actual real, large Christmas tree, festooned with decorations. Despite all the rapes, somewhere in my mind I was curious about what actually receiving gifts on Christmas morning would be like. That rainy Christmas Eve, the Hobsons told me to wait for Santa Claus. I fell asleep quickly, untouched by John or Sara. Unknown to me was that John and Sara spent the early morning putting up a small metal swing set in their obscured back yard. I woke up stunned to see this playground and many gifts waiting for me under the tree. I was further surprised to learn on Christmas Day that the Hobsons did not allow me to take any of the presents home to be shared with my siblings. It did not seem right to me, and it confused me greatly. The gifts ceased to have any meaning, and I retreated to my dark world of muteness that the Hobsons had forced upon me.

Because of the first six months of trust the Hobsons calculatedly built with the Salazars, my family had no reason to worry about the sexual abuse of their children. Because of their firm belief in John's and Sara's kindness, it took almost two months to take in the increasingly visible effects of my solo visits. I was losing weight. Instead of being able to chatter with my siblings and mother, I had returned to muteness. I emitted mere guttural sounds, often accompanied by silent, deep tears as I tried to control the pain racking my small body. I could tell that from the weekend of my first rape, both Petra and my sisters were starting to worry about me. I could answer none of their questions. I had been learning to speak with a strong and capable voice, only to be locked into the silence from which I had so proudly escaped. I could no longer say the names of my siblings or my parents. I had no words to describe the ongoing evil. I knew I felt a deep shame, a sense of profound failure to my family as to what I had become. Even though there was not a moment in which I did not feel assaulted, it somehow built in me a will stronger than I knew I possessed. And I had resisted and tried to escape. But I was locked in a child's prison of pain, of abject silence, with no way out. By the end of December of 1959, even my father had agreed to have all visits to the Hobsons stopped.

It was the early part of February 1960. A full month had passed since I had seen the Hobsons. During that time, various older brothers and sisters were given direct responsibility to make sure that the Hobsons were not allowed to take me from our home. No children were supposed to go with anyone outside the family unless my father was home and directly gave his approval. The Hobsons had lived in our projects, in our same courtyard. This meant that both John and Sara were intimate with the full layout of the buildings; but even more important, they knew the exact location of the alley that was directly behind our home. My siblings and I had already been instructed that I was not to leave the house with the Hobsons ever again. But the Hobsons came for me. They arrived silently in the late afternoon. They drove into the alley behind our unit. Our back screen door had been left unlocked. I was in the living room, and I heard them call my name. Slowly I approached the back screen door. First Sara, then John insisted that I open the door to speak with them. "Just open the door, Tony." I initially refused because I was aware of the new rules imposed by my family regarding them.

After much insistent imploring, I stepped outside on to the back porch, staying 6-8 feet away from the car. I approached no further until John, who was driving with Sara in the passenger seat, emerged from the car and opened the back door. John stood there and told me we were going for a special ice cream run for my family and I needed to come along to the ice cream parlor. John also told me to bring out my sister Virginia, three years older than me, but I hesitated. John took a few steps toward me and ordered me directly and with false patience to get into the back of their car. Virginia must have overheard the Hobsons, and she rushed out the back door to intervene. John quickly grabbed me and threw me in the car, and then he reached for Virginia to put her in the car as well. My brother Rudy, then a nine-year-old, had been placed in charge of watching the other younger children and me that morning. He rushed to the Hobsons' car and threw open the door, grabbing my sister from the rear passenger seat. I was completely on the other side of their vehicle, and Rudy could not reach me before the Hobsons tore off with me.

As soon as we sped off, I realized without any doubt in my mind that the visit to the ice cream parlor was a lie. I knew something terrible had happened to me and my family, but I could not comprehend what that meant at the moment. I recall weeping quietly in the back seat and for what seemed the first time, neither Sara nor John screamed at me to stop. I had learned to cry silently at the farmhouse through the shock and torture of the cold showers I was forced to take after each assault. But now my grief had no limits, no boundaries.

But I recall that on our overnight trip, we seemed to drive endlessly without stopping. Sara had carefully packed snacks for all of us. The Hobsons already had a trunk filled with suitcases and personal possessions. I had only the clothes on my back. But I do know I wore the black tennis shoes they had purchased for me months earlier, a crushingly soul-searing image of the event that forever shaped my life.

CHAPTER V

California Burial Grounds

AFTER THE HOBSONS ABDUCTED ME in early February of 1960, they rushed me overnight to California. Apparently, Sara and John had carefully prepared to immediately introduce me to her mother, Mrs. Mathews, and for John to meet his three spinster aunts in Hemet, California. Hemet is in the heart of the agricultural Inland Empire, forty-five miles outside the City of Ontario, and an hour and a half from Los Angeles.

I remember the ride into California with great clarity. I could not sleep until the early morning, watching instead intently out the back window looking back toward my home. I don't recall the model of the car, but it was likely from the very early fifties, with a bulbous, black exterior and enormous rounded fenders on the outside and four doors. It had an interior that was light, with soft gray upholstery. The window in the back was relatively small. I simply knelt, never looking out the side windows but just backwards until dawn, when I slept. I somehow knew that going backwards was the way home and that going forward was to an unknown place called California.

I had no understanding of what was happening in those initial hours. My muteness was solidified, locked in and I was frightened to death over what was occurring to me at that very moment. My voice only emitted guttural sounds, most of agonizing worry and a feeling of paralysis seeped into my brain, like what had occurred during my sexual abuse in Phoenix. I simply wept quietly throughout the night, with the Hobsons not objecting or screaming at me as normal for crying.

Throughout the long evening and morning trip, the Hobsons made no attempts to reassure me as they normally did when I cried. They remained completely cold, silent except for their conversations between themselves in the front seat. The priority was making it through the night to California, not remotely focusing on a quietly crying child whom they had just kidnapped. I was grateful that in my mind, they had left me alone in the backseat, almost as if I did not really exist, yet at the same time I knew that the Hobsons were planning something terrible.

I was offered food during the ride, but I continued to eat nothing offered to me. Although this generally led to full out hysteria as well as common torture on their part for my refusal to eat, in the car the Hobsons just fumed silently, with certain fury, but they contained their anger and left me alone. In the front seat, Sara and John spoke in soft tones, urgent, worried and in their own world. Even so, their contained hysteria permeated the car. They provided no information to me during that overnight ride.

We arrived in Hemet in the early morning, then a town of about twenty thousand people. The Hobsons urgently desired to reach Hemet because that is where John's very affluent three spinster aunts shared a home together. On the first day of our arrival, we rented a room in a basic single row motel located on the small main street, so that John could visit his aunts who had lived much of their lives in Hemet. I was introduced to them later, but not for the first month. Only two days passed before John was able to arrange to see his aunts. On the same day, Sara had arranged to see her mother, who lived in the California working port city of San Pedro, the place where Mrs. Mathews had moved during World War II from Houston, Texas with her physician husband, Sara's stepfather.

By the second day, Sara seemed visibly relaxed. The Hobsons had planned the day carefully to allow for two key events to occur on the same morning of the second day. Sara by then had returned to speaking Spanish to me after nearly two days in which she spoke English, a language I completely did not understand. Sara told me in Spanish that I was going to meet her *madre*. Hearing the word "*madre*" meant a tiny ray of hope for me.

We met at the motel's restaurant. It covered the front of the motel and held about fifty people or so comfortably. Soda counters circled the kitchen. There were multiple booths covered in dark green vinyl and checkered vinyl floors, complemented by bright white paint on the walls. The restaurant itself was surrounded by sunny windows along the walls fronting the entrance and along the entrance of the motel parking lot.

Sara and I sat at the soda counter waiting for her mother to arrive. Sara ordered a plain donut and milk for me as we waited. I refused to eat or drink, making Sara angry, but she was in a public place about to see her mother and made no disturbance. Mrs. Mathews arrived in an enormous, gleaming white car with a black interior. She opened the side restaurant door, and I saw a fancily dressed, elegant white lady. Mrs. Mathew's hair was almost blonde, her figure fuller than Sara's, and she had a face of determination as she entered the restaurant. She met me for about fifteen seconds, moving quickly away as if I were nothing to her, which I indeed was.

Sara and her mother left me behind at the counter, and they went to a nearby booth. At that time in the mid-morning the restaurant was not full. I was now the only person sitting at the soda counter. No waitress approached me. Everyone noticed that I had been walked in accompanied by a white woman, who was subsequently greeted by another, older white woman. I could sense I was a curiosity since as a Mexican boy in an all-white restaurant, I was out of place.

Sara and her mother met for what seemed like a very long time. I just stared in the mirror in front of me above the counter holding the fountain machines, the coffee and order pick-up. I kept watching all the activity while monitoring Sara's and her mother's reflections in the soda counter mirror. Sara and her mother were seated only two booths away at the most from where I sat. Their conversations appeared friendly, although there was some conversation that became very softly spoken, whisper-like, with enormous anxiousness coming from Sara's mother. The conversation ended, they both stood up, and Mrs. Mathews paid the bill, leaving money on the table. Mrs. Mathews approached me, took one last brief stare at me, looking very disturbed about something. At no time did Mrs. Mathews embrace me, pat me, or touch me on the shoulder.

She showed no signs of kindness toward me, this small, sad brown child her daughter had brought to her.

Sara followed her mother out for one last conversation, leaving me at the counter with my untouched milk and donut. Sara retrieved me to take me outside and told me to wave to my "abuela." I may have done so. I do recall seeing her car pull out of the parking lot at the side of the rear entrance door. I wondered briefly what she might have told Sara.

Sara and I returned directly to our motel room. She seemed deliriously happy, something that I had not seen before. Sara blurted out as soon as we entered our motel room that she had fought with her mother who had offered her ten thousand dollars to take me back to Phoenix, but she had refused to take it. This is a tale I heard hundreds of times from an early age as proof of her sacrifice in "adopting" me.

I had no idea then what she was talking about other than the word money, but it had no further meaning to me. I did not understand that for a moment I had a chance to return to my home and Sara stopped it. I became scared of her unbridled manic state, not knowing why she was acting this way. I had already lost any hope that Mrs. Mathews would ever help me.

John returned from his visits to his aunts soon thereafter, and he also was in an extraordinarily good mood. Both regaled each with their respective successes to a point of self-satisfaction where their nervousness visibly started to subside. Whatever meeting he had with his aunts seemed to lighten his worries. Soon thereafter, the Hobsons were able to rent our first house in Hemet. John returned to his trade as a general contractor, building a few custom homes in the Hemet area. Sara, who was deeply committed to her writing, stayed at home, writing her pieces, ones that were never published.

We stayed in Hemet from 1960, arriving when I was four and a half years of age, leaving when I had just turned ten. Sara and John's focus was to find isolated places for us to live away from the prying eyes of neighbors. Hemet was still mostly rural, with thousands of acres of fruit trees that defined the area. These were dominated by orange and lemon orchards as well as olive groves. These provided secluded locations for the Hobsons' houses. We lived in three separate homes, in an orange grove, an olive grove and in Rio Vista, located two miles outside of Hemet. Rio Vista was a tiny rural town at the time with only a couple of thousand people. We ended up living at the last home on a hill surrounded by hundreds of unoccupied acres directly behind our hillside backyard.

During the first years we lived in a ten-acre orange grove, with our home the only one within at least a half mile in the Hemet countryside. We were there for almost three years. It was a beautiful, original adobe home with the thickest of walls that kept us cool during the summers and warm in the winters. The house was located directly in front of a country gravel and dirt road. The entrance to the property had a small concrete bridge over the narrow irrigation ditch that flowed directly in front of our yard. The adobe home had a spacious front porch with chipped dark green paint, showing underlying layers of old red paint. There were wide white pillars to support the Mexican style roof, with the same white used for the exterior of the old adobe home. We had no backyard to speak of because the orange grove was within thirty feet from the back of our house.

The two-bedroom home had a compact small kitchen in the middle of the house dividing the bedrooms from the living room. The kitchen was covered in antique, colorful Mexican tiles with the kitchen window facing the front porch and the lightly manicured lawn. The lawn was relatively small, covered with grass, with the side lawns filled with thick, overgrown ivy. I found the red bottle brush trees in the corners of the lawn most unusual. I was fascinated, having never seen their thick bristled hanging flowers. I enjoyed walking under them, looking up to see their brilliant, deep red color. Our living room was elegant with its rounded entrance, its graceful fireplace and hearth to the immediate left. The living room had a full set of windows covering the entire front of the room and overlooked the porch with its potted plants and the yard.

I often played by myself under the orange trees, and despite having all ten acres to myself I was too intimidated to enter far into the orchard. My fear was identical to what I had felt in Phoenix at the Hobsons' farmhouse when I looked at the surrounding fields. At age four I had attempted three escapes into the wheat field across from the farmhouse. These failed efforts to escape the Hobsons occurred just prior to my kidnapping.

In Hemet, I remembered with terror that once I had summoned the courage to enter the large wheat field, within seconds I was lost after going only a few feet into the field. I had panicked so terribly that I carried this same fear when I arrived at the adobe house. This fear of being trapped in the orange grove if I dared venture too far inside it, made me restrict my exploration. I chose to stay near my house.

My favorite tree was within thirty feet of my house. The tree had a sturdy, thick trunk. Orange trees generally have heavy leaves when their fruit is in season. Most orange trees, particularly if they are older, provide a lovely low hanging canopy of leaves covered first with flowering orange buds with the sweetest smell on earth, and then with heavy fruit, with some of the branches hanging low, almost touching the ground. My tree moored me to a quiet place, one that unexpectedly turned out to be a safe haven as I survived the years at the adobe house.

My time at the adobe house eventually became defined by two experiences. The first was a source of happiness that led me to my first interaction with my own people since my kidnapping. It was my discovery of a huge chicken farm just down the road and next to our orchard. It was quite visible, located on the same frontage road as our house, and in walking distance. I visited the chicken farm on my own, finding my way there by walking alongside a small irrigation canal.

It was a big operation, with multiple large coops holding up to a thousand chickens each, producing an average of ten thousand chickens for eggs or sale at any given time. I started to visit because otherwise I was completely isolated, never introduced to another child or a family for three years. Neither did I attend school before the age of seven. The white owner was usually present with his white crew supervisors. He asked me where I lived. I was so aware of my limited speech, that I only pointed up the ditch. I was this tiny, harmless Mexican boy, and he allowed me to hang out with his all-Mexican workers.

This was the first time that I was able to return to an all-Spanish environment since my kidnapping. It felt like water on a parched desert that had long ago given up on life ever living on it again. I understood the workers' Spanish, and they were content that I could begin to make halting attempts to respond in Spanish, which made them very comfortable with me. I was always a cooperative, docile child who willingly helped in whatever tiny tasks I might be given. All I needed was just to be in physical contact with them. I tagged along each day, instinctively knowing that I was deeply replenished by being there with them, learning the routine of each day's work and staying out of the way when needed. I reabsorbed every word that I had heard before with the Salazars, learning new Spanish words, listening intently until there emerged a quiet, growing reassurance that I could find happiness just by being among my own people and language. I would seek out this same comfort wherever the Hobsons sent or moved me.

I never stuttered in Spanish with the Mexican crew, something I immediately noticed. At the adobe house, I began to slowly, painfully move from exclusively guttural sounds to the first hint of an English vocabulary. Separate and aside from the sexual abuse and torture I had already endured, I paid a permanent price to learn English. I was barely intelligible with a very limited English vocabulary. I developed a nightmarish level of full-out stuttering that further made me incomprehensible. It added another level of deep shame for me. I had already been profoundly humiliated by my destroyed child's voice, one so damaged from the rapes that speaking beyond guttural sounds was close to impossible for the early years at the adobe house. My stuttering was soul scarring. When I found that Spanish was truly my own language, one that was stutter-free, it gave me a sense of joy.

I simply loved being at the chicken ranch every workday, six to seven days a week. The scents of the chicken ranch never bothered me. I never even really noticed these pungent smells because being with the Mexican crew was far more important. I was so relieved to finally have found anyone at all other than the Hobsons who might see me, might talk to me. I knew that I missed my siblings, but I wasn't conscious that my world included no children. I had ceased to expect my siblings to be there. When I met the Mexican crew, it brought a jarring pain of what I had left behind, but it also returned me to my own instantly recognizable culture.

If I stayed out of the path of farm machinery, mostly tractors to deal with the feces, the worst thing that could happen to me at the chicken ranch was getting a chicken peck on my ankle. I followed the workers around as they fed the chickens in their troughs which surrounded the outer parameters of these enormous cages. It was exciting when I was occasionally handed a scoop of grain I could place in the troughs. This made me feel needed and important. My Spanish improved quickly, and the workers always eagerly shared their lunches with me. I was stunned when eventually they arrived with savory burritos made by their wives who had heard about me. It made me feel very connected, but it also plunged me into a sadness as I connected their generosity to that of my mother and sisters, all intact within the hundreds of images of them in our Phoenix kitchen in the early morning hours. At times, my sense of loss when I returned to my house was heavier than normal.

As I grew older, I learned how to float down the small, shallow irrigation canal fronting our house. It was at the most 4 feet wide, maybe three feet at the bottom where the water flowed at the depth of about 10 inches, more than enough to float. The water ran at almost an imperceptible slow pace, which was satisfying and made the journey feel safe to me. The ditch was barely wide enough at the bottom to fit my slim shoulders and allow me to float. I floated my body down to the chicken ranch. It was a bumpy thrilling ride, requiring me to navigate through tight spots and make several stops along the way. I reassured myself as needed but I mostly tried to avoid the known patches of rough spots where the old concrete irrigation ditch had broken, making floating down these sections very painful. I arrived wet, dressed in shorts and a T-shirt with soaked shoes. Because of the warm spring and summer seasons of Hemet, my clothes dried quickly. I embraced each day with these workers, grateful for the refuge from the Hobsons they provided.

The most visceral memory I have at the adobe house begins at my favorite orange tree. It was old growth, a mighty tree to me, with an unusually large canopy. I used my canopy to make my own private room away from the Hobsons. It was a place where they never came out to visit me, to my great contentment. The Hobsons didn't disturb me while I was under the tree other than to call my name to come into the house. The Hobsons had immediately stopped using my real name of "Antonio," and only exclusively used my new name of "Tony." They knew I was thirty feet from the house and my spending countless hours away from them did not bother the Hobsons in the least. Instead, my refuge provided them a way to keep away from me.

I sought solace, not knowing what to do, but finding my mind and heart turned towards anything that might help me get in touch with my family. I would sit under the orange tree, and eventually I came up with the idea of collecting the spare and broken adobe bricks alongside my home to place under my tree. The adobe bricks were heavily weathered after decades of exposure, old and crumbling. I used these bricks in a way that absorbed most of my attention for the entire two-plus-year period I lived in the orange grove.

I started to form my collection of abandoned bricks into an arrangement that symbolized each member of my family. As I began to bury the bricks near the trunk of the orange tree, I always trusted that I was totally hidden by the tree's canopy, even though I was actually visible to someone approaching the tree. I missed my family so intensely that I wanted to have a way to regularly visit and talk to them, to let them know I was still alive, that I missed them and would be coming back. As I began to build what eventually formed in my head as a burial yard, the inspiration to do so came from some unknown place and quickly took over my imagination. It provided an immense balm to my desperate child's mind, a bruised but never lost identity with a terribly damaged psyche.

I made sure that I had enough bricks for each family member, thirteen siblings and both parents. I laid them out without names since I did not know how to write or read Spanish. I made holes in the ground deep enough to hold each thick brick. I then ritually buried each one by placing them in their graves, using one to two inches of ground cover, then patting the earth down upon each one, and ending the day. I initially buried them in a haphazard pattern.

When I returned to the tree the next day, I began the process all over again. It was deeply reassuring to me and quickly developed into a compulsion. I could never halt this endless cycle of burial and reburial. Only the rain brought a temporary halt to my burying. I had a natural love for the rain, a change of weather that I also found calming and cleansing. I knew that rain was not a good time to work on my burial grounds, but I nonetheless sensed that none of my bricks would be washed away.

As my burial imagination evolved, I realized that I needed to organize the actual burial ground a little better. Suddenly it became clear to me that my brothers needed to be buried as a group, my sisters in their own group, with each of my parents having their own place. I was psychologically compelled to engage in the reburial of my family every day, a ritual that both soothed and connected me daily with my lost Salazar family. Once I realized the need for better reorganization, I experienced an unexpected calmness in my mind. I was no longer so overcome with my daily anxiety about the placement for each of my family members. I went ahead with a burial ground for Petra at the top of my family, only grudgingly giving my despised father Jesus a place next to her; but somehow, I knew that I had no choice but to do so.

I never told the Hobsons about my burial yard, my daily unearthing and reburial or that I talked with my family through these adobe bricks. It was not until we left the adobe house to move to a house in an isolated olive orchard, that I was forced or able to end these efforts. I never repeated the burial again for my family after we moved. I missed my burial grounds, but I had found out about our move with a few days' notice. I used the extra time to make sure my burial grounds would be safe when I left. I believed I had taken care of my family, and I willed myself to endure until the time I could return to them. I never considered a burial space for myself for I believed I would soon be returning to Petra's embrace.

CHAPTER VI

The Adobe House

AS I GREW OLDER AT THE ADOBE HOME, my comprehension of the English language improved greatly. I was slowly emerging from a state of total muteness to a modest speaking voice that was hampered by persistent stammering in English. I had already discovered from speaking with the Mexican crew at the chicken farm that in my own language my stuttering did not exist.

As my English language skills increased, Sara decided to teach me to read. As she began to teach me, I found out that I had a ready mind for learning, despite what I had gone through psychologically during these early years of my kidnapping. My eagerness to learn sustained me during the belittling and cruel tactics that Sara used every day as she taught me to read. Sara taunted me with every reading lesson for my failures. Her methods were truly ego crushing, particularly since I had to learn to read without the benefit of a teacher or classroom and the socialization, which were naturally available with public school attendance.

I felt profoundly oppressed by Sara's debilitating teaching lessons and her irrational pressure on me to quickly learn. Once again, similar to my rapes, I had no other choice but to endure. I did learn to read and surprisingly, reading eventually provided me means to rebuild my damaged, yet still functioning mind. After I learned basic concepts, I almost immediately understood that reading provided me a means for escaping to unknown worlds, entirely outside my own life. It turned out to save me during these early years at the adobe house. By the time I was nearly seven in

August of 1962, I had learned to read at the fifth-grade level. Unknown to the Hobsons, they had inadvertently provided me my first mooring, allowing me to flee mentally from them via my books. Reading remained an essential refuge that I needed to survive a kidnapped life with the Hobsons.

I lived in a world of isolation with rigid rules regarding outside contacts. I was repeatedly threatened to say nothing to anyone about where I lived and with whom I lived, people who were not my own family. There was a desperation the Hobsons radiated associated with the few times I was seen in public, and these were limited to the occasional trip to the supermarket. After the first couple of visits to the grocery store, these visits ceased entirely. Thereafter, the Hobsons purchased all clothes that I needed as I slowly grew, without my publicly going to a clothing store. They even brought back new shoes without my trying them on in a shoe store.

I did go to John's new barbershop to have our haircuts. The visits to the barbershop never ceased to be a moment of paralyzing fear. In Phoenix, the back room of John's barber was used by the pedophile community. It was where I had been raped by multiple men. How could another of John's barber shops be any different? I never settled in while there in Hemet, never took my eyes off the men in attendance or John who yet again seemed so at ease. No sexual rapes did occur in the Hemet barber shop, but each visit remained deeply terrifying based on my prior experiences with John.

I came to expect my continued isolation as these early two and half years passed. In Phoenix during the fall of 1959 when I was barely four years old, the Hobsons had committed multiple rapes and shared me with many older white men. In Hemet, the circumstances of my abuse by the Hobsons were more limited. John now had two major sources of income, and Sara chose to stay at home to write. John's three aunts supported him financially and this covered most of his needs. He initially held on to a number of clients, for whom he built custom homes. Evading discovery of their abuses was all important to the Hobsons as this would bring economic ruin. Their transparent and unexplainable kidnapping of me would also bring unwanted consequences.

Nevertheless, the Hobsons continued to follow the pattern of abuse in Hemet throughout my period at the adobe house. There was one key change in their approach to me. They no longer shared me with other men. John and Sara continued to play their respective roles. Sara prepared the spiked drinks, making sure that I drank them. I now drank her spiked drinks as quickly as possible whenever I understood that I was about to be raped again. I knew about the effects of these drinks. I was aware, though, that in the end it eased my mind during the actual assaults and partially took me somewhere else as the rapes occurred.

As I became older, an idea came to mind. I knew that I was becoming more alert during the rapes. I decided to hold on to whatever level of consciousness my skinny body and fractured mind could muster during the rapes. I now wanted and needed to keep my eyes open during the entire rape, working hard to no longer let myself fully pass out. Although I did not know it, keeping my eyes open inadvertently allowed me to be a full witness to the rapes, creating hundreds of images just of my abuse at the adobe home.

Once I had been satisfactorily pacified, I was stripped of my clothing now often by both Sara and John. Sara's roles were to prepare the drinks and ensure I consumed them. Sara then returned to her essential task of holding my limbs down as my body and mind began to quickly devolve into a desired state of incapacity. It was only when I became compliant, semi-immobile from the drugs and alcohol, that the sexual abuse could begin.

John and Sara rarely deviated from the worn pattern of raping me. Their rapes in Hemet were less frequent, broken up for maybe a month or more between each assault. This was in contrast to my Phoenix rapes which occurred every weekend and usually involved multiple men. Other than the Hobsons slowing down on the number of rapes, there was one more major change for the entire period until I was seven years old. They no longer made any attempts to penetrate me. I did not understand why they no longer did this, but it barely registered in my mind as a change. The overall heinous act was identical to me. Not being sodomized, much less suffering failed penile penetration attempts, meant little to me. I was still being masturbated and John continued to masturbate over my body to orgasm, but these were the new limits that the Hobsons now chose to follow.

I had no idea why they now limited their rapes to me alone without any other men. It may have been that they were already so fearful of discovery as kidnappers that sharing me with other men in Hemet was simply too risky and dangerous. In Phoenix, I never saw them with other people other than their pedophile friends. The rest of their time seemed consumed with securing the complete trust of my family, leading up to my abuse and finally my kidnapping.

The Hobsons had one exception to their rigid isolation of me. John and I made repeated visits to John's three aunts who had idolized him since he was a young man. John always counted on receiving the unflagging support of his elderly aunts. The aunts lived in the middle of town on a street surrounded by homes built in the 1920s through early 1940s. Their quiet residential street was wide with lush shade trees on every side, creating a green, calm setting. They lived on the left side of their street in a charming but small, older three-bedroom home. The Hobsons told me many times that the aunts had lived together in the same home for twenty years or more.

Their primary loving attention was reserved for their favored John. Surprisingly, I was introduced to his aunts within the first month of our arrival. John seemed entirely comfortable with this quiet and contained public display of me with his family. The aunts' house was relatively small with a limited living room, a decently sized adjoining dining room with the kitchen nearby and the three bedrooms located in a cluster at the back of the home. I was enthralled by their living room furniture, old fashioned and dark, and with the mostly dark paintings hanging on the wall. Their paintings in the living room were landscapes. My favorite was one of their largest, taking up one full wall. I later learned that the painting was a seascape of uninhabited California beaches. This painting was dominated by light blue and dark shades of deeper blue to depict the crashing, frothy waves backed by radiant sunlight. This painting would end up with John. It would hang in the living room of our successive homes for about six years.

Somehow the aunts came to know that I enjoyed art books,

likely from John telling them. By the second visit a small cluster of art books was carefully set aside for me to look at. I did so in front of all the adults, immediately lost in the art books, suddenly having no need to further interact with anyone. In subsequent visits I was set up at the dining room table only a few feet away to have more room to spread out the art books. I could hear the murmur of John's contented and unworried voice.

Unlike Sara's mother, the aunts were extremely curious about me and seemed delighted that their favorite nephew now had his own boy. They prepared me a sandwich and chips, with store-bought cookies and milk set aside. Unlike with the Hobsons, I quietly ate voraciously and drank everything in sight. They were so pleased to feed a young boy that they immediately made another sandwich, one which I could take home if I did not finish it. They never appeared mean or angry with me, and John was always relaxed and at his most charming self with them. Oddly enough, John seemed particularly proud in bringing me over on his visits to his aunts, clearly showing me off as his prize, a young dark boy with an implausible adoption story that was unquestionably accepted by his aunts.

I knew they adored John and witnessing their love for him was such a contradiction to the John I knew. It really shattered my brain. This image of an unknown John was terrifying. How is it that a monster could have a nice family who was actually kind and welcoming to me? They never commented on my muteness from what I could tell, and I saw only friendliness in their eyes rather than the perennial violent tyranny reflected in John's and Sara's.

I only recall the names of one aunt, Aunt Florence, but the aunts all acted toward me the same way. I remember the visits because these were the only outside visits I ever had except for my initial meeting with Sara's mother. Mrs. Mathews spent only seconds acknowledging my presence and nothing more. To my knowledge she never visited Sara again, and I certainly never saw Mrs. Mathews again. I had a deeply negative view of her when we left the motel restaurant. Once I quickly determined she would do nothing to save me from my kidnapping, it never occurred to me to think about her, except when Sara talked about her. I was overwhelmed with the loss of my own family.

To my knowledge, Mrs. Mathews never turned in her own daughter to the authorities, despite knowing that her daughter had kidnapped a small, obviously deeply damaged boy. Instead, she chose to completely cut off ties with Sara. She left me there knowing that Sara had committed a terrible crime and that I was a helpless, mute child. I assume in that brief visit with Sara, she never learned about Sara's full participation in my rapes as a female pedophile.

Sara blamed me for her mother's abandonment of her. Sara suddenly would start to yell at me in incomprehensible words, often with extreme anger. I was forced to stand in front of her as these harangues took place. I learned to quickly shut my mind and body down, waiting for her to cease before I could safely leave her presence.

Sara was always the dominant, controlling personality between John and Sara. I never had the ability at that age, much less the will to make any attempt to understand their deeply cruel and paranoid behavior. I did not have the words at the time to describe their tone, their forced isolation of me, but I understood that something beyond my control was seriously wrong with my kidnappers. I began to understand that the fear in the car that had permeated the ride from Phoenix to California, was now present daily. It was becoming the norm at the adobe house.

The Hobsons seemed anxious every day about something related to me. It became so severe that they stopped talking to me, often for days at a time. This oppressive silence further flattened my world. Out of the insanity of my abduction, the Hobsons calculatedly decided on a careful strategy of weeks of nearly complete silence, a fresh layer of dehumanizing abuse.

I was handed meals, which I ate by myself, gratefully, in the kitchen, with the Hobsons turning completely away from me in fuming anger. This silent treatment was unpredictable. I never knew each day when I awoke whether their silence would break. The Hobsons' new decision to often be completely silent for lengthy periods of time at the adobe house was one more damaging form of abuse.

Although I was deeply frightened by the Hobsons' lengthy periods of unexplained silence, I came to welcome them. Anything to get away from interacting was positive. I had by then adjusted to eating Sara's meals, while avoiding drinks other than water and juice. I had no idea that water and juice could also be laced with drugs. I knew the laced drinks were coming. I never doubted the consequence of these drinks, my certain semi-consciousness as I was stripped naked on my own single bed located in the back of the adobe house. There I was raped. After the rapes, and for the first time, I was allowed to shower alone to use soap to cleanse my body from each violation.

As before in the Phoenix farmhouse, I was forced to return to bed by myself, to sleep in the very location of my rape only hours earlier. I felt a crushing darkness as I lay in bed, reviewing the day's rape, conscious enough to be aware of everything that was being done to me. I still had no words to describe any of what occurred; but I knew the rapes, and I knew the physical pain that followed.

As each month passed, I learned to better keep my eyes open. Doing so created countless images, particularly John's humiliating activities that I both felt and watched, once I had been moved from my stomach to being turned over on my back. I carried the full imagery in my mind of John's gray pubic hair, the same erect penis with which I was already very familiar, forced to see every bulging vein of his pink genitals. And I noticed his penis softened after each orgasm, having no understanding of why it would do so.

I did not know how to state in words what I was missing other than the overwhelming desire to simply be sent home. But the Hobsons initially seemed very content to keep me completely isolated from four and half, the age of my arrival in Hemet, until one week after my seventh birthday in August of 1962, when I entered public school.

CHAPTER VII

Little Lake Elementary School

BY THE TIME I TURNED SEVEN in August 1962, I had been completely isolated from the general public for two and a half years. I met no families. I never met a child or played with other children. The missing children weren't something that I really noticed. I lived in a foreign and controlled environment, imprisoned in this unknown world where my kidnapping had landed me. I had no realization at the time that other children could or should be able to play with me.

I did not know how to state in words what I was missing even to myself, other than my overwhelming desire to simply be sent home. But the Hobsons, while we lived at the adobe house, seemed focused on keeping me isolated. It was the first week of September of 1962 when I saw children for the very first time since arriving in Hemet. John and Sara registered me at Little Lake Elementary School at the fifth-grade level without my having any prior formal education. My school records reflect my age and my grade placement. They also show John and Sara Hobson as my "parents."

Sara said she decided on a fifth-grade placement based on her alleged "degree" from Rice University in Houston, Texas. She regaled me with the successes of her own remarkable and rare life in education. Her story, from nearly the moment I could understand her, was the one constant justification for her harsh educational standards. She never failed to remind me at our reading sessions that she had entered Rice University at the age of fourteen, becoming the youngest BA graduate at seventeen ever to accomplish such a feat. It turned out later, via verification of Rice University's own records, that this was a total lie. Sara had only attended Rice University for one year, never to return.

Notwithstanding all the challenges I endured with Sara's daily cruelty of either silence or rigid, uncompromising lessons, I read at the fifth-grade level by the time I was almost seven. When I arrived at Little Lake Elementary school, the Hobsons insisted that I be placed in the fifth grade although I was seven years old only by two weeks and lacked any prior public school education.

I arrived at Little Lake Elementary School completely disadvantaged in every way except for my reading prowess. I was out of place since I had no prior socialization that would have normally taken place through pre-kindergarten, kindergarten, and all the earlier grades. I had not even talked with a child for two and half years. When I first saw the other children, to me they appeared as a menacing and massive swarm that overwhelmed my mind. I willed myself to try to never raise my eyes to look at them.

I could utter only a few words of English, though my comprehension was quite decent, given my reading background and a large written vocabulary necessary to advance so quickly in my reading skills. The problem was that I could not really speak because of my torturous level of stuttering. This made even basic conversations with other students nearly impossible. My lack of prior interaction with children first seemed to me as an insurmountable barrier to my survival. I could not take in that now I was required to also meet the full educational requirements of fifth graders who were normally ten years old with an underlying public school education of at least four full grades.

Upon my arrival, I was quickly noticed by all the students and teachers in the small school. I was a freak of nature, a dark Mexican boy in a mostly all white school who refused to speak to anyone. I was resented by the students based on my placement. Resentment was a feeling I knew all too well, from my life with John and Sara. The teachers seemed to have their own concerns, but I did not know what they were. There was one bright spot. Principal Acton felt an immediate need to be very protective of me. He eventually became the first one to dig into the veracity of the Hobsons' story of how they came to be my "parents."

My fifth-grade teacher was British. I remained in her class for three to four weeks. Mrs. Lee, the fourth-grade teacher, had learned from my fifth-grade teacher and confirmed with Principal Acton that I had no prior schooling. Mrs. Lee had me transferred to her fourth-grade classroom. Based on my age of seven alone, I would have normally been placed in the second grade.

To Mrs. Lee it was important that I learn to be with other children more appropriate for my age, but she recognized my reading level skills. Mrs. Lee waited patiently for many weeks as I refused to talk to any of my classmates, or even to participate in any games held within the classroom. Instead, Mrs. Lee gave me books to look through at my front desk as she attended to the other students. She took in stride my resistance to speaking with any classmate, though I always listened and interacted with her by my nods, desperate to not constantly show my irrepressible stammer in front of the other pupils. I did not want to remind them, as if they needed to be reminded, of my disability. Mrs. Lee never pressed any interaction with the other students other than to offer me the choice each time to participate in the games or to become lost in my books at my front desk. There I was undisturbed by any student. None of these children had my level of reading skill or vocabulary as I sped through every regular book Mrs. Lee handed to me.

I could not participate well in her classroom anyway because my stuttering made me incomprehensible. I became a devoted listener, always sitting in the front row. I was so terribly nearsighted that I could not really see the blackboard, even sitting so close. Apparently, this was so obvious to Mrs. Lee that she spoke with John and Sara about getting me glasses. The Hobsons refused to take any actions to correct my vision during my first year. They knew they had no prior medical records to show any doctor. I had no idea at the time that I lacked medical attention or that this sole visit to an optometrist would be my one and only medical visit during my life with the Hobsons.

The inability to see well that initial year unlocked my mind, unexpectedly showing that I had a natural skill for memorization. I learned I could easily memorize most of what I was being taught. Math was particularly challenging to me, as I had no prior math lessons when I moved to Little Lake Elementary School. I eventually understood the basics of math and it became one of my greatest academic strengths.

Mrs. Lee took the greatest care in encouraging me to play with other children in the school yard playground. I could not cross the outer lines of the playground because it reminded me in the extreme of the basketball games with my siblings, something that had constantly haunted me since my kidnapping. I remembered those cherished nightly basketball games with my siblings where I belonged. The renewed visual pain of seeing the basketball courts in the back of the playground caught me completely off guard. Now I was being asked to enter the playground without my siblings.

This new experience pushed me into a new sadness that I could not control. I arrived under the crushing weight of my inability to make contact, while knowing by then it was somehow connected to the life I was forced to live, the years of sexual abuse, the harsh and unforgiving reading lessons and what turned out to be weeks of stony silence from Sara and John. I had a bottomless shame and sense of inferiority, particularly with these strange new, white creatures called children. The contrast from my home experience was so entirely different from school. But I had kindness I could rely upon from Mrs. Lee. Mrs. Lee took extra care with me, fully aware I could barely make myself intelligible.

I refused to enter the playground for weeks. When I did enter, Mrs. Lee always stood by me at every playground moment with her reassuring presence. She came up with an idea that slowly instilled in me some confidence that I belonged on the playground with the other children. We started slowly, always one on one. She began to teach me tether ball. I learned to hit it pretty quickly, doing so often with the bottom of my curled fist. I was attracted to hitting it as hard as I could because doing so unknowingly released some of the pent-up anger and helplessness I felt with the Hobsons. Then Mrs. Lee introduced me to the two square game. I was enthralled because it was a game I had secretly envied from the sidelines. We started the game very slowly to my great relief. I loved the feel of the two square ball, something which I had never seen or touched before. I, who had no toys of any kind, was particularly attracted by the softness of this pinkish ball. It was so easy to bounce high, thrilling me from the moment I first touched it. I found out that the lovely Mrs. Lee, a woman possibly in her late forties or early fifties with a generous figure, could be a killer two square player. She patiently taught me many tricks, and it pleased me to see myself becoming a capable player. Finally, Mrs. Lee placed me in the four square line with the other children, always holding my hand. Once Mrs. Lee and I reached my turn, she let my hand go and said it would be "OK." I was initially more than intimidated by the other three players once I entered the four square game. But Mrs. Lee had taught me all her moves, and I turned out to be well prepared for the game. I immediately played hard, low, and fast.

The fourth through the sixth graders, who all shared a playground, noticed my skills. Suddenly my classmates wanted to play with the stammering Mexican kid. This broke the ice. It was wondrous to me, so unexpected. My classmates now seemed content with my athletic prowess, which provided them a slot in which to put me. Now everyone seemed eager to play four square with me on their team. This opened the door to a much better year. I realized that all this occurred without my needing to talk with any of them. I could simply play without the burden of multiple language barriers. My absolute refusal to interact with any children eroded once I accepted the threatening playground as a safe place.

It was such a relief as I slowly came to be comfortable with my classmates and to play with them without Mrs. Lee. I was reassured that she would be there watching, and I now took security in her presence as I played with others.

Even though I loved playing four square, the thought of participating in the daily dodge ball game was still intimidating. I knew not why, but I certainly didn't want a ball attacking me, thrown by classmates who were all older, stronger, and more talented at the game. Even my four square successes did little to provide me with the confidence to play dodge ball. Mrs. Lee was yet again incredibly patient with my refusal to participate in this much coveted fifteen to thirty-minute game held during the lunch hour. Mrs. Lee finally told me, "Go and show them how fast you are." I knew already I was a good runner before I arrived. I had learned earlier of my speed through my visits to the Mexican workers at the chicken ranch on fall and winter days when it was cold. I enjoyed running to the chicken farm a quarter of a mile away. I did stop regularly for rests during these runs, but I was always determined to get to my Mexican friends as quickly as I could.

Once I had the courage to enter the game, my speed and athleticism were evident. Soon, I was playing dodge ball with all one hundred twenty or so fourth to sixth graders. We all lined up in an elongated square using painted sidelines for the dimensions of the dodge ball game. Once I adjusted to the playground, there was something glorious in seeing all the students line up to enter the arena with only a few older students remaining initially on the outside to throw the dodge ball, hoping to get one of us out. As each person who had entered the middle of the dodge ball square was eliminated, we soon had scores of students on the sidelines whose role was also to throw the dodge ball at the remaining players. To me the sight of all the students eventually lining up the sidelines was impressive, exciting to my eyes. Due to my speed, I was often in the top tier, the last three to five students to be eliminated. I delighted in this achievement.

I'll never forget my best day of the dodge ball game where I nearly won as the second to the last to be eliminated. We had all returned to class. Before we started Ms. Lee commented at the front of the classroom on what a great day I had representing the fourth grade, and my classmates cheered. I had already fallen in love with Mrs. Lee, but hearing her say this, as well as my classmates cheering made me both proud and embarrassed, my face flushed and tears welling in my eyes. Somehow the praise relieved a bit of my persistent agony. It gave me something that I knew I had desperately been needing for three years. What a contrast to the misery at the adobe house, where only silence, rape or recriminations awaited me! I was able to grab control of myself, desperately hoping that no one saw the tears from my front row seat. I know that Mrs. Lee noticed. The image of my first public validation made me feel for the first time included, recognized: the rarest of feelings and an image that I could carry inside me.

Little Lake Elementary School provided me with my first saviors. Key among them were not only my beloved Mrs. Lee, but also the extraordinarily kind and caring Principal Acton. Principal Acton, who had already adopted ten children from around the world, became the first genuine protector I encountered in my life.

Principal Acton was a young white man in his late thirties or very early forties. He was unlike any other white man I had known. He sought no sexual exploitation of me. Instead, he was the first person in a position of authority who was suspicious of the Hobsons, particularly now that they were officially listing themselves as my "parents" without any attendant documentation. As an experienced adoptive father, Principal Acton was fully aware of the strenuous effort and voluminous paperwork required for a legal adoption. Obviously, since I had been kidnapped, John and Sara were unable to produce anything.

Principal Acton apparently did not accept their explanation of why I had no prior public education and why I was placed at their insistence in the fifth grade. I had been given a reading test to prove my advanced reading skills at the fifth-grade level, initially leading the school to accept the Hobsons' requirement that I be placed where they wanted. Principal Acton, within only a few weeks of my assignment to the fifth grade, coordinating with Mrs. Lee, ordered me moved from the fifth grade to the more appropriate fourth grade level.

Principal Acton was deeply appreciated by the school district. He had an outstanding reputation with his teachers and was admired for his community involvement. He immediately took a laser beam focus on me and the Hobsons, one that endured for my entire three-year period at his school. Principal Acton advocated for me the entire time I attended Little Lake. Unknown to me at the time, there were massive warning bells going off that were obvious to an experienced administrator such as Principal Acton. He simply never believed the Hobson's wild story about how I had innocently come into their good Samaritan hearts and lives.

Principal Acton's worries and disbelief were so severe that he called John and Sara into his office to discuss my future at the school. He formally invited the Hobsons to release me for adoption into his own large family and to take me off their hands. John and Sara discussed this option at home while I was present in the same room for what seemed to me like several days of open discussions.

Their discussions at night were always accompanied by more than their normal excessive drinking. At the time, Sara and John only drank Johnny Walker Black or Red, and their bar was always fully stocked. They both smoked a combined seven packs a day of filtered Benson & Hedges. Sara put her cigarettes out at the halfway point, only to start immediately on a fresh cigarette. They rarely emptied the numerous ashtrays, and it was common to see countless cigarette butts overflowing onto all the tables. Neither did they stop smoking while they ate. Their smoking created a heavy acrid scent painting visible light layers of cigarette smoke on the walls and leaving a bitter dominating smell in the interior of their home.

I was always in the room as if I did not exist, overhearing and now understanding virtually everything they said. All I really knew for certain was that it was a real opportunity to escape from the Hobsons and go to my protector Principal Acton and join his family of children from around the world. I desperately wanted the Hobsons to agree.

Even though I had been kidnapped by the Hobsons, in their crazy world, they stunningly seemed to actually think this adoption might be a good idea. They negotiated between themselves as if I could really be dropped off at the Actons, without any further consequences. They initially thought, as I overheard their arguments, that they would be finally free of me, a burden that seemed increasingly unbearable to them. Then the Hobsons refused Principal Acton's initial offer to take me off their hands. Principal Acton continued to approach the Hobsons at the beginning of each fall semester with the same offer. The Hobsons went through the merits of his annual offer with the same identical worries they had previously discussed in prior years. They always decided to keep me to themselves.

My first nine months at Little Lake Elementary ended in June 1963. With Mrs. Lee and Principal Acton as my advocates, I had experienced kindness and even some feelings of success and inklings of happiness on the playground. I then found out on the last day of school that the Hobsons were sending me for the entire summer by myself to a guest ranch in Northern California.

CHAPTER VIII

The Ranch and A New Mexican Family

IT WAS THE SUMMER OF 1963, and I was seven years old. Without warning, Sara and John sent me to a premier dude ranch vacation site for many Californians. It was situated in a deeply forested area of the northern California county where it was located, relatively close to the Nevada border and off the main highway at a small town. Although most guests came from every corner of California, there was also a significant West Coast presence from neighboring states. The Ranch was an attractive one- to two-week stay for families and provided an excellent dude ranch experience.

I was told only on the evening of the last day of my fourth grade school year about the Hobsons' summer plans for me. They said I would learn to ride horses. As proof of my imminent departure, the Hobsons retrieved an old, dark khaki green Samsonite suitcase. Sara opened it up to show me that I had nothing else to do but get ready for tomorrow's big day when my horse-riding lessons would begin.

Hearing this, I was briefly, modestly hopeful about the proposed guest Ranch, knowing that like everything else, it could and would likely be taken away from me. Learning to ride horses was something that I had never imagined before. At my age, I had never experienced the love of a pet, particularly the loyalty of a dog, a source of pleasure that would have helped me immensely in my forced isolation. For some reason, the Hobsons, albeit dog lovers, never allowed pets. This was despite Sara's claims to have previously raised a line of two pure-bred collies, Squire I and Squire II.

I had already been abducted for three years by this time. I

instinctively remained very suspicious and uncertain about what the Hobsons were really planning. As evening approached and bedtime came, I barely slept. My doubts now began to overtake my mind. I held on to this new dream of riding horses, but I was already fearful of the airport flight, surely accompanied by John and Sara to meet their contact in Reno.

The only saving grace to that long night was that I suddenly realized it would be the first time that I would be without the Hobsons in three years. I found that this realization of finally being away from them gave me the courage to face the guest ranch. At the same time, I knew I was being sent to an unknown fate, something that had defined my life since the moment of my kidnapping.

Sara told me that I would be meeting one of the Ranch owners, "Mrs. R", in Reno, and she would drive me to their dude ranch in upper Northern California. I had no other information. I did not really understand where I was going, whom I would meet, what kind of white people I would face, particularly men, but I had some vague belief that Mrs. R. at least might be better than Sara. I also allowed myself a glimmer of hope that maybe this would actually be the last time I ever saw the Hobsons.

During the May and June prior to my departure, the Hobsons were very vocal about their money worries. Suddenly, they became sufficiently flush to buy a relatively rare and expensive Volvo. We drove to the airport in this new car as I became increasingly worried about what lay ahead for me. The Hobsons never told me until the ride to the Ontario airport that I was going unaccompanied at age seven to fly to Reno. Throughout the car ride, both John and Sara seemed as deliriously happy as I had ever seen them, almost glowing in self-satisfaction. Although they continued to emphasize that I would be learning to ride horses, I did not trust them. How could I when they promised to get ice cream for my family when I was four years old, insisted that I accompany them on the ice cream run, and then kidnapped me and took me to California?

Somehow, I was not shocked when the Hobsons said they were not going with me, not even one of them to make sure I made my connection in Reno to be retrieved by a stranger. When we arrived at the Ontario Airport, their mood became completely cold, another wall of silence instantly reinstated, identical to the weeks of silence they periodically forced upon me. I knew it for what it was, an absolute shut down and lockout of me where I was nothing more than an inconvenient object to quickly dispose of at the airport. The Hobsons did not even walk me to the gate. Instead, they approached a flight attendant and placed me in her care. I knew from that moment that something was seriously wrong.

I recall the flight to Reno, both scared and enthralled by the plane. I was not seated at the front or anywhere near it so I could be easily observed by the flight attendants. Instead, I was assigned to my own empty row, about five rows back from the wing, on the left-hand side. The takeoff was difficult for me to handle, but I found its speed and power a positive thing, understanding it as necessary to get off the ground. As we began to fly, surprising cloud-like white fumes spurted from the wings, a sight that was thrilling for me to watch. I tried to settle into my seat and shut out my abandoned circumstances.

The trip turned to terror when we began to fly over an enormous body of dark water. It was foreboding and made me panic because I had no way to understand this new frightening thing far below. I had no understanding that when I looked down to this vast water mass, it was something called Lake Tahoe. My deep shock at seeing this threatening dark mass could have easily been avoided. All I needed was an adult who was accompanying me to explain the profound beauty of this natural wonder.

The flight had already been an emotional disaster for me. I had never flown on a plane. I was entirely alone in a confined setting with all English-speaking passengers. I stammered badly when stressed, so I was not able to communicate well without a patient listener, and I was embarrassed and ashamed by my obvious disability. I don't know if I would have spoken to a friendly passenger if they had sat next to me. Instead, I was by myself in an empty row, never provided with the opportunity to have someone approach me.

I was greeted by a matronly white lady in her late forties or early fifties, with graying short hair, around five-foot three-inches in height, similar to Sara's height, with a roundish face. She simply approached me at the gate, as I was the only child on the plane, much less the only dark seven-year-old to emerge. Mrs. R. was slightly overweight, wearing stylized cowgirl clothing. In addition to her jeans and cowboy boots covered with a slight layer of dust, she provided my first sighting of a cowboy belt buckle. It was bejeweled with small blue and red stones, with a fancy metal cover for the actual tip of the leather belt. Her blouse was white, thin for the summer heat, and she wore a cowboy hat. Mrs. R. seemed anxious to leave the airport.

She drove a rare VW, which was not the classic "Bug." I was familiar with a Bug since one of the younger teachers at Little Lake had purchased one and drove it to school every day, to the children's delight. But I had never seen a car shaped like this VW before in my life. It had an elongated sloped roof with enough room to hold the suitcases. Mrs. R. loaded my suitcase for me. It turned out to be the rare VW Fastback, a two-door vehicle. The car was newish, and its unique shape for a couple of crystalized moments diverted my mind from the uncertainties of the trip itself. By the time we were on our way, the car had ceased to be relevant. Instead, the scenery of the ride dominated the trip.

As we drove into California from Nevada, we crossed the California state line. The only other state line I had crossed before was on the overnight frantic trip from Phoenix to California on the night of my kidnapping. By this age I understood the overall shape of California, where Hemet and LA, as well as San Francisco and Sacramento were located on a map. The area where we were crossing had no similar identifiable landmarks for that region of California that I knew, so I had no idea where I was geographically. I just quietly noted the ominous California state line and what crossing it had meant to me earlier in my childhood.

Mrs. R. had taken pains to provide a car fully stocked with snacks, drinks, and candy. The ride from Reno to California was friendly but mostly consumed by the scenery, not the small talk of Mrs. R. I had come from Phoenix, and I had never been exposed to large fields of tall, vibrantly green grass that appeared to go on endlessly to my great contentment. We traveled through grass-filled valleys with farms of all sorts of animals, each one thrilling to my eye and visible from the road.

The ride was less than an hour from the border, and it passed quickly. As we approached the turn off to the Ranch, the terrain suddenly changed to large, forested areas, something that I had never seen before. Although I was familiar with the agricultural environments of Phoenix and Hemet, the forest ranges near Hemet in the mountainous area of nearby Idyllwild were unknown to me. I quickly learned that the Ranch was adjacent to a national forest, which was about hundreds of thousands of acres.

The entrance to the Ranch's private valley was at least a mile up the road into a secluded forest. The end of the forest opened up into a stunning valley of almost 1,000 acres owned by the Ranch. The pastures were dominated by thick fields of long grass, burbling tiny brooks, and carpets of wildflowers that were breathtaking in color and variety. The natural beauty of the Ranch could not be denied and provided an ideal location in which families could very comfortably vacation and enjoy nature.

The top of the Ranch held a dozen or more cabins, along with extra cabins to meet in, a dining room to easily hold eighty guests and a spacious commercial kitchen run with great loving discipline and efficiency by a matronly woman called Annie. Annie was in her fifties, with fully gray short hair and strong upper arm muscles that always flapped as she worked. I found her look totally endearing. Annie had been a cook for twenty-five years prior to her arrival at the Ranch. She had a warm demeanor and was naturally kind to children, experienced with them from raising her own family. Annie showed me only kindness and invited me from the first day to sit in her kitchen with her all-Mexican crew. The food servers were jobs reserved for white women. I could not believe my good fortune. I was filled with a warmth similar to being with my mother and sisters in the early morning. The kitchen staff spoke to me in Spanish, and I embraced my first language again, now for the second time after my coveted chicken farmworkers.

I also found out that the Ranch had a Chicano cowboy, called Jaime or Jim in English. He was young, recently married to Maria Elena, and they lived in a small house at the bottom of the Ranch that was provided for the resident cowboy. They each spoke both languages well and used them with me, but mostly relied on my obvious comfort with Spanish. Both Jaime and Maria Elena, along with the Mexican kitchen crew and Annie, became very caring towards me.

I did not fully grasp why I was at the Ranch, but I knew I was not in the category of guest, more as unpaid child ranch hand doing the necessary chores for co-owner Mr. R. I remember that the Hobsons gave me only ten dollars for the entire summer. They told me that was all I would need since my housing and meals were already taken care of. My chores proved to be a lifeline, starting in the corral with the horses at 6:15 AM. There is where I initially met the cowboy Jaime, someone whom I connected to instantly because he was also a dark-skinned Mexican, similar to myself and my family. Jaime was my father Jesus' height, five foot ten or so, slender and incredibly strong. Unlike my father Jesus, Jaime had a ready smile, a warm and gentle face and he liked me. He was still young and childless, and taking me under his wings seemed to please him.

I loved my cowboy family. I also found out that I instantaneously identified with horses, and that being with them was calming and healing. I had read about the occasional horse and did not have an instinctive fear of these large, graceful animals. Initially I watched in the barn so that I could learn to stay away from the hooves of the horses as they emerged from their stalls. The majority of horses were allowed to roam by themselves in the adjoining field, but it was the more difficult ones who stayed in the stables for their own protection. We always had at least one or two proud geldings at any time. Proud geldings are relatively rare but often exist when their castration has been delayed. These geldings have tempers that can be as feisty as stallions. If left alone they fought with each other, as well as with the horses who were not troublesome. That summer one of the proud geldings had caught his front hooves in the barbed wire fence and was kept in the stalls at night from that moment. Nevertheless, these fierce geldings were ridden by Jaime during the trail rides and by the experienced rider cook who always accompanied our outings. Guests were not allowed to ride them, but there was excitement each day in seeing that in strong and capable hands, these horses became compliant along the rides and did not cause problems.

My second task was learning to stay away from the hind end legs of all the horses to avoid being kicked as they emerged from their stalls to be groomed, fed, watered, and saddled. I was happy to help in these chores, always with Jaime doing the majority of the work with great efficiency, but I took great comfort in a shared task. After I had learned the basic rules and was entirely comfortable with the corral and the barn, I was allowed to brush the manes of the horses. They already were tied up at various holding posts, based on size and height. I was assigned to the children's smaller horses, but they were not small ponies; they were just smaller and shorter in every regard and tended to be very cooperative. Although I could not always reach the top of their manes because I was too short, I made every effort to do the best job I could.

Brushing their manes gave me my first great joy as I felt their necks, with their long yet maintained manes. I thrived when I touched their warm bodies. Their necks were so impressive with so many large, long, and supple muscles where I could feel their blood pulsing through their veins. I simply reveled in the nurturance they provided, not yet knowing the real treat with the animals was just around the corner.

I soon had a role in feeding the animals, which took me directly to my quintessential experience with the horses. I came into contact with their muzzles, incredibly soft, with an array of horse hairs sprouting from each side. They were eminently pettable and doing so was reassuring to the animals and a source of surprising pleasure for me. Jaime always made sure that we had enough apples cut in quarters and in halves for the twenty or so horses. We gave them their treats as the bridles were placed over their heads, the treats keeping them both happy and easy to work with. Although I was too small to fit bridles, I carried the bucket of apples, and the horses were always eager to lower their heads to take another piece of apple from me. I fed them with open hands as taught by Jaime and I avoided ever being bitten as I fed them. The visceral touch of their soft muzzles and the apple munching were something I looked forward to every day.

In the first week, I was learning so quickly, both in the kitchen with Annie and her Mexican crew, and in the corral, that I felt an odd sensation, long buried, that I might actually still be alive some-where in my body and that I had finally found a small way to return home in my mind to the world the Salazars had given me.

The morning barn deadline was to have the horses fully fed, saddled, and watered by 9:00 when the first ride began. Seeing

Jaime at breakfast was a big draw for the guests as he drank his coffee, ate his prepared breakfast and made sure I ate with him. The ride was divided between the adults and children under fourteen. Jaime led the trail rides, along with an outdoor cook.

I remember the first time that Jaime placed me on a horse to prepare me to accompany him on the daily trips. He had already given me my own horse, a beautiful small brown gelding with black hooves, quite calm and easy to manage. Jaime and I knew that I could not accompany him on their daily rides unless I could ride safely. Jaime returned from the ride, and I was there to greet him and to do anything he asked me to do to get the horses fed and watered, with the majority being let out to open pastures.

After we were done putting everything away after the daily rides, his riding lessons would begin in a now empty corral. I was placed on my horse the first time by Jaime, so the issue of actually mounting a horse on my own was something I did not have to worry about. He then quietly led me around the corral, showing me how to keep my heels down, my reins held to gently control the horse with a loose but firm touch. I learned his preference for a snaffle bit, one that was not hard on the horse's mouth. The snaffle bit allowed the horse to chew and play with the flexible bit in their mouths, something comforting to the horses but impossible with a standard rigid horse bit. After this was carefully explained to me by Jaime, I never considered again ever using a rigid bit on my horse. Jaime also taught me how not to dig my heels into the horse with harshness and to take time in keeping the horse calm but working.

Those first few days of training in the outer corral led me to my first unforgettable horse ride. I was able to walk down the middle of the ranch's pastures to visit Jaime and Maria Elena on foot in about fifteen minutes. I enjoyed the beautiful tall waves of grass, the discovery of even more small brooks and walking past our small herd of cattle that were kept in their own large fenced in area, maybe sixty head at the most.

My first ride from the stable to the house was with Jaime at my side. Although I was a little scared being on my first trip outside the corral, I was determined not to fall off and had confidence that I would neither disappoint nor be hurt by Jaime. I was now learning the very skill I had been promised by the Hobsons, but I quickly swept them from my mind as we rode. Jaime's small cowboy home as seen from my horse was so romantic, so picturesque that night against a wide opening beautiful summer sky surrounded by five hundred thousand acres of untouched forest.

My fresh view of their side yard was equally striking. I knew that they had an open stream surfacing in their side yard, and that some exotic plants surrounded it. They turned out to be watercress. But from the horse's height, I saw for the first time the sheer size of the water cress, some almost one foot tall, fed by the natural spring. The water was at least five times larger than the size of their home. As the plant was explained to me and identified as watercress, Jaime said that he too had never seen anything like it before, but he thought it was beautiful. Upon hearing his words, the watercress that surrounded this idyllic little cowboy home became a piece of paradise in my mind.

On that night Maria Elena had made a memorable meal. She was an excellent Mexican cook. It was a meal that covered the table with all the homemade Mexican food I sorely missed. When I saw the filled table and ate their familiar food, it was a shining moment and became all important to me. At the same time there was a barely suppressed pain upon being treated so well. I remember that night Jaime taking me back in his old truck to the Ranch in what was only about a five-minute drive, feeling secure and full as he dropped me off to sleep by myself in my cabin.

I had been shown my first kindness following my kidnapping when I entered Little Lake Elementary School and met Mrs. Lee and Principal Acton. Their intervention in my life gave me the initial hint of affirmation in an unknown world. But that evening's ride was the happiest I had been since losing my family. It was a moment of pure joy, unsoiled by my kidnapping, becoming a pillar for my survival. It became my most important, sustaining memory after losing the Salazars. Jaime and Maria Elena provided me with my first sense of home since my abduction.

Coming from the misery of my life with the Hobsons, these first three weeks at the Ranch were glorious. The Ranch was a dream world of graceful, powerful animals and warm new Chicano friends. I had learned to ride by the end of the second week with Jaime's daily lessons. Once allowed to join the daily ride, generally five hours in length at a time, I was introduced to the wonders of the National Forest.

We were nearly always on our own dedicated trails that avoided contact with other people in the towering forests. There I was introduced to pinecones appearing in the branches of millions of sharp-needled pine trees, providing cool shade between intermittent shards of sun that illuminated our trail. Generally, there were about twenty of us on the trail rides. I remained with the eight to fourteen year old riders. The Ranch did not allow younger riders because of the length of the trip and their nervousness around the horses. Instead, they were left at home to play in the rec rooms, eat their lunch, play supervised games, or go for walks to the fossil hill directly abutting the small, heavily stocked lake.

My favorite part of the day was the time we spent in the forest's upper valleys. There we rode through valleys much larger than where the Ranch was located, some more than ten times the size of our one-thousand-acre Ranch. Crossing the scores of brooks along the valley trails was the only dangerous aspect of the rides. The valley's brooks could often be a dozen feet or more in width, although they were under a foot deep. Our horses knew how to either walk directly through them or to sometimes jump across the smaller brooks, to the initial shock of the guest riders. These moves initially startled all of us novice riders but by the second ride, even the children became secure that the small brooks could be safely crossed without much worry.

The valleys displayed green foliage of multiple varieties, the plant names unknown to me. I did enjoy each time seeing the tens of thousands of tall yellow flowers, roughly three to four feet tall, with tough sticky stems. One could touch the stems, similar but much rougher to the touch than sunflower stalks and very unpleasant to handle. What changed my view of them was the horses' reaction themselves to the spiky plants. We usually ate our lunches in these valleys with the cook doling out anything that needed to be heated, like the pot of beans cooked over an open campfire. The horses were released, but they were well trained and did not wander far off, always easily collected again by Jaime, often three horses at a time. As the horses rested, slightly away from the ranch guests, they drank deeply from the running brooks. I expected them to eat the rich grass that filled the valley. Instead, they focused on the yellow flower heads of this unusual plant. They ate dozens of these flowers, seeming happy to do so. After seeing them eat so contentedly, my perspective on the valley changed from just wonderment to feeling pleased to see the horses revel in their flower heads. Each day, I now looked forward to these verdant valleys, not only for the thrill of the ride, but knowing that the horses were looking forward to their tasty lunches.

Every week we took a trail ride directly to the top of the mountain to see the forest ranger. The forest ranger was a nice young man, pleased for our company in his isolated environment. In front of the ranger's cabin was the California bear forest sign announcing the risks of fires in the area, a familiar sign that was strewn along the major trails. His cabin impressed me, and after the first visit I imagined becoming a fire ranger, if I could do so as a cowboy. The wood cabin was small, sparsely furnished, with a radio to communicate fire alerts. On all sides, one half of the walls were windows providing him with unobstructed views of the surrounding forest. His cabin was perched exactly at the clearest, unobstructed site looking down to the forests below. Within twenty or so feet from his home was an enormous wooden watch tower, with a large stairway going directly up to the top. There was an open-air lookout station on top that could easily hold a dozen people. All the children could climb these steep stairs with the ranger showing us the way. I remember being mesmerized by the view of the unblemished forest that stretched forever from this viewpoint. It made the forest appear not intimidating but beckoning in its beauty and sheer mass.

Twice a week, the Ranch held evening hayrides. It was rare that any guests stayed back at the ranch during the hayrides, because they were considered one of the highlights of the week's activities and were coveted by adults and children alike. We traveled in two large, rugged trucks designed to hold twenty-five or so adults and children. Accompanying us were the cook who would be occupied throughout the evening, along with a guitarist to lead us in camp songs. Mr. R. never failed to show up for the big Saturday evening hayride, one meant to be grander than the midweek hayride, as this was the last day before most of the ranch guests left for home. The cook prepared all the beef ahead of time and brought along plenty of hotdogs for the guests to roast over the open flames. There was the standard fare of egg and potato salad, cowboy beans with bacon and fresh cornbread made earlier that day. Also, to the delight of the crowd, the cook served an enormous sheet cake for dessert that had been baked that day by my friend, Annie. Mr. R. was always dressed up in working cowboy boots, a fresh cowboy shirt and a clean, cream-colored hat with an outsized Western oval belt buckle. His role was to regale us with camp stories, all meant to charm the guests and to make him the center of attention as the revered ranch owner.

On our hayrides we traveled up on the old logging roads, always heading for the highest valleys in the area. Every time we chose a valley location that was generally about a thousand feet from the surrounding woods where we unloaded the guests, as well as the ample food that would be cooked or reheated. This allowed us to safely make multiple fires for the cook and the guests, to both prepare food and to serve as campfire gathering spots for the guests. I particularly enjoyed watching our staff work and then mix with the guests as they ate their dinners together, to the shared delight of the guests. One campfire was reserved for the parents as they assisted their children in making s'mores. S'mores were always in high demand, and I was allowed to join in, which was reassuring and greatly increased my comfort with the children.

I still had my uncontrollable stammer in English, but somehow the kids knew that I understood them and their parents, and more importantly, I was with the cowboy, Jaime. They seemed content with my role. They also valued the speed and agility I had discovered at Little Lake. This made me a perfect partner for hide and seek and tag. I was able to show them everything the Ranch had to offer. I knew they were impressed with my taking them to their fossil searches, always successful given the millions of tiny fossils embedded in the hill beside the Ranch's tiny lake. I never let a child leave the hill until I helped that child find a fossil to take home. This combination of skills, despite my disabilities, overcame the children's hesitations about me during their quick vacations at the Ranch.

When I was assigned to live by myself at age seven, I was not concerned with being left alone, other than the fact that my cabin was the farthest away from the other cabins. At night when I always returned unaccompanied, the path was barely lit, scaring me as I rushed to my cabin with the tall trees now blackened, looming giants that surrounded me.

I initially found contentment, simply because I was away from the Hobsons in a perfect place for a young boy to explore. I had a manageable situation and the first, slow easing of my mind in the full embrace of my new Mexican family at the Ranch. Everything they did reminded me of Petra and my siblings, and for that brief period, they started to fill the bottomless void in me. Although I idolized Jaime and Maria Elena, the welcoming kitchen crew with their little treats for me were important. Each one of the Chicanas had children of their own and knowing this made me feel instantly safe with them. I was secure in sensing that the betrayals I had experienced were ending, and I embraced the dream of being a cowboy.

CHAPTER IX

Darkness in the Forest

I HAVE AN EXTREMELY HARD TIME WRITING about the three summers at the Ranch from 1963 to 1965. There I found the best of human beings providing me much needed love and protection, as well as a reaffirmation of my Chicano identity through language and culture, the taste of my mother's food once more on my tongue. My new Mexican family there showed me the human kindness that deeply replenished my soul.

I don't want to overwhelm you with sorrow. At the same time, the three summers were dominated by systematic abuse. I need to write it down, both the good and the bad. I am sorry if the reading is difficult, but I need you to remember that I experienced this as a child from ages seven through ten. My soul was recognized and rebuilt by the love of my Mexican family, as well as the intervention in my third and final summer, where my abuse was halted by a caring, gay white cowboy from San Francisco.

My cabin was identical to the other cabins at the Ranch. The cabins were spacious and had two full-size beds, with portable cots available if needed. There were two large comfortable chairs with a modest round table between them for smaller items or drinks. The cabins had their own good-sized bathroom with pre-formed corner showers with glass doors. Long blocks of stripped wood framed the cabins' exteriors, with the interiors made of regular drywall. The furniture was country themed, carved pine beds and bed stands, along with simple drawers and closets large enough to accommodate the belongings of four guests. Large families arranged to have cabins rented alongside their main cabin, often allowing a group of ten or more to visit the Ranch at one time.

No one ever told me why I was living alone. I never had anyone check on me at night for which I was grateful, as I wanted no evening intruders. Unlike other guests, I was also responsible for cleaning my own room every day, something that my father Jesus had already engrained in me with his rigid rules.

Mr. R., the owner of the Ranch, started to come by my cabin in the late afternoon, an hour or so before dinner. He told me he was there to check in to see how I was doing. He was quite affable in appearance, grandfather-like and always came with a drink in hand. He just sat there, mostly talking about himself and taking slow sips of his drink, creating a forced cheeriness I had seen all too often. During those first three weeks he did nothing to touch me except tapping my legs on the way out, telling me to head on up to the kitchen for dinner.

Since I first met him, I never for a moment felt comfortable with Mr. R. He simply looked like every older white man, and I knew what such men were capable of. My initial reservations about Mr. R.'s true intentions were blunted by meeting Annie and her crew, along with Jaime and Maria Elena, who immediately absorbed my attention as well as my heart.

By the end of the third week, Mr. R.'s visage had changed. He arrived drunk, just like John did on so many occasions. Mr. R. had a heightened sense of nervousness, but with an obvious leer and determination appearing in his eyes, a look I instantly recognized for what it was. He brought me a milkshake, a drink that was not offered at the camp. How had he heard about using milkshakes for my rapes? Even at my young age, I knew that the only way he could have found out about using milkshakes would have come from John. I recalled that John had introduced me to the milkshakes laced with the pills and liquor to numb me prior to the assaults.

Just like in the barber shop, it took me only seconds before I returned to seeing the milkshake as a way out, one that had worked during my rapes at the barber shop. At Mr. R.'s first assault, I just wanted to go blank, to be utterly removed from this world. Whatever he had placed in my drink subdued me quickly, but it did not knock me into unconsciousness. As I lay on my bed, I was able to stay somewhere alert in my mind and by now knew to keep my eyes open, just as I had taught myself during the Hobsons' assaults at the adobe house in Hemet.

I heard the knock on the door. Two men whom I recognized as weekly visitors from the camp entered. They were slightly younger, maybe in their late forties or early fifties. Both had children I already knew. Mr. R. sat in his chair and greeted the men, one who had a liquor bottle in hand, as well as their drinks. It was the younger man who undressed me as I lay immobilized in my bed, my eyes capturing their faces as their assaults began. So here it was. The Ranch, however beautiful, was just another station along my trail of sorrow. I suffered a repeat of the assaults by the white men that had started in both the Hobsons' farmhouse and John's barber shop in Phoenix. I added the Ranch abuse to the two- and one-half years of the abuse at the adobe house, the months of pure silence, the harsh reading lessons, the Hobsons' solitary rapes and my near total isolation from anyone for nearly three years. Abuse was nothing new.

The only thing that changed at the Ranch was the pattern of the assaults. Unlike the barber shop where I was constantly photographed by the men with their flashing lights, no cameras were present. The initial assault involved Mr. R. He did not touch the bed other than to stroke my body from the edge. He eventually stopped, sitting himself back into one of the cabin's two chairs. As the two men reached their heights, he accompanied them, leaving himself fully dressed, but with open trousers.

The pedophiles were blessed with complete privacy and had every reason to be secure as they carried out their assaults. All the conditions were favorable for Mr. R. and his guest rapists. My cabin was isolated from the other cabins. The owner of the Ranch was present and a full participant. The likelihood of authorities being alerted in this hidden and distant area was non-existent. The men always took the time to prepare the room. They took great care to carefully relock the door and to rearrange the print curtains, displaying cowboys on bucking broncos, to make sure they covered both the large front window and the window at the back of the room.

I averaged being assaulted every two weeks, usually by two separate sets of men, each with their close friends, always with

Mr. R. present. The men all shared the same physical traits with their disturbing odd pubic hair and pink penises, as well as the bitter smells of their emissions. Unlike the previous rapes, when I had no idea what was happening to me, I knew where and why the pain was taking place. I now understood every step; maybe not the reason, but every step of how their assaults would be carried out.

All that kept me going was my knowledge that it would eventually end. I knew I could see Annie and her crew after my mind turned back on, and if I were lucky, Jaime or Maria Elena would invite me to their home. I had my horses with their warm manes and soft sides to lean against. I would be able to return to them, speaking our own language. Surviving these attacks was crushingly difficult, but unlike all the prior years, I had the warmth of my Ranch Mexican family to support me.

I never told them what was going on, feeling an even greater shame. I felt I had let them down, our dream of a new Mexican family now likely impossible to sustain. I had already told them about the Salazars. My Ranch friends knew the names of my parents and siblings. They were aware that I had been "adopted" by the Hobsons and that the adoption was the reason I was no longer with the Salazars. Telling them anything about what had just happened to me was too painful; I lacked the words, and I instinctively knew that although they may have wanted to help, my silence prevented them from doing anything.

After the first rapes during this summer of 1963, my mind began to freeze. I no longer knew how to relate to any white adult male. I could barely acknowledge the children whose fathers had just raped me. I stopped all interaction with the children that was not absolutely required. Although only a small percentage of their fathers would end up raping me, I was now fearful of each white male, however kind and genuine his approach might be, because the next day maybe he would be the one knocking on my door.

Most terrifying were the men, often in pairs, who came to the Ranch without their wives and children. Ours was not a ranch which offered hunting. It was not a usual place that groups of men sought to carry out their sport. We instead offered basic trail rides, hayrides, and campfires. There were no reasons that single men would normally be attracted to stay in such a placid vacation spot, unless there were another motive for their visit. I was almost never wrong about these single men, often sharing a two-bedroom cabin with a close friend. Invariably it came down to them arriving to assault me with their roommate and at Mr. R.'s invitation and full participation.

My dream of an ideal summer vanished in an instant. There was no lingering doubt about where I was, what I was there for and how the Hobsons, apparently in great detail, had shown the Ranch owners the way to subdue me via the doctored drinks. Mr. R. had followed John's directions to the letter, and knowing this fact caused my soul to add another layer of utter hatred of John that never diminished in its intensity.

I have no way of knowing what level of remuneration the Hobsons received for this first summer at the Ranch or how much these pedophile guests paid Mr. R. for these dark privileges. Even without this information, I knew my body had basically been sold to the R.s to do whatever they wanted to me. It was a brutal assessment for any child to make, but a child can eventually connect the dots that he is nothing more than a sexual slave. I just happened to be "rented out" for the summer, but at the time I had no certainty I would ever be able to leave the Ranch.

My life was divided into two realities. I worked desperately to keep them apart, but I failed. I had the world of hidden assaults at the Ranch and their devastating impact on my psyche, just as I had begun to relax and feel that I would not be betrayed there. The other world was dreamlike, providing desperately needed reassuring time with my new Mexican family, my horses, and my coveted chores.

After the initial assault, I never left my Mexican crew out of my sight, particularly Jaime. The problems occurred by the second assault, when I was told to stay at the Ranch skipping the daily ride, leaving me without Jaime's protection. The rapes occurred while Jaime carried out the full day rides that returned about 6:00 PM. My assailants preferred the full day trail rides because sometimes I was drugged so heavily that it took me hours to become completely alert after being abandoned in the room. The pedophiles who had children in attendance sent their families ahead on the trail rides for the full day, giving them more time to indulge in their obsessions.

I was always left undressed on the bed, generally with a sheet thrown over me. Although I was explicitly required to change the sheets, I would have done so anyway. I could not bear their scents, their sweat, or the crusty liquids on the sheets. I changed the sheets for me. I changed the sheets because the stains were visible, with darkening blood. Mr. R. gave me specific instructions on how to dispose of my sheets. Their contents could not be discovered or associated with my cabin. I was to gather the sheets, place them carefully inside a pillowcase and leave it outside my door. Sometime that day, it was removed, but I never saw by whom. I worked to complete the cleanup in a daze, still half-naked, wearing only underwear that had just been stripped from me. I took my shower and clothed myself, now falling with full force into the same deadening trance I entered during my prior abuse at the Hobsons' home, before my arrival at this first summer at the Ranch.

The ritual of cleaning was soul scarring. My perfect little cabin had slowly started to evaporate during the first three weeks of Mr. R.'s late afternoon visits. By the first assault it turned into a cabin of horror, at once matching the life I had been living with the Hobsons. At the same time, in the evening, it remained my refuge. My night cabin provided my mind with a tiny shield because I knew I could lock my door. I took enormous comfort in the locked door, wholeheartedly believing that the simple latch was unbreakable. No one ever entered at night. Although I suspected something could happen, I had a locked door to protect me.

Unlike Phoenix and Hemet for my first three years, I had immediate access to friendly and compassionate adults, my Mexican family at the Ranch. On these long days of the all-day rides when I was held back for abuse, I always missed lunch. Annie and her crew would offer me a sandwich and drink as soon as I walked into the kitchen. I occasionally ate a bite or two of the sandwich, but mostly I just thirstily drank liquids. No one ever chided me for not finishing the small lunch. They sensed I was now in a different world, slowly emerging, barely functioning, often wobbly. My shattered condition must have been apparent to all in the kitchen, but it was always Annie who seemed the most worried. Annie was gentle when she approached my table where I sat in a daze, serving me my late lunch. Her eyes implored me to speak up, but I never said a word. The Hobsons had engrained in me that if I spoke up, I could be institutionalized and would never see my family again. But I did not step out of that kitchen or dining room until I could look out the kitchen windows and see the trail riders coming in at 6:00 PM.

I had only seen Jaime at 6:15 AM that morning for the preparation work required for the Ranch rides. Every time the riders returned on these long days, I rushed down to the corral's outer elaborate gate. It was framed by an enormous beam so high and thick that it looked unbreakable to me. The Ranch's display of its cattle brand hung below the large beam by chains. Under this were large metal gates, maybe eight feet wide on each side, placed on well-oiled hinges. The gates were easy for me to open, and it brought life back into my body to see these gates open wide after my near psychological death experience from the assaults I had undergone that day. I felt a consuming desperation to see Jaime on these days. Only focusing on his eventual return gave me the strength to hold my mind together. No people were more significant to me this first summer than Jaime and his wife Maria Elena whose affection enabled me to survive. They saved me.

The Hobsons visited the dude Ranch only once in the middle of the summer, after weeks of assaults had already taken place. When they arrived around lunch time, I was waiting at the large front porch outside the wood-clad dining room and kitchen. The R.s told me to wait there for the Hobsons. I remember seeing them get out of their car, a brand new 1963 Volvo model 122, white with black interior. Only in May the Hobsons had expressed countless money worries in front of me, yet they had acquired this brand-new car right before I was sent to the Ranch.

I did not leave the porch to greet them. Instead, I watched them amble up to the dining room in visibly high spirits. When they approached me, they were artificially cheery for the one minute or less that they said hello. I said nothing in response. They seemed to take my silence in stride because they were looking forward to the lunch with the R.s, and they insisted we go in immediately. I followed inside to find the dining room completely full since it was lunch time, except for the table where the R.s sat waiting for John and Sara. The R.s sat on one side, and I was told by the Hobsons to sit between them. I willed myself to endure the lunch. I said nothing, and I ate nothing. This was not a private lunch; this was not meant to be a private moment with me. Instead, it was designed to be conducted entirely in public with no risks of outbursts. It was the creation of the appearance of caring "parents" visiting their child at the Ranch.

The Hobsons exuded a sense of contentment, and the R.s were as cheery as any two people could have been. The guests who surrounded us in the dining room were just a few feet away. There was zero privacy to be had, much less sought. At the lunch I was not even asked the basic question of how I was doing, as this seemed meaningless to all the adults at the table.

I had an overarching worry as soon as I heard the Hobsons were coming to the Ranch. I was worried they would do something terrible. The worst would be to take me away from my Mexican family. It did not matter to me at that moment that more rapes would continue if I remained at the Ranch. All that mattered was not being taken away from the new home I had created with Jaime and Maria Elena. After all, if I returned to the Hobsons in Hemet, it would be back to their abusive physical and psychological hell anyway, something I had learned I could not prevent. I knew that the rapes at the Ranch would continue, but this was also my certain fate in Hemet. I preferred staying under the protection of Jaime and Maria Elena at all costs. I knew not how at the time, but at least it was a hope that I held onto during the lunch.

The Hobsons stayed barely an hour or so. During the visit it was immediately clear that I didn't really exist for them at all. It was merely a quick stop to see the R.s. As the Hobsons were getting ready to leave, Sara as always reached for her purse to get her compact out to put on her lipstick. It was a fancy woven bag, yellow cream-colored with small sunflowers sewn on the outside, with a matching clasp connected to the purse with large gold colored clips. It was a bag I had seen before, and I recognized it instantly. When Sara opened the bag, I noticed a large thick envelope stuffed with something. I could not see its contents because it had been sealed and to me appeared very hefty in size. In retrospect, I have often thought that the Hobsons only came to the Ranch to pick up a payment for providing Mr. R. with a child to sexually exploit.

I was grateful for their utter lack of attention to me. It further solidified my hatred for them, as if that were even possible. I knew they were solely responsible for every aspect of the trauma I was suffering at the Ranch. They knew it would be identical to the horrors that they had already carried out since I was four years old. I was thrilled to see them leave without me. I could remain with this new Mexican family, which is all I cared about. As they departed there was as usual no invitation for hugs, but I worried they might try it for appearances' sake. When the Hobsons left it was a great relief that they attempted no false affection. It was something I had hoped to avoid, finding their touch always like a direct burning flame on my flesh. As they were leaving, I remained on the porch watching them depart.

This does not mean I was numb to the rapes that followed or any of the rapes that had preceded the Hobsons' arrival at the Ranch. I was just so familiar with every contour of this darkened life that started when I was four years old. I was now just seven, and I knew what men would, could and did to overpower me, no matter what struggle I could put up. I began to close my mind off almost completely, to try to divide the horror of my assault at the Ranch from the gifts the Ranch provided me. I had hoped I could keep them separate, but they immediately intruded upon each other.

My Mexican family was now seeing the changes in me after each rape. They saw the state of mind I was in. I became obsessed with overwhelming worry that if my Mexican family knew of my secret, I might now be rejected. All my mind could hold onto was that if I maintained my silence, my new family would not abandon me. However, I was quickly swept away as my two realities collided, forcing me to absorb the physical and mental anguish on my own. I had become so numb at the end of the summer of 1963, that what-ever mental control I might have had initially upon my arrival, was eroding daily. I did manage to hold on as the summer passed, saved only by the quiet but consistent reassurance and love of Jaime and Maria Elena, Annie and her crew. Their acceptance enveloped me and helped me to hide a small part of my emotional torment, as well as the physical pain I endured.

My assaults remained unknown to Jaime and Maria Elena, thanks to the rule hammered incessantly upon me by the Hobsons. The Hobson's rule was absolute: I could not ever speak with anyone about what the Hobsons did to me. This had been engrained in me with threats since I was four and I had tried to escape through the farmhouse's wheat fields. I fully believed their lie about how I came to be kidnapped. Once I was five and a half years old, a full year into my kidnapping, I better understood the English language. The Hobsons began to scream at me that the kidnapping had been entirely my fault. They incessantly told me I had been taken from my family only because I had broken their key rule of complete silence with the outside world.

As the very early years passed from ages four to seven, I came to believe this as true, and I made sure that I never risked disclosure again. I was by then absolutely paralyzed with fear for my personal safety having been ravaged without stop for so many years. I worried about what the Hobsons might further do to ensure I never saw my family again. The Hobsons' fantasy that I was somehow able to speak with my family about their abuse immediately before the kidnapping occurred was completely impossible, but this is the story that shaped my entire future. Forcing this lie upon a broken boy as his truth destroyed my identity and affected my entire outlook on life. I never questioned what they said, but blindly accepted it as I realized my own actions were responsible for the loss of my entire family.

I did not return to muteness even once after my initial assault at the Ranch. I was too familiar with the detailed steps of the Hobsons' rapes and with hundreds of images of their abuse at the adobe house. More importantly my mind and English vocabulary were quite developed. I had finally begun to make sense of some of the pieces of my abuse. Although I became quiet, my voice remained intact. I began to slowly interact with people because I sensed the R.s were increasingly nervous that I had become so withdrawn, although not muted by the assaults. This reminded me of the Hobsons' fears that I could expose them. I retained an obvious ability to speak, albeit with an extreme stammer. I had stopped speaking with the Rs, but fearing more negative attention, I started to communicate with the children through their mothers on the daily horse rides. However, I no longer played with the children when we returned to the Ranch. I no longer went to the rec room, no longer swam with the other children. My prized fossil searches were now conducted in solitude without any children in tow. I did enjoy the twice-a-week hayrides because they felt safe. I was within a large crowd, and I did not want to be left alone after the kitchen help had gone home for the day. I knew that Jaime would be remaining at home with Maria Elena, as he was not needed for the truck transport. If I remained at home at the Ranch during the evening hayrides, I would be a mile away from his home, without his protection

I do not recall the trip back to Hemet after that first summer at the Ranch. I was so overwhelmed at the loss of my Mexican family, so anguished to be returning to the Hobsons, so uncertain of what would come next, that these moments are lost in the intense mixture of deeply bruised memories and grief. As I returned from the first summer, my Ranch Mexican family was instantly out of reach, but I hoped that at least the strange men at the Ranch would not follow me to abuse me. I was aware that I was returning back to the Hobsons' house of hate and pain. Fortunately, I returned to Little Lake Elementary School. I entered the fifth grade, having barely turned eight in late August. There I had the watchful eyes of Principal Acton and my classmates to provide some buffer. I had my joy in learning new things at school and my school yard games, when for fleeting moments I was just a child.

Then the fifth grade ended, and it was the summer of 1964. I was given no choice by the Hobsons. I was going back to the Ranch for a second summer. This was a terrifying thought to me, but at the same time, I urgently needed to return to my dear Mexican family who would be waiting for me, as well as my horses. My mandatory return to the Ranch for the second summer had another benefit. I realized that while I was forced to return, it was the only way to get a few months away from the Hobsons. I had long abandoned any hope that I had upon my initial trip to the Ranch that maybe it was the last time I would see the Hobsons. Instead, I knew that they would not end the cycle of abuse no matter what I did. I knew I would be raped, but I felt fatalistic about it. All I truly knew in my heart was that I was not going to lose my new Mexican family.

I could pay any price to have that.

I returned for the second year at the Ranch when I was just eight years old. I traveled from Hemet to Reno Airport to again meet Mrs. R., a woman fully aware of the pedophiles at her ranch. She drove the same VW Fastback model in which she had first picked me up. We drove for hours in silence to the Ranch. I refused any cheery invitation to talk. During that second summer, I never received a single visit by the Hobsons.

I was greeted with great fanfare by Annie and her Mexican crew. But nothing buoyed my spirits more than seeing Jaime and the promise of being at his side every day. I also held on to my fantasy that maybe Jaime and Maria Elena would adopt me, and I could live with them, anywhere but at the Ranch. Jaime was visibly moved to see me again and quickly took me to his home to see Maria Elena. She invited me for meals with the food from my Salazar life throughout the summer. I returned to my glorious chores at 6:15 at the stables with Jaime. I was assigned to the same cabin of the previous year, living alone.

During my second summer I could stand on a large box, built for assisting shorter people or children to get themselves on the horse. Jaime taught me how to bridle the smaller horses. I began to work with the children's saddles, much smaller and lighter than the adult saddles, and I was assigned to attend to the horses that were smaller and docile. I was thrilled that Jaime always checked on everything I did, always hoping I did the work correctly. I was never embarrassed to be taught and I never had an unkind word from Jaime.

The major changes in my duties occurred for the daily horse rides. During these rides, the children rode within ten to fifteen feet of the adults. I had previously ridden with the children as a participant. Now, to my great surprise and glee, Jaime told me I was ready to "lead" the children's group as we rode. I was immensely proud to be handed this honor and responsibility. It gave me a sense of accomplishment, of stature that I had never had before. On the trail, I took point with the children, often going alongside them to ensure that the riders at the back kept up. I also saw that the kids took notice of me daily, following my garbled instructions with my necessary hand movements to keep them pointed in the right

direction. Now that I was leading the children's rides, I fully identified with the Mexican workers.

I half believed that my new assignment might reduce the
number of assaults, but this did not occur. Unlike the rapes of
the first summer when nearly three full weeks passed before the
assaults began, this second summer the assaults began on the
second weekend. The pattern never changed, just the faces of
the older men in their forties and above. The rapists no longer
used doctored milkshakes to subdue me. Instead, they served
me a prepared small glass of nauseatingly sweet liquor. I learned
to throw it back because it was the only way to escape what would
happen next.

When I could not visit Jaime and Maria Elena for the evening,
I stayed around crowds of people as much as I could. This meant I
attended every movie night, every large evening activity without
fail, solely to be protected from the men at the Ranch. I went back
to my isolated cabin unaccompanied in the dark, along dimly lit
paths and slept in the bed where I had been raped that morning.
At least the sheets were fresh, and my door locked. I generally fell
asleep trying to think only about the Salazars or reassuring myself
that my 6:15 chores would come around soon, bringing me to Jaime.
That summer I again experienced a bewildering mixture of pain
and compassion, the horrific rapes contrasting with the kindness
of my "Mexican family." I was whipsawed, divided, and living on the
thin edge of sanity.

CHAPTER X

The Third Summer

WHEN I HAD COME BACK TO HEMET at the end of my second summer at the Ranch, I knew that a return to the Hobsons offered no reprieve. They would continue to inflict physical and mental abuse. The Hobsons were very nervous when they met me, palpably fearful at my arrival. Out of nowhere, the Hobsons rushed to get me a dog for my return to their olive orchard home. Sara had often told me about her prized collies that she had raised for years and how she would only accept purebreds. Her earlier collies were called Squire I and Squire II. Since I was five Sara had for some reason taunted me that I would never get a dog, much less a dog that was as exquisite as her well-bred collies. These definitions meant nothing to me other than I had always wanted a dog to play with, and Sara would deny me this. Having one would have been such a balm for my soul, something I could nurture and who would love me back. Despite living in the country in isolated homes with vast orchards, that was still not enough for them to provide me a dog.

Unexpectedly, I arrived home to meet Squire III. I had of course no choice in the selection of the dog or the naming of the dog, but I was instructed to be reverential. My dog was valuable because he was a pure-bred collie. I couldn't have cared less about John's or Sara's insistence that having a dog with an alleged pedigree was remotely important. All I knew was that I had a beautiful, fully grown dog that I instantly adored and who became my best friend. I now had the ability to care for an animal every day. I could not believe my first good fortune with the Hobsons, and I was not going to miss out on it for any reason. I believed Squire III was looking for a boy. I knew I had been looking for him for a long time.

I also found, when I returned from that second Ranch summer, that the Hobsons were gripped by a bewildering panic. I got caught in the crossfire of their frenzy. By the end of the school year, John's alcoholism was dominating our lives. The only essential thing during my fifth grade that sustained me was the protection of Principal Acton and the sanity of the school routine that Little Lake Elementary School provided. John began to renege on his building contracts, paving the way to the Hobsons' financial ruin. They became increasingly out-of-control adults. Sara pleaded constantly for John to stop his drinking, all the time drinking with him every evening. As John deteriorated after my return from the second brutal summer at the Ranch, my touchstones continued to be Squire, and Little Lake Elementary School.

I was now nine years old and entering the sixth grade. I continued to be a talented student. I studied with intense discipline, striving to reread until I understood as best I could the school's material. I had the benefit of a much higher reading capacity than most of the arriving sixth graders. The teachers had taken early notice of my advanced reading levels and provided me with my own adjunct library of books appropriate for my level and interests. I began to gain confidence for the first time at Little Lake. Although I had done well in the fourth and fifth grades, I came to realize that I excelled, just noting that no one else arrived for class better prepared than me, despite my verbal limitations. I began to feel my first internal hint of my intellectual strengths, maybe even an emerging ego despite the Hobsons' criticisms. I slowly and tenderly emerged from my shell with the loving care of Mrs. Lee and Principal Acton, who became my staunch advocates during all three years at their school.

This year Principal Acton started to notice that John was an uncontrollable alcoholic as he occasionally was the one to pick me up, maybe once a week, completely drunk. I thought John's constant visits to the drunk tanks after his arrests in the skid row of Hemet were somehow hidden in this small town. But with John's public drunkenness at my school, I knew that his condition could no longer be kept secret. John invaded my one sanctuary from the

Hobsons. All the staff seemed to notice, particularly the office staff he might run into during these stops. He never halted his habits. I was now publicly humiliated, drawing me further into myself. But as always, the staff at Little Lake threw me a lifeline, and I willed myself to arrive at school for a few hours of peace away from John and Sara.

Principal Acton was profoundly worried about my state of mind and my change in personality as each summer passed and I returned from the Ranch. Every year Principal Acton met with my parents to encourage them to allow me to be adopted into his ten-child adoptee family. And the Hobsons each time reviewed the merits of his offer at length, doing so in front of me. Since my English was now strong in these later years, I better understood their worries and had fully accepted that the Hobsons would never let go of me or acquiesce to any legal adoption. Their main fear was apparently appearing in court for the adoption process. I had no idea what that really meant, I just understood they didn't want to appear in front of someone called a judge.

In June of 1965, after completing sixth grade and graduating from Little Lake Elementary School, I was sent to the Ranch again. This third summer everything changed. I arrived to find that Jaime and Maria Elena were no longer there. I was crushed to learn that the core of my newfound family was gone. My dream of eventually being adopted by them was now impossible. Just like the absolute loss of my Salazar family, the break in connection was a severed rope. I had no way or understanding of how to contact them. I felt the same helplessness that flooded me from the day I was kidnapped. Both Jaime and Maria Elena were gone. This pain was profoundly familiar to me, the rent in my heart now another unhealed wound like the one from the earlier loss of my family in 1959. As this summer passed, the full breadth of their absence became clearer to me. I became consumed with worry that this third summer would prove to be my undoing, without anyone to anchor me. In the absence of my Mexican family at the Ranch, I no longer had any hope for getting home to Phoenix.

When I discovered that the entire kitchen crew, filled with the kind Mexicanas/Chicanas who had their own large families, had been replaced by white workers, I was further heartbroken.

I realized that I had no one to continue to assist me in sustaining my own Spanish language, much less provide any further access to my reclaimed Chicano identity. In addition, my beloved Annie the cook had been replaced, leaving me without a kind white woman who was always generous in her affection towards me. I had barely any relationship with the new kitchen crew as they were all white and did not speak Spanish. Although by then I understood English quite well, there was no nurturance to be had from the new white cook. She was always busy, quite competent in making a menu dominated by preferred, bland white meals, with never a nod to Mexican fare.

Roy, the new cowboy, was probably in his early fifties and was from San Francisco. When I met him, I was relieved that he had the same name as my youngest brother, Roy, called Rogelio in Spanish. Roy was a large white man, with a full head of graying hair and a winning smile. Although I did not have the word to describe him at the time other than he was extremely funny and entertaining, he was openly flamboyant from the moment you met him, with sweeping gestures, a ready wink, as he was continually amusing.

It was only 1965 when Roy arrived at the Ranch. He had an unspoken openness as to his identity, and everyone knew he was from the notorious San Francisco. I had no idea what being from San Francisco implied. Despite some of the guests' initial hesitations about Roy, these seemed to quickly evaporate as Roy was accepted in his role as a gentleman cowboy. Most of the guests came to adore him and appreciated Roy's large presence. Everyone, including the R.s, seemed pleased that he was such a good fit, as well as obviously being a very competent ranch hand. The only thing he did not do was to castrate the horses or butcher the goats in early August, as this was now done by a crew that had been brought in for the day.

When I met Roy, his kindness oddly enough seemed sincere. It was a little like the kindness I had encountered with Principal Acton, as well as some of the white male teachers at my school. Roy was assigned to my cabin to sleep with me in the second bed. Roy was the first roommate I had been given in three summers. I took the risks of my new roommate very seriously. I was very cautious as to who Roy might really be, what he might become and certainly what assault risks I might have alone with him in my cabin. These were the questions I faced upon Roy's arrival. For some unknown reason, though, here was a white man who was clearly totally disinterested in any sexual aspect that might involve me. His zero sexual interest in me made no sense, given my prior experience with white men. Even though I could barely trust my instincts, Roy seemed to be a man who was not going to terrorize me with his assaults.

Each night Roy transformed into an exaggerated vision of what a gentleman cowboy could look like. He confidently knew how to work a crowd and to be the center of attention, bringing a fresh brightness to the evening's dinner and the activities that followed. Roy wore regular work clothing and cowboy boots during the day but seeing him change his clothes every night was a fascinating moment for me. It was exciting to watch his preparations for dinner. Roy perused his closet filled with a multitude of elaborate outfits that he had carefully carried from San Francisco. Each of Roy's garments had arrived covered in large clear plastic bags, something that I had never seen before, but that made his clothes even more important and rich. Roy also had an impressive collection of intricately tooled Western belts and stand out cowboy hats protected by hat boxes kept in the closet. He seemed to me to have walked off the screen from a Western movie.

Although I ached for Jaime and Maria Elena, I felt a sincerity in Roy's heart early on. I was initially hesitant to accept Roy, given my prior experiences with pleasant men suddenly turning on me. Instead, Roy became almost instinctively protective of me, sensing that something was deeply wrong about my background. He was the first adult other than Principal Acton of Little Lake Elementary School who I could tell did not believe entirely my story of the adoption. I also didn't understand why Roy's mysterious San Francisco background was an apparent tip off to the adults, that it meant something to them that I didn't understand. Once I became increasingly trusting of Roy, I began to accept the sincerity of his companionship. This was an enormous step for me to take, but one that became essential to my survival during this third summer at the Ranch.

Nevertheless, the routine of rapes by the men who visited my cabin returned in full force. These now always occurred during the day-long trail rides when Roy was occupied. Again, I was held back at the Ranch and by mid-morning the drugging and the rapes began. Afterwards I could no longer rush for comfort to Annie's kitchen and her crew as they were no longer there. The current cook was not inviting, obviously unhappy as I initially tried to shelter in her kitchen. She preferred that I keep to myself in the dining room or just leave the premises altogether.

I started to go down to the corral, pet the small number of horses there and begin to do the minor chores for Roy until he returned home. Just like Jaime, Roy was patient with me, but it simply was not the same. Although he always tried to be kind to me, by this third summer with my friends gone I could feel myself losing my grip. Even with Roy's reassuring help, I was becoming mentally lost. I had banked that my Mexican family would be there as always, making the trip worth the devastating assaults I would endure. Without them, I had none of the previous solace that I once had.

Roy continued to build on my trust throughout the summer. At the beginning of August, Roy ensured that I be allowed to enjoy one of the great adventures to be offered in cowboy country in our region. Held in early August of each year, the County Rodeo was the biggest event of the season. Roy took me to the rodeo twice on my own during his days off, something that shaped my cowboy imagination all my life. It was thrilling to see my first rodeo, every competition from bull riding, barrel racing, lassoing, and tagging, along with all the colorful parades with flowing banners and flaw-lessly groomed horses with intricately carved saddles and bridles, often embedded with gleaming silver decorations. I was thrilled with the farm animals which I took enormous interest in, feeling completely drawn to the pigs, sheep and the much-prized bulls, the air filled with the intoxicating scent of their temporary metal stalls. There was so much to see in this lengthy rodeo, covering nearly two weeks of championship events. But this event, this joy, was so fleeting, just a gloss on the torment, insufficient to stop the dark passage forced upon me.

By the end of the summer, I could no longer cope and was without virtually any hope, other than what I perceived to be merely a thin reed of support that Roy offered. After one of the rapes, I decided that the only thing that made sense was to hang myself in the shower. The suicide attempt occurred before my August 21st birthday. I was only nine years old. I had no desire to ever see the Hobsons again. Instead, I wanted to rush into the arms of my Salazar family, and this was the only way to reach them. To my mind, my suicide was my way home to the Salazars.

I was determined to carry out a plan that had suddenly, unquestioningly, popped into my head following that day's rape. I decided for the first time to disobey Mr. R. and not change my soiled bed. I just wanted people to see what had happened to me by leaving the sheet stains obvious and exposed. As the drug wore off, I remember getting out of the shower and putting on clean clothes and shoes so I would not have to be dressed for burial. I had already created my own burial plots at the adobe house, which I had rearranged compulsively for nearly three years under my favorite orange tree. I had some idea, albeit incomplete, about death. I then walked into the bathroom with both my used towels and a large handful of fresh towels that I kept with Roy's in our shared closet. I wiped down the entire shower, taking great care to dry the interior shower floor. I then dried the floor outside the shower stall.

For some reason it was of enormous importance that the shower be clean and completely dry. I remember stretching to reach and dry the shower head, throwing a towel over it to make sure it was as dry as I could make it. I was familiar with lariats and ropes, one that had been given to me by Jaime, as well as the stored ropes in all sizes in the corral. The lariat Jaime gave me was very stiff and not meant for a shower, but for horses and cow wrangling and practical uses on the trail. Instead, I used a small, pliable rope, slightly thicker than what you would use for hanging your laundry.

The shower pipe was very thin with a small waterspout where the water came out in sharp, rapid bursts, rather than the gentler types of shower sprays. I carefully tied my rope maybe five to six times around the narrow pipe. I had already been taught basic rope techniques by Jaime, something in which I took pride. I did not make a formal noose, as this was both too difficult and unnecessary with strong slip knots. I made a loop big enough to reach over my head from the ample remaining rope. I entered the shower fully dressed with my shoes on. It was vitally important that I have my shoes on because I did not want to be buried in wet socks or shoes or force my family to change them. I needed to be completely ready and that meant being dressed and dry.

My focus on the shower and its potential to help me do what I wanted to do was extreme. I desperately missed my family, and at that moment I had lost any hope of seeing them alive. I could not handle the fact that my Ranch friends were gone. I was frantic to contact them, but I was helpless to do so. Neither could I believe that my dream to be adopted by Jaime and Maria Elena would ever occur. I was sure no one would or could help me find the Salazars, or that I could reach them other than through my death.

I felt that I was doing nothing automatically, but instead I believed the steps to kill myself were a fully conscious plan and only choice. I needed to get this life over with, never doubting for a moment that doing so would somehow reunite me with my family. I was caught up in a shattered nine-year-old mind and psyche. The rest of my thinking perhaps occurred in a fugue state, but I had no idea what this state of mind might have meant in my choice. At the time my thought process, although born of despair, seemed clear.

My hope was that the Hobsons would now be forced to contact the Salazars, even though I sensed that this was an unlikely scenario. I also might be allowed to return in some way to Little Lake Elementary School via my death. I knew that Principal Acton would have to find out about my death when I did not show up for school. I wasn't sure what this would mean, but I took comfort that he might lead the way for the Salazars to pick up my remains.

I entered the shower, satisfied that everything was dry, and the rope arranged. I then put the noose over my head and neck and pushed myself out from the wall to let myself fall to a premeasured level that guaranteed I would not land up on the shower floor. I immediately felt myself starting to choke, but I had traveled to a place that I knew I could endure until I suffocated. I faded from consciousness, only slightly panicked and somewhere more relieved that I was being successful, that I had chosen correctly and now I was on my way home.

Crack! Suddenly there was a crashing sound and I fell to the floor. The thin, cheap shower pipe had broken. I hit the back of my head when I fell and my body was in a heap at the bottom of the shower floor, with the rope still tight against my neck and the strands of unused rope spilling out onto the floor. I was dazed and choking and realized for some reason I had fallen. I finally saw the broken shower pipe.

Nevertheless, the rope had already made marks around my small neck, something I was totally unaware of, and that Roy would see almost immediately upon his return to our cabin. The rope marks had not fully cut into my flesh in any severe way, but instead left a thin trail of rope burn marks around my neck.

Oddly enough, I suddenly became hysterical that I would be blamed for the broken pipe. At that moment nothing else mattered to me. I had to find a way to explain to the R.s, to Roy, what appeared to be an insurmountable crisis of blame and maybe physical discipline that briefly shut out my initial disappointment that I was not dead. I had no explanation to offer other than the truth, and I dared not share that with anyone.

I decided that since it was the late afternoon, I should clean up the bathroom messes, along with our bedroom and stay in our cabin knowing that Roy would soon be arriving from the corral to shower and change into his dinner dress outfit. By the time of his arrival, I had cleaned the bathroom, placed on fresh bedding and waited, deeply anxious about his response. In my thoughts I returned to my fragility in the wheat field in Arizona. I remembered that my escapes to the farmhouse's wheat field had failed, and I had been caught by the Hobsons when they saw the wheat spurs in my socks. I had been totally traumatized by the Hobsons' reaction, and I was not entirely trustful of what Roy might do to me in this crisis.

Roy returned from work, said a friendly hello and went into the bathroom to shower. He came out with a worried look on his face. Then he noticed my neck. It shocked me to realize that the marks were clearly visible for all to see. Roy sat me down with great compassion and asked me what had happened. I told him I did not know how the shower had been broken. But then he asked about my rope burn marks. And there was the crushing evidence just feet away of the shower pipe broken entirely in half. I could not let go in my mind that what I had done was the equivalent to the end of my world.

Roy brought his face close to mine. I could see both fear and pain in his eyes, and he teared up. Roy was so kind to me at that moment that for the first and only time during my three summers, I began to sob uncontrollably. He simply stayed with me for an hour or so until he felt I could be outside. We went down to dinner, having missed the regular dinner service. The kitchen staff had as normal gone home by 8:30. The guests were watching the evening movie in the gathering room, a good distance from the kitchen and dining area. Roy entered the kitchen, taking cold cuts and milk out for me to eat. He simply stayed with me all evening, never leaving my side. At that time, I unknowingly found from him all that I needed for the rest of the summer.

I never told him what had happened, and Roy chose not to press it. He had seemingly made up his own mind about the incident. But he must have known I had tried to kill myself and that some of the fears he had instinctively picked up from me early on, had in fact come true. I do not know what Roy did or said to the R.s. I was no longer left at home during the day-long rides. I was never abused again at the Ranch.

I had only ten days or so left before I left for Hemet. Roy did his best from that point on to never leave my side. As always during these summers, I would have another birthday, and on August 21, 1965, I turned ten years old. I returned to the Hobsons as always on the last day of summer just before school began.

I was mentally fully captured by my suicide attempt, both at the Ranch and thereafter. Throughout the remaining days at the Ranch, I began to fantasize about a sturdier way to kill myself, to hang myself from something that would not break. My dreams revolved around the grand entrance of our corral main gate. It was tall, with an enormous thick overhang of solid wood. I knew that I had no hope of scaling up to a beam maybe sixteen feet high, but in my fantasies, it was ideal, as sturdy and unbreakable as the enormous trees of the National Forest. I would take a much thicker rope from the corral, sling it over the top several times to make it secure so it would not slip. I would have a ladder, anything to get me up six to eight feet, which was as high as I could go in my mind. The suicide noose dangled conveniently in front of my face. Once it was securely around my neck, I would kick my legs so that the ladder would fall out from under me and I would die, bringing me back to the Salazars. I could no longer halt these non-stop suicidal thoughts. They enveloped me and continued throughout each waking hour. I now also had suicidal nightmares in which I tried to reach my fate with death, the sole, obvious way to escape from the life I had been forced to live.

Roy returned to San Francisco at the end of the summer, two days before I was sent back to Hemet. Once at home my suicide compulsion followed me. I needed to find a way home, and I continued to believe that my death was my only way to return to the Salazars. It never occurred to me even as I grew a bit older, that my being dead might prove to be a bad strategy as this meant I would no longer be able to communicate with them. I simply did not make the connection. I was boxed in, and I took a strange comfort in my certainty that death was my answer and that I really had very little to live for. This belief existed alongside whatever small successes I had experienced in school.

CHAPTER XI

The Hobsons' Decline Brings Moves and Separation

THE HOBSONS' DECLINE was in full motion by the time I had graduated from Little Lake Elementary School in May of 1965 and returned in August from my third summer at the Ranch. John's building projects were not bringing in any money since he had reneged on most of the building contracts he held. Whatever remuneration the Hobsons had received for the sale of my body had ceased. My close call with suicide at the Ranch undoubtedly terrified the Hobsons. They must have known that the child they kidnapped and exploited had almost succeeded in killing himself, leaving them perilously close to exposure to the authorities. As a result, I was never sexually abused by the Hobsons following my 10th birthday, although their calculated psychological torture of me never abated.

After John reneged on his contracts, his only remaining source of money was his three spinster aunts whom he had reconnected with when the Hobsons reached California following my kidnapping. John and Sara had often regaled me with stories of the aunts' generosity over the years since I had met the aunts, and even at my young age, I had sensed John's reliance on both their emotional and financial support. For John, his aunts had always been his safety net, a trio of spinsters whose love appeared to have no limit.

But even they ceased to support him at this juncture. What did the aunts find out about John so that their rejection of him, after decades of support, was complete? Was it due to his countless visits to the drunk tank over this three-year period in Hemet where he was picked up on skid row or thrown out of cheap dives? In such a small town, it was easy for these events to become the subject of public gossip. John's failure to meet financial obligations was not new to them. He was a general contractor by trade and had about twenty-five years' experience as a skilled builder of custom homes. In 1960, when John came to Hemet, he won at least a half dozen large contracts for building ranch style custom homes. He completed work on three of them. I heard his and Sara's anxious conversations about the money that John had already taken from the additional homes in the form of large deposits. Apparently, John merely had workers lay the foundations before walking away with the money for three of the homes he had under contract. John was in the throes of severe alcoholism, unable to function or meet his contractual obligations. John was sued for the theft of the money, left town for long periods, and may have declared bankruptcy.

Even with these facts, the question remains about what pushed his three elderly aunts over the edge to abandon their favorite nephew. It had to be something major, something that they simply could not accept in their lives that caused their rejection of him to be complete. What had broken the pattern of love and dependence, of adoration and ample funding for whatever John needed? The aunts had long been aware of John's heavy drinking. They may have overlooked the "bad luck" of his multiple arrests for drunkenness. And I had heard stories about times when the aunts had saved John from prior business troubles with bailouts. Why wasn't a bailout offered to John when he reneged on his building contracts? What did the aunts find out about him that was enough to lose their love for John?

My surmise is that they discovered something that completely shook their image of their beloved nephew. There is a strong possibility that his homosexuality was somehow revealed to his aunts inadvertently, either via arrest or other forms of exposure. At some point the venom from the daily wars in our Hemet house regarding John's sexuality could have leaked far enough to reach them. During our visits to John's aunts, he was the very picture of a charming, adoptive father. At this early stage, the aunts did not know that John was also a predator of young boys, a malignancy that undoubtedly led to my kidnapping and systemic rapes over many years. In 1965, being gay was not generally accepted. The aunts may have felt betrayed by the façade John presented them: heterosexual, married with a son. Something finally broke the strands of their relationship. It unraveled, making it impossible for them to continue to support their formerly cherished nephew. Although the full circumstances are unclear for this permanent breach, the combination of his sexuality, his financial ruin, coupled with unbridled alcoholism may have been enough. Perhaps the circumstances of my own life with John and Sara may have somehow been revealed. The aunts' pillar of financial support and profound adoration ceased in its entirety, allowing them to turn their backs on John permanently. John never again received financial support from his aunts, and to the best of my knowledge he never contacted them again.

John's break with his aunts was an added toxin to the bitter mix at the Hemet house. The loss of money added to Sara's accumulating rage, fueled not just by John's financial recklessness, but also his extended absences. By the time I was eleven, John had a multi-year pattern of abandoning Sara and me. Beginning with his repeated arrests for public drunkenness, John started to disappear for days, weeks and then months at a time. His alcoholism broke any remaining layers of self-preservation he had, leading him to defraud clients. During his absences, none of his contractual work was carried out. He returned penniless, having further depleted the Hobsons' financial resources, adding fuel to Sara's hurled accusations.

It took me a while to piece together from Sara's tirades why John kept leaving three to five times a year without notice. It turned out to have little to do with economics but his compulsive need to be on his own. By the time I was six, Sara had become very vocal in denigrating John as a homosexual. Their relationship, which I witnessed for years, was defined by Sara spewing anti-gay hatred toward John from every pore of her small frame. Sara tried to shame John by telling me in his presence about his homosexual past. Sara made a point of insisting that John had been arrested for solicitation in the San Pedro docks. Sara repeatedly stated that the sole reason John had not served in any capacity during World War II, despite being age eligible, able-bodied, and well-educated, was the discovery of his homosexuality, perhaps via an arrest record. Sara's accusations of John's homosexuality were unrelenting, oil-soaked fuel for her drunken rages. She belittled John at every turn as less than a man.

I heard the battles regarding John's sexuality as a constant refrain, never understanding what being a homosexual meant or why it was disgusting. Instead, I believed that our crisis was about money and my discovery by authorities. John's repeated abandonment of us for weeks or months every year was the more pressing reality of the latter Hemet years. While I was aware of Sara's strident claims about John's sexuality from an early age, John's homosexuality remained an unclear concept for me.

John's exit pattern never changed on the days he chose to abandon us: He arose cheery with a cup of coffee in hand, in a gregarious mood, walking out the door as he headed to "work." He then would not return for two to three weeks at least, but he generally averaged being away close to two months. According to Sara, John depleted all the checking accounts for his travels, leaving her without any funds. John's regular abandonment of us began before I was six years of age. Each departure of his was welcomed by me after I came to realize that no sexual abuse occurred in his absence. This was the simple equation I made, and but for Sara's horrific torture of John upon his return, I would have considered it a non-issue.

Sara's behavior toward me during John's unexplained absences was abusive. Sara initially was insular and depressed. She gave me her silent treatment as we avoided each other. The house became like one that had been left deserted, heatless, with no roof to protect from the elements. The stillness shattered as Sara morphed into fury against me for being present in her life. Her resentment was explicit, and she made every effort to make me understand I was the sole cause for John's absences. Sara often told me that if I were not there, John would not have left her. I already knew that the Hobsons considered my existence an immense burden on them, but her unrelenting screaming shook me to my core. I had no way to escape her wrath and no ability to respond to her threats or blame for ruining their lives. Sara took pleasure in never letting up on me during John's absences. She visibly gathered her strength to launch new verbal attacks, bringing herself to a level of uncontrolled viciousness against me that she apparently thought was her due.

I was trapped in Sara's madness, isolated except for school, and bound by the promise to never tell anyone what was happening to me after nearly six full years of abduction. Sara herself was a heavy scotch drinker, and she was at her most malignant and repulsive self every evening as she drank alone with only me in the house. Her attacks were amplified by alcohol, and except for the lack of physical abuse, she was unrelenting in trying to tear my emerging ego to shreds.

John always returned, broke, unkempt, and wiped out from weeks of drinking. Sara never rejected his return, whether it had been for only three weeks or a full two months. John came back to Hemet to a desperate and financially strapped Sara. Each time he returned from his long, unexplained absences it was a mixed blessing. There was the hint of possibility that he could generate income, but mostly it was John returning in a state of open defeat and depression. Sara's sense of relief upon John's return was palpable before she unleashed her anger against him.

John returned to heavy drinking without missing a beat, following a well-worn pattern of behavior. John was a quiet, docile drunk, always choosing his favorite chair in the living room where he often passed out. Sara also drank with him at the same time, building her own drunken rage. It was in this setting that Sara began her torture of John. Sara perpetrated her unbridled attacks in front of me, making me a permanent witness to her intense cruelty.

John never fought back against the onslaught of physical abuse that Sara carried out almost ritualistically against him. Sara began by slapping him as he was semi-comatose but alert. This was followed by her throwing her drink on his face as she smoked incessantly, pacing the room in circles as she surrounded his chair. She eventually started to put out her cigarette butts on his forearm, to his screams and protests, but John was unable to move from his chair. I saw all of this. Sara's torture of John when he returned from an absence was routine; eventually the scarring from the cigarette burns became visible to the naked eye. Even so, despite John's weak protests, he never struck her, never fought back or did anything but weep as she tormented him.

Sara's untethered cruelty in her physical attacks never altered, the sequence of slapping to burning of his flesh was carried out with great discipline. I could see her visceral hatred of John in her eyes, with no fear that he would ever fight back. In Sara's tirades she spewed streams of poisonous hatred toward his homosexuality and his physical abandonment of her, leaving her without any financial means to support her, much less me.

Oddly enough, John never denied his gayness. John never lifted a finger to either describe his activities or to acknowledge where he had been. Instead, there was a silent belligerence, almost daring her to find a way to make him admit to something. John was fierce in his refusal to answer her questions, simply leaving the charges unchallenged, to her great fury. I saw her entire body shake repeatedly in rage at him for being gay and his refusal to stop abandoning her at will. John was immoveable. He accepted her wrath and had another drink.

The Hobsons' situation was untenable, and so once again I was uprooted, moved like a piece of unnecessary and unwanted spare furniture. Three weeks after my third stay at the Ranch, Sara and John fled Hemet in fumes of suspicion and fraud, emerging penniless and going their separate ways. Sara had not worked for years, instead spending her time writing fiction at home. But the Hobsons were broke, and Sara had no means of support. Her sole choice was to seek a job on her own, and she found a position in Chino, California. She and John either divorced or separated. All I knew was that John was gone.

I was ten years old at the time of our departure from Hemet. My English was excellent, albeit with a stammer, but my comprehension was more finely tuned than the normal child due to my horrific experiences with the Hobsons. I had a maturity forced upon me by the years of abuse, and I had learned to listen to every word of their vicious fights. I was acutely sensitive to the state of their hysterical worries, not necessarily the substantive reasons behind them. But I was guided by their open discussions of their accumulated financial losses and their increasing sense that they were about to lose control of everything they had created for themselves.

I was a used-up child, never having recovered from the rapes at the Ranch. Nevertheless, my will to survive continued to grow. I had built a more sophisticated private world in my mind that separated me from the reality of the Hobsons' home. I had a burgeoning sense of faith in myself that allowed me to create a more adult and comprehensive resistance to my life with John and Sara. My hatred of them enabled me to ignore them, a mental trick that served me well in most circumstances. I endured their life as an outsider looking into my hell. It did not diminish my feelings about Sara and John, but it allowed my steel wall to be continuously built and fortified between us.

The fact that John and Sara had separated was mostly meaningless to me. Although I fully identified John as the perpetrator of the rapes, I had acute feelings about Sara distinct from John. I blamed her for her mental cruelty, the viciousness of her character and her seemingly unfilled need to humiliate me in any way she could. For me, Sara was the instigator of all the evil I had faced. This had been amply proven to me by the psychological aggression she carried out against me during John's long absences.

Sara secured a job as a counselor at the California Institute for Women in Chino, California. She and I moved with my dog Squire III to Cucamonga, California, located about forty miles closer to outer Los Angeles, next to Ontario. At the time, Cucamonga was sparsely populated with thousands of acres of orange orchards dominating the landscape. When I learned that Sara was taking me from Hemet, I was struck with a paralyzing fear. I knew that I was in the hands of a mad woman who could not control her rage and took little comfort that John was gone, but I was pleased with his departure. But as we arrived in Cucamonga, I was filled with trepidation that I would be left alone with her without anyone to intervene.

I needed a bridge to walk across to allow me to survive. I found that bridge once more in the public school I attended, with its caring principal and teachers. When I entered Cucamonga Junior High School it turned out to be a place where I flourished. On the first day I met with my new principal by myself, along with a new English teacher. He told me that Principal Acton had called him and told him all about me and my successes at my old school. I have no idea whether Principal Acton took it upon himself to mention his deep suspicions of the Hobsons as my "adoptive" parents, but given his deep distrust of the Hobsons, this could have easily occurred.

Whatever Principal Acton may have shared with my new principal, he managed to open a completely welcoming environment for me at my new school. My acceptance by the school and its teaching staff was immediate. There were very few other Mexican students in this predominantly white school, but I don't recall any instance of prejudice. Like my arrival at Little Lake, when I showed up at the new junior high, I was a source of great interest to the other students. The students knew I was young for my grade, and my small size confirmed it. I had confidence in my physical prowess, however, and I joined our school's baseball team. My reception quickly eroded my shyness, and I began my first friendships with two boys in my class. My stammer was coming under much better control, and I encountered only the occasional inability to speak. I was assigned the most caring of teachers, particularly in English and history, who carefully fed me additional books and texts to read to my heart's content.

My mental wall of steel was increasingly strong, allowing me to separate as best I could my existence from Sara. In John's absence, I found myself increasingly able to live outside Sara's cruel orbit. Sara and John had spent years refusing to talk to me for weeks at a time. This level of mental cruelty towards a young child was incalculable in its potential for permanent damage to one's soul. I had to learn at an early age to simply leave their world during these periods and to stay in my own world of the adobe graveyard and the chicken farm with its Mexican workers. It was not a sophisticated defense; it was all that I knew how to do. In Cucamonga, choosing silence against Sara was effortless by my age. Silence was my weapon of choice: my first and last resort and it gave me my first sense of power over her. Without the threat of sexual attacks from John, I felt I could outlast her. I did not see John again for nearly two years.

Sara enjoyed her work life at the California Institution for Women, and she chose to work long hours. Her work involved the assessment of incarcerated women and their eligibility for parole. Sara took pride in her reports to the Parole Board where the now

California Senator, Dianne Feinstein, presided. This gave Sara a sense of prestige since most of her recommendations before the Parole Board were accepted. Sara was a now single woman in her early fifties who had left a ten-year relationship with John. She had scant attention for me, a fact for which I was very grateful. Sara left early in the morning to commute twenty-five miles to Chino, which was then a predominantly agricultural area that surrounded this vast penitentiary for women. I visited her work only twice as she picked up papers and I remained in the parking lot. I never saw the inside of the prison, but the female prisoners were in full view in the yard. Viewing these prisoners in their uniforms was chilling to me. It reminded me of the threat that John and Sara had made to me often, that if I spoke with anyone about my kidnapping they would go to prison and I would be institutionalized or assigned to foster care, never to be found by the Salazars. It was not a stretch for me to envision Sara as a prisoner, but I was so fearful of foster care, of being permanently lost from my family, that my silence remained absolute.

On the job Sara made friends with her African-American colleagues. I do not know much about these friendships, but I was intimate with her colleagues' interracial affairs. This was the mid-1960s and interracial relationships were both condemned and hidden. Sara decided to use our tiny two-bedroom apartment as a place her friends could use for sex during their days off in the middle of the week. Sara provided these couples with a key to her apartment. I remember two sets of couples coming repeatedly and perhaps one more couple briefly using our home. I returned from school at 3:00 PM and often found complete strangers in my home. I was alone with them except for my dog, Squire III, who never left my side as these guests visited. The couples stayed in our apartment until Sara returned home late from work. My bedroom was immediately adjacent to Sara's bedroom, separated by only a small bathroom. When the couples were present, Sara's bedroom was filled with alcohol-tinged fueled laughter and the grunts and groaning of sex, sounds of which I was all too aware. I inherently knew the rules: silence was required, secrets were to be kept.

Sara went ahead with these sex arrangements without regard to the eleven-year-old boy who was left on his own to meet complete strangers in his home. I had already been brutalized by adult sex for over five years. Of course, dumping me in the midst of these trysts meant nothing to her. Indeed, after each couple had left after a contented bout of sex and drink, Sara never raised the issue of their presence with me when she returned home. She never asked me how I felt about these strangers and their couplings, nor did she explain why they used our apartment. I was nothing to her. I expected her indifference to me regarding these couples. It was just a continuation of her bizarre and unexplained behavior.

I knew without ever being told what the couples were there for. Since they were staying in my home for hours, I had to achieve some balance, some way to not be entirely lost while they were present. My only way to make these visits tolerable was to try to connect with these visitors. I was already seasoned at sex, I knew its dangers, but the couples were clearly not focused on having sex with me. This fact alone created an opening for me to interact with Sara's guests. My interactions with these couples were easier to accomplish than I initially feared. I realized that they were just as nervous about me and my reaction to their presence, as I was about them. The couples were quite embarrassed at first, trying to pretend everything was normal. I appreciated their attempts at warmth, particularly by the women who always introduced themselves as coworkers of Sara. The men were more awkward, not sure what role to take on with a strange eleven-year-old but wanting to ensure I did not get in the way. At no time were the men ever threatening or angry with me, placing me at modest ease with their presence.

I survived their visits on my own, shaped profoundly by this experience as I was shown another explicit window into adult sex. However, I was able to make the connection that whatever sex was going on was not against someone's will and more importantly did not involve children. As I adapted to these visits over a year, I concluded that these sexual encounters were ultimately not a direct threat to me. I survived my initial fears of the visits without great damage to my emerging strong will and efforts to maintain my independence from Sara.

If I had not created my own world outside of Sara, I would not have been able to survive the pain I had endured during my two years of isolation with her in Cucamonga. My junior high school transformed my life, gave me a sense of identity, and made me secure enough, despite my language issues, to give the class address for my graduation. I was starting to make friends with girls, and I came to love the weekly Friday noon dances. I had my first success at popularity and respect by my fellow students, treated not as an oddity but as an equal.

On one occasion I was unusually worried about a test I had just taken. I was accustomed to getting very high grades, and I was obsessed as a student about my performance on a daily basis, routinely asking my teachers about my latest test scores and worried about my grade point average. My history teacher was one of my favorites at the time, and I remember that he asked me to walk with him to his car. He just took me aside and told me to "just slow down" and that I "would be all right." He said that he knew I was going to be a success no matter what I did. I already had a relationship with him, but this quiet moment of absolute reassurance came at a critical moment for me and still gives me strength.

I had survived Sara's erratic behavior and her vicious mental manipulations for nearly two years before John returned to our lives. Sara claimed that she had seen John walking alongside a local freeway when she was driving. She said she recognized him and had no choice but to stop and take him home. That was the only explanation of their encounter that I was ever given when John reappeared only one month before I graduated from junior high.

When John arrived at our small two-bedroom apartment he was a physical wreck, with his face and neck deeply sunburned and unshaved. He had only the clothes on his back, wearing a windbreaker for warmth and soiled khakis. He was derelict, sweaty and needed a shower. I recognized him, but he looked completely defeated. Sara immediately got him to shower, handed him a towel to wrap around himself, and told him not to leave the bedroom until she returned. Sara rushed to wash his clothes in the apartment's public laundry and brought a quickly made sandwich to their now shared bedroom. Sara headed out for a quick shopping to buy clothes and shaving products.

The next day John awoke weary, with blurry eyes and needing a drink. He had little interest in food. The days passed as he made a slight attempt to dry out. Sara quickly returned to her own pattern of heavy nightly drinking with John. They both returned to the same old world of alcoholism that I had endured for years, only interrupted by John's two-year absence from our lives.

My resentment at John's return was extreme. I never believed Sara's story about finding him on a nearby freeway, convinced that she had sought him out. My hatred at his return would have totally enveloped me except that it was the last month of junior high. I had come through two years of increasing acceptance and had recently been voted class speaker. This was my first public address, and I was of course worried that my stammer would return during my speech. My focus was finishing school, giving my speech, and taking care of my adored dog.

Two days after graduation the Hobsons took Squire away from me without notice. I was told that they had found Squire a better home on a ranch for him to live. I was destroyed. Squire was the only source of uncompromising love I had encountered since being taken away from the Salazars six years earlier. I relied on his presence as absolute, finding every aspect of him reassuring. He was loyal and soothingly soft to the touch, my life's only source of physical affection. Squire adored me, and I loved Squire more than anything else that I had in my life.

Squire was irreplaceable, and I sensed that I would never again have another dog to protect me from the horrors of the Hobsons. When they took Squire from me, I was so wounded that I felt I was falling without any guard rails to protect me. I never doubted for a moment that the Hobsons were lying to me. I had no doubt that they did this callously, cruelly. It was an act that I believed was willful, calculated to eviscerate my increasing resistance to them. The sudden loss of my dog, my one reliable friend of nearly four years, was searing. I thought I had become strong and independent, but nothing prepared me for this permanent loss. For the moment, the Hobsons had won, and I fully returned to my status as a helpless victim.

Sara had done well at her job at CIW. I had no idea that she had applied for a position with Sargent Shriver in Washington D.C. In May of 1967, coinciding with the end of junior high, she received word she got the position. Sara was thrilled, but it required her to move to Arlington, Virginia. Once again, I was dragged along to a new place like a worn and battered suitcase. John accompanied Sara with the promise he would get a job in the building trades while she commuted to work in Washington DC to be part of Sargent Shriver's team.

I entered Hammond High in Arlington just after I turned twelve by a week. East Coast schools in 1967 were generally regarded as being one year ahead of West Coast schools academically. This time I had no Principal Acton to pave my way. I was just another student in the sea of a massive student body. I had just been torn from Cucamonga, leaving a supportive community behind. I was in mourning for the loss of my dog. Given my younger age for my grade and the more advanced freshman year curriculum, this first year was very challenging, but I was determined not to stumble in my studies.

The school numbered thousands of students housed in an enormous two-story structure a block in length, with large sports facilities attached to the school. It was a formal public school where the boys were required to wear sports coats and ties every day. The slight mixture of diversity in the student body was negligible. I don't recall meeting another Latino. My difficulties stemmed not from academics but were based on my extreme alienation from the other students due to my age and lack of physical maturity. There were two overpowering worries that I suffered from at Hammond High that made any connection with the student body impossible. I experienced new and unexplained social barriers, mysterious and overpowering to my mind and body. I was suddenly extremely attracted to the girls in my school, everywhere: in my class, the hallways, or large general assemblies. My eyes and mind were caught up in the pure romanticization of these girls. They were entrancing, with their soft skin and long hair as I ached to make sustained contact with them, talk to one or even make a female friend. I quickly realized, though, that no matter how bright I was, I simply could not compete with the older and larger boys. I was too young, barely a pre-teen among teenagers. I remained an oddity at Hammond High with these girls, never having a real chance to approach them.

I was frankly intimidated by the size of the boys in the high school. We had boys from age fourteen to eighteen years old, large strapping young men, some with full beards requiring daily shaving. I was acutely uncomfortable in the gym with these young men. I was still a young boy, with no signs of puberty. Back then we were required to change into our gym clothes, wear jock straps and take public showers. I walked down the middle of the unending rows of metal gym lockers, seeing these giants, often with their white penises visible. I did my best not to flee from this sight that flooded me with so many terrible images of white genitalia. Between the girls and these young men, I realized that my age made it impossible for me to fit in. Instead, I stayed by myself, neither acquired nor sought any friends, and worked hard at my studies.

I returned home on the school bus to encounter the Hobsons' familiar nightly drunken quarreling. I was still adjusting to John reentering our lives, something that I greatly resented. However, I was blessed with my own bedroom and unlimited books. I retreated to my room, apparently to the great satisfaction of Sara and John, who always seemed more content when I was out of their way. We were living in a two-bedroom middle class apartment, one of scores of identical units in suburban Arlington. Sara proudly drove to work in her Volvo every day to what she described as a very important executive position. The arrangement with John was that he was to leave the house with her every morning to look for work as a contractor. John swore that he spent every day looking for work and said that the construction trades were not hiring. This contrasted with the truth as Arlington was in the midst of a building boom in 1967. Nonetheless, John's lies persisted until April of 1968 when the next terrible crisis hit.

In just one evening in April of 1968, my world again crashed around me. I had days earlier received my grade point average for the year. I had a solid B if not a B-plus average. I achieved this despite my young age and all the circumstances of my home life. Within a few days of receiving my grades, Sara and John viciously pounced. It was a Thursday night in Arlington, and I came home to be told that we were leaving that night. Sara and John informed me that we had to leave because I had humiliated them with my grade point average. I was now a public disappointment, giving them no choice but to leave immediately that evening. I believed them.

I later found out that we left only because Sara had just been fired by Sargent Shriver's office. John had never sought work for even a single day while in Arlington, preferring to remain in his favorite dives. Nevertheless, the Hobsons never altered their story about my being solely responsible for their urgent departure. Instead, it now became part of their canon of abuse, a threatening refrain that but for my academic failure, we would have never had to leave town.

I watched as they finished packing in a frenzy, and I dutifully walked to my room to gather my clothes. It was not midnight when we left, but it was quite late. We drove out of town, heading to California, but stopped within two hours of our departure. John and Sara were tired, apparently broke and wanted to save money by not renting a motel. I remember staying awake most of the night in the back of that car, like the night when I was kidnapped at age four and taken to California. I couldn't understand why we needed to sleep on the roadside, rather than stay in a motel. I understood we were trying to save money, but it just seemed so odd to me to pull over and wait for dawn to break.

Once again, I knew something was terribly wrong and that our sudden departure made no sense. When we returned to California, my life was beset by the Hobsons' unrepentant alcoholism and stays in cheap roadside motels in Lodi and Stockton.

CHAPTER XII

Lodi, Stockton, and Room 204

IN APRIL OF 1968, the Hobsons decided to completely avoid Southern California and to instead locate in Northern California where they might find jobs. John and Sara were no longer young and vibrant. By 1968, John was sixty years old with a face showing the wear and tear of decades of uncontrolled alcoholism, his face blotched, his nose reddened and his eyes watery. John's darkly handsome good looks that prompted comparisons to Clark Gable were long gone. Sara in her fifties was mentally sinking into her own world, unable to accept the loss of her dream of working in Washington D.C. where she had just been fired by Sargent Shriver. Sara's face was aged beyond her years, with her own alcoholism taking its toll through premature wrinkles. Her lips were thin to begin with, but the decades of smoking four packs a day created deep lines around her mouth that dominated her face. Our only possession was the Volvo and the clothes we had packed. All of the furniture from our prior homes was lost to creditors, auctioned off, leaving not a shred, including the beautiful seascape painting we had lived with for years.

John and Sara heard there were jobs to be had in the Stockton area, located forty-five miles south of Sacramento. Sara held out hope that she could find work as an executive director of another organization, and John was confident that with his contracting and construction skills, he could again be able to secure employment. Sara remained permanently unemployed for the rest of her life. John was able to secure a job in Lodi, California, just twelve miles north of Stockton. Both Stockton and Lodi were located on the main regional freeway, Highway 99. It turned out that I would live on the frontage roads alongside Highway 99 in derelict motel rooms for the next four years. I never lived with the Hobsons again in an apartment.

We lived in the first motel for nine months. Its forty rooms were in a U-shaped structure made out of shabby beige painted slender bricks and spread out over an acre. It cost approximately fifty dollars a week. The motel had a large, generally empty parking lot. There was little highway traffic to draw in new guests to add to the approximately five or so permanent guests who lived there. We had a corner unit, with a decent size kitchen, one room with two large beds and a bathroom. It was a shock to me to live in a motel rather than an apartment or house, but I understood that the Hobsons were broke.

John never worked again as a general contractor. I overheard that he had problems with renewing his general contractors license and that he may have lost it following the multiple breaches of custom home contracts on his record. Instead, John's first job in Lodi was at the Johnston Tire Company, which made molds for tires used throughout the United States. A rare hint of normalcy arrived when John was hired as a quality control inspector and seemed content to work every day in a job that for him was easy.

It was from this isolated motel that I repeated the 9th grade during my first year at Lodi High School. I was both embarrassed and alienated by where I lived. I was unhappy about my school in general. I avoided speaking with anyone other than my teachers during the first year. I remember my isolation as I waited for the school bus to arrive. There were many homes surrounding our falling apart motel, so a half dozen or more students waited at the school bus stop. I refused to join them, both out of embarrassment about where I lived as well as my inability to explain the insanity of my "family" situation with Sara and John. This meant that for an entire first year I stayed across the street on the frontage road away from the other students, even during the rain when I had no umbrella.

I got on the bus and spoke with no one, knowing that there was little risk of anyone trying to reach out to me. The only positive for me on the bus is that I was introduced to popular music, a form that had been completely vilified by Sara and John. In our home they allowed only classical music or jazz. On the bus I heard rock and roll for the first time. It was Creedence Clearwater Revival and in that one moment, I was swept away by intoxicating music which spoke to me.

I was also out of sync by the clothing that the Hobsons mandated that I wear to high school. John and Sara insisted that I wear only black slacks and a white shirt every day, identical to the clothing I had worn at Hammond High School, but without a sports coat and tie. Lodi was an agricultural town with students who dressed informally. I stood out from the other students, the boys a sea of jeans, boots and white t-shirts, and the girls in mandated skirt lengths in the three permitted colors, blue, black, or white. In contrast, I dressed like someone ready to attend funeral services.

I had one overwhelming mental barrier which dominated my first year at Lodi High with its four-thousand-member student body divided by two campuses. I could not accept that I was having to repeat the 9th grade even though I had been only a month away from completing my freshman year at Hammond High School with either a B or B-plus average. I was furious that Sara and John yanked me out of school on a fake excuse. This made me lose a year of high school, delaying my progression to college and, more importantly, my plans to escape. I fixated on the loss of my freedom, forced to endure another needless year of high school and the Hobsons' torment. My attitude toward John and Sara was deep rage and embarrassment as I was forced to retake courses that I had already completed in Arlington. I never told my fellow students that I was repeating a full year, too ashamed to admit that I had failed to live up to the Hobson's oppressive standards for their "adopted son."

Lodi at the time was one of the most conservative grower towns in California, with its predominantly German and Italian population. Lodi was also one of the wealthiest towns per capita in the United States since large growers did their banking in Lodi. But its enormous wealth was limited to an elite, the rich grower community. The rest of the white community was divided up by a small professional class of teachers, attorneys, and doctors while the remainder of this population had average working class lives based on the Pacific Coast Producers, which in season employed over two thousand cannery workers. A limited number of Mexicans were allowed to work in these factories, considered by our community as the plum jobs in the region.

Lodi is famous for being the largest producer of Tokay grapes in the world. Growers routinely had tracts of grape fields well over five thousand acres, with bountiful rivers running alongside which were used for easy irrigation. During the picking season in Lodi, there would be an influx of hundreds of migrant workers to pick the grapes in the nearby fields. The Lodi growers were violently anti-union and considered the United Farm Workers' Union to be their nemesis. For years they threatened severe physical consequences if the UFW approached their workers. At the time, the UFW was focused on other more accessible areas of the Central Valley and Salinas, where unionization would eventually be won with great sacrifice and physical harm.

Racism was woven into every fabric of this wealthy town of approximately 22,000 people. In Lodi, no Mexicans were allowed to live within the city limits. We were relegated to living outside the city limits or to live in two nearby campesino-dominated towns of Acampo or Woodbridge. Throughout my time in Lodi and beyond, no African-Americans were allowed to stop in Lodi to even purchase gas. Somehow, they were always spotted in Lodi and immediately one to two police cars then showed up, refused them service, and immediately escorted their vehicles back to the freeway following the cars out until they had left our city limits. These racist policies were well-known to all, and for years nothing could break Lodi's monolithic racial walls.

Emblematic of its conservative roots was Lodi's tolerance of outright racist organizations that had a violent ideology. One example is Lodi and its neighboring town, Galt, which permitted a right-wing military-style militia to exist for decades in the region. This militia was a proudly white supremacist, ultra-right national association whose mere presence and acceptance of its race-baiting was not only tolerated but allowed to flourish.

Lodi carefully sustained policies with negative racial impacts in its educational system. I attended a high school of 4,000 students, each with a graduation class of 1,000 students. In my class about

200 were Chicanos. Lodi High had a system of educational tracking. This was the prevalent educational method of sorting students into curriculum tracks based on their future occupations and supposedly objective testing criteria, but in reality, it was a system of class and race internal educational segregation. It resulted in severely restricting Chicano student access to either honors or college advancement courses. In my year only two Chicano students were allowed access to these courses, despite the large number of Chicano students who could have prospered in such a program. I surprisingly enough was immediately designated as one of the two students.

This racist structure meant that for all the four years, I was only one of two Chicanos in honors or advanced placement college courses, surrounded by affluent white German and Italian students, some of whom had adopted their parents' and grandparents' racist views. There were exceptions that made this situation livable since many of the honor students were from more middle- and working-class non-grower environments, and they had the common sense to be genuinely concerned with the racist conservatism of their school. My close friends would come from this pool of people and eventually sustain me once I opened up in my sophomore year.

There was one other important saving grace about my education at Lodi High. There were many new and talented teachers who did not come from the region, many instead being from the more progressive Bay Area. These excellent teachers provided a fresh liberal view of the world built on the social movements of the day. By doing so, this small retinue of progressive new teachers provided an effective antidote to Lodi's racist culture.

My self-isolation in this first year from other students had the effect of making me focus intently on my studies. I was so upset at repeating the ninth grade that I had an even heightened state of anxiety about the need to be a perfect student or risk failing another grade again. At home the Hobsons continued to ridicule me for my alleged failures in Arlington, grinding away at my ego. They were both hysterical at their economic position and their housing situation and it was convenient for them to use me as a whipping boy for their own failures. This environment was there when I woke up and greeted me when I returned from school.

My only answer to their sadistic attempts to make me the focus of their troubles was to excel in school. I could tell that I exceeded the expectations of my teachers, and they took notice of me. The attitudes of my teachers changed from tolerance of my Chicano presence to recognizing that they might have a student worthy of their attention. I took nothing for granted, but I was smart enough to embrace the teachers' newfound confidence in me. As before with my education, I read every textbook twice and discovered a new form of effective note taking, bringing me more success on exams. I had the benefit of an advanced vocabulary; I could write adequately for my grade. I was driven to never be caught out as unprepared.

My initial resentment at being placed in the 9th grade began to fade as I saw that I was going to have a successful year. This did not mean that I talked to my fellow students. They learned that approaching me was fruitless. I responded to their overtures by nodding my head or making the most limited responses possible. The students were aware of my academic abilities, and my limited interaction was somehow understandable given my younger age and my circumstances. I was obviously not a mean person, just one who came off as being deeply insecure, out of place and working hard just to survive in this bewildering new environment.

I finished my first year at Lodi High with solid grades and an emerging sense of confidence in myself to survive the 10th grade. Despite all of the hardships of this first year, my life had the first hint of becoming stable, something I could work with. John was employed, Sara seemed more under control, and I was looking forward to summer school. It took only a moment before my life was severely altered and we would plunge into further poverty. John was fired from the Johnston Tire Company for alcoholism. We had no source of money. The Hobsons had to find an even cheaper motel immediately. They chose the cheapest motel available for twenty miles on Highway 99. It was called the El Rancho Motel located directly on the frontage road abutting the freeway on the edge of Stockton.

When we moved into the El Rancho Motel in May of 1969, it cost three dollars and fifty cents a night or twenty-five dollars a week.

The El Rancho remains unchanged to date, still intact and in business. It is located on the frontage road of Highway 99 and has a tall, arrow-shaped electronic sign that was lit with bulbs at night. It is an L-shaped motel, single story, made out of bricks painted white, with large square pillars of brick in front of each room holding up the roof. The El Rancho has a pseudo-Mexican look, holds about twenty-five rooms, had a small pool surrounded by a lawn and ample roadside parking for truck rigs.

We lived in the motel's sole corner unit, Room 204, for three full years. It was about two hundred square feet with limited furnishings made from pinkish colored metal. Our dingy cream-colored room held one large armchair, one small metal chair without arms, an outdated tv, and a metal chest of drawers with a pullout table for eating. The two beds, one regular size, the other a single bed were only eighteen inches apart from each other and had matching pink metal bed frames. There was the smallest of corner kitchens, maybe six feet by six square feet at the most. One corner was so limited it could only hold a skinny four-burner stove. On the other side was a small white metal unit that held a tiny wash sink, two drawers for utensils with cupboards underneath and metal cabinets above. The room had one tiny closet. Our bathroom was about eight feet square, tucked away into an awkward alcove, with a cramped shower in the corner, a toilet, and small bathroom basin. The bathroom looked out on the ten acres of walnut orchards located directly behind the El Rancho. I spent hours in this orchard, exploring its beauty, enjoying its much-needed privacy as I walked along the large irrigation channel that ran beside this property.

In the middle of the motel was a small, wood-paneled office, with heavily worn furniture that was musty from years of use. Yet even this office served as a refuge from the confines of our room. I was intrigued by the ancient telephone system with a full plug-in board to connect with each room. In my free time, the clerk, usually one of the two married managers or their bored grandchildren, allowed me to work the telephone board as an operator to my contentment.

John and Sara fared very poorly at the El Rancho Motel. Their lives were now defined by poverty, obvious mental illness and rampant nightly alcoholism often ending in the familiar torture of

John. We only survived by John picking up weeklong jobs on construction crews or evening jobs remodeling and repainting offices.

John's fall from grace reduced him to an almost unrecognizable state of a poorly dressed, unkempt man. The contrast with his former self was severe. Even during the Hemet years, John, when he wasn't disappearing for months at a time to return diminished from his benders, had been a careful and prideful dresser. Each workday he had worn carefully pressed khaki slacks and white or blue dress shirts. During the fall and winter months he took care selecting from a large collection of lightweight Pendleton wool shirts, beautifully tailored with flaps covering the pockets. But nothing could compete with John's dress clothing, which he favored for the Hobsons' trips to Palm Spring with its glamourous cocktail clubs and jazz orchestras. John had a profound interest in music. He was an accomplished pianist, playing the classic standards and show tunes to accompany his rich baritone voice. John also played the guitar and had some basic knowledge of the saxophone. John was driven by his music and had a passion for ballroom dancing, which he performed with a lightness and grace. When he went out to clubs, John had donned the most expensive suits, fresh dress shirts, and gorgeous embroidered or tightly woven narrow knit ties common to the day. He was fastidious in his tailored look. John's tastes were sophisticated, much ahead of the limited scope of Hemet but perfect for their jaunts to the nightclubs of Palm Springs.

For these outings Sara had dressed up in luxurious cocktail outfits, often matching jackets and tuxedo pants cut slightly higher above the ankle, or rich linen or multicolored silk dresses, paired with intricate jeweled evening bags. During their Palm Springs visits, I was usually limited to watching them as they walked out the door in their elegant dress, leaving me alone. I did accompany them three to four times. I have no idea how I was even permitted to enter these clubs given my age, but the Hobsons were persuasive in insisting that I be allowed to stay. They then ordered me a Shirley Temple, a non-alcoholic sweetish drink as I sat between them in large, curved red vinyl booths surrounding the stage. My introduction to big band and other jazz styles of music as I watched these acts perform eventually helped form my own identity as a future musician. I usually drifted off to sleep during these Palm Spring evenings, generally overtired, yet at times awake enough to watch our return during the fifty-mile trip back to Hemet.

John's perspective on wealth came initially from his very affluent life in Indianapolis, Indiana where his family had started a successful trucking business that crashed during the Great Depression. At the time, John was in the midst of attending Purdue University as an engineering major and told the story that he left because of the Crash. John equally emphasized that he chose to leave Purdue after his junior year to devote himself to automobiles and to the activities surrounding the Indianapolis 500. John eventually moved to the West Coast to live the life of a playboy, occasionally interspersed with his career as a general contractor for custom homes and buoyed by handouts from his aunts.

Sara, during her early daily writing days in Hemet, took her look equally seriously. She always took great care in her dress, with pressed blouses, tailored slacks, and the most expensive shoes available in our region. Although Sara, a short, slender woman, was not a natural beauty, she had an exotic quality enhanced by her unusual green eyes, beautifully cut stylish short hair, and an eye for selecting chic clothes. Sara continued her refined sense of elegance dressing for both her counseling jobs at the California Institute for Women for two years as well as meeting the formal dress requirements of her work with Sargent Shriver in Washington D.C.

Sara's expensive tastes were also based on a very affluent background, one that even eclipsed John's access to wealth. Sara came from a wealthy Southern family headed by her stepfather, Dr. Mathews, who was in charge of tuberculosis eradication for the State of Texas. Sara's mother was an early example of women elected to public office, serving as the first woman on the Houston School Board. Sara's wealth continued when she married Jim, a Standard Oil executive. They lived among the ruling class in Colombia and Venezuela for nine years. Jim died of throat cancer shortly after their return to the states in 1950. Sara did not remarry for about three years until she met John in San Pedro, where her family lived. They quickly married and after some years moved to Phoenix.

Sara recalled those Latin American years fondly. She often boasted to me about the large custom homes she had built from the ground up, preselecting every piece of furniture before the two of them moved in. In Latin America, ruling class women such as Sara not only had a host of servants, but also open access to the finest tailors in the country. Such women were immaculately dressed, perfectly coifed and pampered, carrying the region's famously supple leather bags that completed this classic Latin American look.

Both John and Sara had complete disdain for middle class people but fetishized the "working class" as part of their leftist ideologies. They fancied themselves some version of communist or Trotskyist; this aspect of their past was never really clear. What dominated was their ruling class attitude and their genuine disrespect for my family of origin, the Salazars.

By the time we arrived at the El Rancho Motel in the Spring of 1969, the façade of wealth had evaporated, and the Hobsons were caught in the growing realization that they were trapped. Near poverty became their permanent new status. The Hobsons realized there was likely no hope of returning to their previously affluent life, having lost all the possessions they had accumulated over the years. At the El Rancho Motel, things fell apart quickly for both John and Sara in their appearances. John no longer wore pressed khaki or ironed shirts to work. Now being forced to work as a mere carpenter on a crew rather than as a general contractor, John began to wear old work trousers, wearing the same shirt several days in a row. He began to shave much less often but still continued to wash daily and make himself more presentable in the evening before he started to drink.

Sara's reaction instead took the darkest of turns, spinning out of control with nothing to hold her increasingly depressed mind together. My most graphic and deeply disturbing images are of the complete deterioration of Sara's personal appearance. Sara no longer had fastidious daily or evening outfits. Her wardrobe had been reduced to what she had managed to pack in our small Volvo car as we returned from Washington D.C.: two large suitcases of clothing and a sack of shoes. Sara allowed herself to become completely disheveled, so different from the elegant woman whom I had known for so many years. She had dentures available to her, but upon our arrival she refused to ever use them again. Seeing this crazed white woman, toothless by choice, unable to control her frustrations and anger, made her almost unrecognizable to me. She became agoraphobic and rarely left the confines of Room 204 for close to two years.

Sarah only got dressed and showered about two days a week. She engaged in a disturbing ritual that showed how far her mind had slipped. Sara always disrobed in the same manner with what seemed to me to be a clear sense of angry rebellion against her circumstances. As a young adolescent, particularly given my six-year history of the Hobson's sexual abuse following my kidnapping, I was repulsed by seeing her willful display of nudity. I was helpless to stop her glaring eyes peering off into her inaccessible world. Sara always started to disrobe in the middle of our tiny motel room until she was completely naked in front of me. There was no place for me to avoid her disrobing and nudity, either when I was alone or when John was present. Once out of the shower, Sara took her time to slowly dress in front of me as she put on her bra and underwear, managing to look at me for a reaction out of the corner of her eyes.

She never failed to try to shock or affect me in a negative way as she carried out these aggressive acts. She was openly arrogant about her full nudity being exposed to her thirteen-year-old boy. It seemed to me such an act of mental violence, and I tried to purge the sightings of her body from my mind, but her pattern never changed as she antagonized me with her nudity, knowing I openly despised her. These scenes were profoundly disturbing to me. I considered her nudity as another example of the sexual abuse I had lived with. I had seen the penises of John and his pedophile associates since the age of four, but I had never seen a naked girl or woman. Seeing the body of a fully grown woman, one that was heavily aged, coupled with her deteriorating face and constantly moving eyes was about as frightening as I could handle from her. I was stunned that this had occurred even once, but to have it become a theme for all three years, repeated over and over again, was a level of visual abuse that was particularly difficult for me to overcome.

At the El Rancho Motel, Sara seemed to have actually lost her mind. I felt helpless as Sara became increasingly forlorn, actually pathetic in her gripping depression. Sara and John drank every night, with John sitting in his chair, working his way into his preferred stupor state of mind while drunk. Sara always joined in every evening, excessively drinking her scotch and smoking heavily. Sara and John filled our small motel room with smoke from the seven packs of Benson & Hedges they smoked each day. When money was scarce it was my job to make cigarettes for them. They bought bags of tobacco and two-dollar cigarette rolling machines, and I made cigarettes by the score.

There was little room for Sara to pace, but she used what few feet we had to walk back and forth so that she could hover over John. Her true intentions never changed. Sara was at her core a sadist, and she gleefully returned to torturing John in the identical manner that she had been doing since Hemet. She started to again put her cigarettes out in his forearms, already heavily scarred from her prior burning of his flesh while drunk. But she began to use a truly chilling new torture, one that caused blood to run down his arms, staining his shirt and clothing. Sara had a small paring knife. She decided that she could control the tip of it sufficiently to allow tiny stabs in his arms, occasionally moving to his upper chest. They miraculously never seemed to go very deep, often just enough to break the skin and cause blood to drain out. John then cried uncontrollably, not moving while Sara in a crazed state took obvious delight in hurting him with the knife. I had become accustomed to years of her relentless torture of John in his helpless drunken state, but I could not absorb her newfound depravity. Sara's madness, John's drunkenness and these assaults that went on for all three years defined my life with the Hobsons. Despite all the terrible things the Hobsons had done to me, they had impressed upon me over the years that they were my "adoptive parents." And from the age of four on, they were the only adults who were consistently in my life. Indeed, on each new school application throughout my life, I had the humiliation of them identifying themselves as my "parents," rather than Jesus and Petra Salazar. Now they had carried me to a place that was so brutal, emotionally destructive and impoverished in every way that I was at the edge of an abyss. All I knew was that I had to find a way to survive and ultimately to escape from them.

I could not study in room 204. There I was surrounded by abuse and alcoholism. I had to find a quiet, warm place to study at the motel. It turned out that the motel's laundry room was the one place which offered that possibility. This became my main place of study every day for the next three years. The laundry room had a long narrow passageway used for storing old beds. At the end of this semi-darkened hallway was a washing machine and dryer for the guests to use. The machines were located in a room with space enough to hold only one commercial washer and dryer. This little room was brightly lit, made warm by the machines. I did not resent studying there. I was just grateful to have this quiet place where I could get away from the Hobsons' rapidly deteriorating mental condition. I liked to sit on the dryer when it was not being used. If it was being used, I sat on the washing machine waiting for the drying cycle to end. For me, the drying cycle made this tiniest of rooms warm and cozy. It did not matter to me that I never had a chair or a table. I simply ran with this opportunity as a place of my own that allowed me to intensely focus on whatever material I was studying. As guests used these facilities, I moved out of the way, saying hello at this short disturbance and feeling grateful when they left. This laundry room was my place of refuge from the Hobsons, even from the motel itself, because I could find privacy, something I needed to survive the twisted life the Hobsons were living.

There was one other family who lived at the very front of the motel for several years, consisting of two elderly grandparents and their uniquely beautiful granddaughter, Cathy. She was seventeen years old and had long auburn hair, a wide, welcoming smile, and piercingly clear blue eyes. Parked in front of their tiny apartment was a perfectly conditioned light blue 1962 four-door Cadillac with a white interior. I came to greatly admire this Caddy. Their tiny apartment was in my eyes so superior to our Room 204. They had a miniscule front room where you could actually sit and talk to everyone at the same time, with two separate bedrooms. The family was very friendly to me, and Cathy took me under her wing. She was considerably older than I, determined to go to college and clearly saw me as just a young kid. We never left the motel grounds but took walks in the walnut orchard and went swimming in the small pool together. I took comfort in knowing her, felt pangs of sexual attraction, but knew my age placed me out of her league. Instead, I was grateful to have another young person, especially a friendly older girl, living at the motel. Cathy was someone to whom I did not have to explain my circumstances but instead shared my life at the El Rancho.

Other than our two families, there were two resident truck drivers who used the motel as their home base for trucking gigs. The El Rancho was known for miles on the Highway 99 route as the cheapest place in the area to accommodate Central Valley truckers and their rigs. This meant that most motel guests were truck drivers seeking shelter for the night and a place to heavily drink themselves into a stupor as they greeted other truck drivers on the identical routes they had just traveled. These truck drivers were all men, earned better than average wages and had money to spare to hire prostitutes. It was common that the motel was flooded in the evening with prostitutes arriving in the truckers' rooms for their private parties. I remember the faces of the women who arrived, never hiding their presence but with a level of comfort and sense of security as they worked the motel. All the prostitutes were white, and I never met a non-white trucker who was allowed to stay at our motel.

Although I technically now lived on the outskirts of Stockton rather than Lodi, the Lodi school district had a school bus stop across from the motel. Lodi High's district extended to this area which included the nearby affluent Morada neighborhood where scores of Lodi students lived. Their homes were some of the richest custom homes in both Stockton or Lodi, often appearing as mini estates on two-acre sections of land with pools and land-scaped yards. I befriended the daughter of one Mexican family who lived just outside this neighborhood in a middle class home. Other than this one family living on the margins of Morada, everyone else was white. Surrounding this very affluent region was an exceptionally large working-class area which abutted the inexpensive lands alongside Highway 99. Here the homes were filled with teachers and workers living in everyday homes that you might find in a barely middle class rural neighborhood. My closest friends would emerge from these two neighborhoods, pro-viding deep and unquestioned friendship and support that we have shared together all our lives.

I was humiliated by where I lived. I could not conjure up any excuse for my dire home surroundings or how far we had fallen financially. To stand in front of this cheap, obviously suspect motel with its well-known reputation was terrible. It was September of 1969, when my sophomore year began, and I recall my embarrassment as I waited for the empty school bus to arrive in front of the towering motel sign. Charlie, the young white bus driver for the next three years, took an instant dislike of me. This may have been based on Charlie's racist views as well as his resentment at picking up a poor child at such a location. Although I was always the first and last one on his bus, Charlie's behavior made it abundantly clear that I was cheap Mexican trash, who lived in the cheapest motel in the area, to him. I was unworthy of even basic conversation. When I was alone on the bus, Charlie ridiculed the motel where I lived and shamed over the notorious truckers and prostitutes who used the El Rancho motel. I had the oddest of reaction to this bus driver's attitude toward me. It was only by my own internal insistence that I not rise to the bait of his taunts that I endured his rough treatment of me.

CHAPTER XIII

Field Work, Cesar Chavez, and Trotsky

DESPITE MY DIFFICULT LIVING CIRCUMSTANCES, in the summer of 1969, I was not defeated by the Hobsons. I was not a broken adolescent. I had already managed to recapture the fortification of my identity, and I gathered all my strength to survive. There were areas in which I was leagues ahead for my age, the brutality of my kidnapping and abuse forcing me into an advanced maturity about the world and its evils. This maturity gave me an edge to figure out new ways to exist on my own and block out the Hobsons' madness. I reached back to the blessings of kindness I had received from my Salazar family who taught me how to love. I called on the memory of the unequivocal support from the principal and teachers at Little Lake Elementary School, and the love of Jaime and Maria Elena, my Mexican family at the Ranch. I remembered the kindness and support I received during junior high, where the principal and teachers built my academic confidence.

I had finished my first year at Lodi High, and I had done well. I had my foundation in place. I knew that I was no longer the four-year-old mute, terrified child the Hobsons had abused at will. I was a thirteen-year-old with a voice, and I would speak up. I placed the Hobsons in a mental box that created for me a well-designed permanent distance from their downfall. My north star had never changed since my abduction. I wanted to go home to the Salazars to see my family again, to greet my brothers and sisters. Most important to me was to see my mother Petra and to tell her I was back home. My north star was practical. Survive three more years, abandon the Hobsons by going to college and then never see them again.

The summer of 1969 came together more naturally than I ever thought possible. I had the opportunity to return to my Chicano roots through my discovery of a new Mexican family. I also began a profound political transformation that I carried with me all my life. As before in my moments of profound crisis, I needed a bridge to cross to a better place in order to survive this new hell of the El Rancho Motel. Again, I was saved unexpectedly by a Chicano family who lived in a small two-bedroom single row trailer located directly behind the last room of the motel. I met the Ramirez family within a few days of my May 1969 arrival when school had just finished. The Ramirez family consisted of two very warm traditional Chicano parents with four children, some younger and others close to my age. Wattie became my close friend, a rotund, friendly eleven year-old boy, with a warm and funny personality. We hit it off right away. This family embraced me and became the substitute Salazars for me in these exceedingly difficult times.

Mr. and Mrs. Ramirez welcomed me into their family, as if they sensed my deep need. I told them about the Salazars, and they were saddened by my story but reassured by our connection. My farm-worker roots made me one of them and they essentially adopted me for the period I was at the El Rancho Motel. They invited me to share every meal, to spend time playing with their children, and to use my Spanish. Within two weeks, the local picking season began, and they had me ask Sara and John whether I could accompany them to the fields. Sara and John were so wrapped up in their own world of worry and financial downfall that they eventually overcame their initial deep racist resentment that I choose to pick fruit. They did not grant permission without their pound of flesh. They screamed that after all they had done for me that I was now choosing to be a farmworker, just like the filthy Salazars had done all their lives. I was called a familiar word used by them, an ungrateful "Spic" and that there was nothing worse than being a field hand. Despite their all-consuming rage against me, they were more content to have me away from them during this initial summer. They allowed me to go with this family every day. It provided me with the essential alternative family and Chicano identity that I needed to survive the Hobsons. Just like being at home with the Salazars, we followed an identical wake up and departure schedule. I was never late and looked forward to every day, no matter how difficult and tiring the farm work might become. Señora Ramirez made the familiar breakfast and lunch tortillas for me and her family. We had a similar station wagon that we drove to the fields.

Most of the children spoke both English and Spanish, but the conversations throughout the day were always in Spanish, allowing me an opportunity to continue to use my language and grow my vocabulary. Although I often carried out a private internal dialogue in Spanish as I described to the Salazars, particularly my mother Petra, where I was, what was happening to me so she would understand, I had not had Spanish available to me for over two years. This had deeply affected me, as Spanish sustained my spirits and preserved my identity as a Chicano. When I returned to my Spanish and natural Chicano culture with the Ramirez family, it provided such a wave of relief that it soothed my grief from the loss of the Salazars.

I was grateful that this farm work was carried out without the abuses we suffered at my father's hand in Phoenix. In the Central Valley the Ramirez family and I were obviously there to work and to make as much money as possible. At the same time, we did not have the pressure of Jesus' abusive timekeeping and the belittlement and cold treatment he gave his family that had made each workday miserable. Instead, Mr. Ramirez was kind to both his wife and his older children who worked the fields alongside me. He worked hard, but unlike Jesus, he treated us well, had a friendly countenance, and sense of humor throughout the workday.

The Ramirez family worked with a contractor in a crew of about forty other workers. The contractor determined where we worked on any given day or week, and we followed wherever he took us. It ran from fruit picking for the commercial market to fruit dumping to preserve artificially high prices for such produce. One example was a three-week assignment where we worked a cherry orchard that was about one hundred acres in size. We were told to arrive earlier than normal at 4:30 AM and to immediately turn off all lights, particularly car lights and to keep quiet.

At the first hint of breaking light, we were instructed to rush quietly out into the cherry orchard, given tall ladders to pick the fruit in utter silence for the entire day. There were none of the familiar cat calls, the friendly ongoing conversation which nurtured us during the long days of work. The usual blaring of competing radios playing our favored Mexican Norteñas and Rancheras to keep us alert and productive had to be silenced. As workers we had no choice but to work in this alienating work environment or risk losing our jobs to be immediately replaced by other workers.

Multiple bulldozers were placed through the cherry orchard. They had already dug most of the two-hundred- to three-hundred-foot-long trenches that were about five feet deep. Our role was to pick the fruit in silence and dump our filled buckets in half ton crates. Once both sides of a large cherry row were completed, the forklifts arrived. They took each of the half-ton boxes which were filled with perfect, sumptuous cherries ready for market and approached the large trenches alongside each set of major rows. We witnessed our fruit being dumped into the trenches, fruit in perfect condition that had required our hard labor to pick. We looked with astonishment initially as we saw our hard work being discarded. We were not allowed to take any of the surplus fruit for our families. This is something which seemed natural to do, but even this small gesture was not permitted to the workers who had picked the fruit.

During this first summer, Mr. Ramirez never asked for or took a cut of my wages, despite my surviving on his food and his family's goodwill. I would have gladly handed all my money to him because I was so grateful to be included. Surprisingly, Sara and John never asked me about my wages or asked me to give them the money I earned. Since this was the first money I had ever had, I was extremely careful in saving nearly every dime. I kept the money I had earned in my shoes, allowing myself two dollars a week to buy soda and candy from the motel's machines.

I made one major purchase with my first summer's wages, buying something so unusual that it surprised even me. I somehow managed to get a ride with a set of the Morada students, many of whom were in the same honors classes I attended. Although everyone in the area knew I lived in this derelict motel, I had conjured up a lie to cover up why we were there. I told them that

John and Sara were managers of the motel. I thought this just might be considered an acceptable story to explain my circumstances. I do not know if the honor students ever believed my story, but it went unchallenged. Throughout the three years I remained at the motel, no friend ever raised a question about my family's situation or questioned me about why I was living there. Instead, my friends picked me up at the frontage road. It turned out that in the four years of living at the two motels, I never allowed a single student to enter where I lived.

I felt a rare pride going shopping with my newfound friends with my own money to spend. They seemed much more attracted to regular student clothing, such as jeans, shorts, tennis shoes and equivalent items for the girls, than the students in the much more formal high school in Arlington, Virginia where sports coats and ties were required. I had spent my first year at Lodi as an oddity standing out in my black slacks and white shirts the Hobsons forced me to wear each day. I wanted a different look, but I was unsure what that look might be and where to acquire it. It turned out that this Stockton outdoor mall where we were shopping had a traditional store for men. We all walked in and no one else bought anything in the store but me. I saw a light brown suede sports coat, and I was overcome with its beauty and sophistication. The correct size was available and fit my slim frame perfectly. It cost ninety-nine dollars, and I bought it with my summer earnings. I then wore this jacket every day from my sophomore year on. I was the sole student to wear a sports coat at my school, and it became my signature look.

We were also looking for cheap surplus army clothing. It was available and popular given the ongoing Vietnam War, with army wear considered a cool style. We went to the heart of downtown Stockton and found a block with two or three army surplus clothing stores. They were filled with sailor pants, blue and brown work shirts, and army jackets, as well as portable water jugs and eclectic military surplus gear. We did our best to clear the stores out because we were drawn to the look they offered and the incredibly cheap prices.

It is here that I found the second half of my look that would carry me through my high school years, always replenished each year by new clothing items from these same surplus stores. I bought several identical brown and blue work shirts, long sleeved with collars, along with a couple of jeans. My look was coming together, and it made me much more accessible from my sophomore year on. I came to take my new look very seriously as only a young man can. I knew my circumstances, both the good and the bad. I had to create a completely different identity, a fresh persona entirely distinct from the Hobsons. I needed a way to return to Lodi High, showing through my clothing alone my newfound confidence to survive in a conservative, affluent and outright racist high school.

My experience picking fruit that first of my four summers doing farm work became a defining moment, a catalyst that began my radicalization as a young man. We worked in terrible conditions, often with a belligerent contractor who felt confident of his God-like authority. We worked with limited filthy portable bathrooms, causing the men and women to often relieve themselves in the field rather than face the disgusting conditions of the toilets. Cool water was always in short supply as it was kept warm in metal corrugated containers and had a metallic taste to match. Picking fruit is hard, unforgiving work, involving overworked backs, tired legs and heavy arms needed to delicately pick the fruits as determined by the grower. The growers did nothing to improve our working conditions. They seemed oblivious to the sacrifice workers made to just survive and earn barely enough to feed their families. Emblematic of their total lack of basic humanity was their constant use of carcinogenic pesticides, often sprayed as we picked the Central Valley's abundant produce. The workers were just inputs, like seeds, fertilizer, and other costs of bringing crops to market.

My resentment at these deeply oppressive work conditions was familiar to me. I remembered the farm work carried out by my Salazar family, the wretched work conditions as we picked vegetables and fruit in the oppressive heat of Phoenix. In the Central Valley the conditions were no different. The rows of cars lining up to work were the same rows of cars in the Phoenix fields I saw as a baby at age two and a half. I remembered the exhaustion of my family when they came home every day, making clear the connection with their working conditions and my conditions in California.

I decided to fight back in the only way I could imagine. I knew I needed to somehow improve our conditions in the fields. We as farmworkers needed more protection from the pesticides, as well as better toilets, to be permitted to use our full breaks and lunch periods, and most of all to secure fair wages. Although my thoughts were not remotely fully formed given my age and experience, I was determined by this first summer of picking fruit to become some kind of representative, maybe a spokesman for farmworkers. I did not have any idea what role my advocacy might take. I just knew that I had to do something in my life about injustice in the fields, something to protect the Salazars, the Ramirezs and others like us as we worked. I had no idea where this journey might take me, but I had an idea where it would start. I knew that finishing my education in order to help farmworkers was key to helping our people.

My choice to publicly become pro-farmworker in the overwhelming anti-farmworker towns of both Lodi and Stockton, turned me into a reviled student by the Lodi High School administration as my views became well known. I had already heard about the United Farm Workers' Union in the fields where I worked, as their unionization attempts throughout the Central Valley were legendary. During this first summer, I began to seek out contacts in Stockton so I could become part of the UFW movement. For Lodi, my interest in the UFW could not have been a stronger repudiation of the overwhelming anti-union views held by the powerful growers.

My radicalization during this first summer was also a product of the Vietnam war as the United States was convulsed in controversy, with thousands of our soldiers dying in battle. The anti-war movement was growing in strength throughout the country, even affecting our conservative Central Valley. I began to learn of the scope of the division within our country by reading the local paper, *The Stockton Record*. In the motel office, I could borrow that day's newspaper and catch up on world events, which often focused on the anti-war movement. Although an anti-war position was considered radical for the entire Central Valley, an anti-war position made sense to me. I realized that nearly everyone had a position on the Vietnam War and that protests were taking place across the country, particularly in San Francisco.

I read about an anti-war demonstration to be held in Stockton. It would be the first demonstration of many that I attended.

I convinced my Morada friends, some of whom were quite liberal, to attend this event. I was surprised by the number of people who showed up near the university to protest. It was a combination of students and regular people, maybe numbering five hundred to a thousand. To me it looked both overwhelming and exciting. I listened to the rally leaders speak against the war and was convinced that resisting the war was the only correct thing to do. I was not alone in this feeling because the liberal students with whom I had attended the rally were cautiously becoming anti-war as well.

At the rally there were many banners, several veterans against the war and eloquent speakers whose rally cries and chants were intoxicating. Then Cesar Chavez came to the stage, and that moment was a turning point in my life. When he began to speak, he immediately captured the complete and almost reverential attention of the protesters. I absorbed every word delivered with his quiet immoveable determination, the clarity and certainty of what I immediately recognized as a shared cause that was central to my own identity. Hearing him tell the history of the sacrifices of farmworkers, the lengthy protest fasts where he placed his life in danger for La Causa, reached me to the core. I listened intently to him as he described the violence in the fields, the efforts to improve conditions via unionization and his invitation to any and all to support justice in the fields. I did not know that in a short time, I would have the honor to meet him, to tell him the story of the Salazar family and that he recognized a strength in me that at the time I did not know I possessed. I did not meet him that day, but I stayed with the farmworkers present and knew that the UFW would be the vehicle I would use to advocate for my people. I met Cesar within a few months, and I had no idea that I would have a relationship with him spanning over twenty years.

One more major thing occurred by happenstance at the rally which further refined my new radical identity. At the demonstration, I met both Stockton liberals from various churches as well as radical left-wing organizers seeking to recruit new members. I came across such a group that was extremely friendly to me. It was the Socialist Workers Party, "SWP," a Trotskyist organization. To me, these Trotskyists presented a logical and refined understanding of the world. They explained the basics of Trotskyism, and I was deeply impressed that Trotsky was assassinated in Mexico for being against censorship in any form.

I did not realize at the time I was looking for a model to understand the world. The SWP presented an all-in-one ideology, their world view simplified for recruitment purposes. I was ripe for the plucking, recruitment as a young socialist giving me an identity that I needed at the time. I was offered a free subscription to their newspaper called *The Militant*, along with encouragement to sell their newspaper at my school. I decided to accept their offer and soon I was receiving twenty-five to fifty packets of newspapers every month or so. I was instructed to try to sell them at twenty-five cents apiece, but to not worry about actual sales. Instead, my role was to explain their headlines, mostly anti-war at the time and to just give away *The Militant* if there was any discernible interest in reading it. I took this responsibility seriously, and I daily sold the paper or gave it away at my profoundly conservative high school for my remaining high school years.

Prior to returning to the 10th grade in the Fall of 1969, I was focused on how to shed the black and white uniform forced upon me by the Hobsons during my first year. The Hobsons were hysterical about my new clothing purchases and made every attempt to try to prevent me from wearing them. But I had already crossed to the far side of hatred for both of them. I decided I would just dare them to physically challenge me, to leave my face bruised to be potentially exposed at school. I called their bluff in this pathetic, suffocating Room 204. The Hobsons realized they could do nothing to force me to wear their preferred uniform. I built on this successful rebellion as I did my best to navigate away as far as possible from their crushing lives.

To return to high school I still needed a visible physical protective layer to survive, to distinguish myself as an outsider at Lodi High School. I was intent on ensuring that I wasn't seen as one of them, but instead a Chicano that the administration could not ignore. For me, it meant creating my own version of a militant uniform, using farmworker clothing as well as wearing the popular anti-war protester's look that I had adopted. I took my new radical look very seriously, planning out my wardrobe with only the attention that a teenage boy could muster. I wore the same blue or brown work shirts I had worn in the fields with my jeans and my suede sports coat. At the summer demonstration I had purchased anti-war buttons but also two brass collar pins with clenched revolutionary fists depicted. I placed these pins on both sides of each shirt collar for the entire duration of school.

Wearing this outfit, selling The Militant, reading about the San Francisco anti-war marches, created a new world for me in which to survive. I now had an ideology, a purpose for completing my education, knowing I would find a way to somehow better protect my own desperately ill-treated people. I knew that I would become deeply unpopular not only with the administration but with some of the teachers as well who came from grower families. Nevertheless, I refused to change my positions, refused to be silent in this racist school filled with nearly a thousand voiceless Chicanos who were denied honors courses or access to a college preparatory education for their four years at Lodi High School based on their race. Given my singular, newly developed radicalism, and my unquestioned belief in the righteousness of my causes, I knew that I would encounter forces at school where newfound barriers were be placed in front of me as my deserved punishment.

CHAPTER XIV

Friends and Girls and Chicanitos and Chicanitas

AFTER THE SUMMER OF 1969, the next three years passed quickly as I was able to create distance from my horrific life with the Hobsons. Although forced to live with them at the El Rancho Motel in our tiny Room 204, by the end of my first summer my rebellion against everything they stood for was in full force. I managed to successfully call their bluff on their prohibition against my new farmworker-based protester clothing. I took this victory and ran with it. After this, my life with them was never the same. I discovered the power to reject their lives and to create my own separate world.

To survive the Hobsons, I used a strategy they taught me by their own example. I turned the tables on them. I had learned from their decade-long history of weeks of prolonged silence as their preferred form of punishment toward me. I now chose nearly complete silence against them. I might respond initially each day to a few of Sara's crazed questions before she became aggressively hostile. I then stopped speaking to her, held my body straight up and looked directly into her eyes, denying her the satisfaction of visibly hurting me. For the remaining three years, John and Sara endured in disbelief my ability to carry this off. I learned well from their disciplined cruelty, and I wasn't going to let go of my effective strategy against them.

When I returned to Lodi High School as a sophomore, I was a transformed student. I was girded for battle with my militant beliefs and my signature daily outfits supporting the UFW and the anti-war movement. I became visible and outspoken in my political views that were fed by the current Vietnam War. These stood in sharp relief to the Lodi growers' obsession with avoiding its grape pickers' unionization by the UFW. I followed my own construction of what I imagined to be the responsibilities of a radical student. I sold *The Militant* every day and approached students who I thought might be responsive, carefully avoiding the many white male students involved in Lodi's extravagantly funded sports department. I had everything planned out and well organized. I knew with that full certainty of youth what my militant obligations and life would become.

And then I met a girl. It was October of 1969, and I was invited to a Saturday morning English Club meeting to see if I were interested in their annual journal, *The Pegasus*. When I arrived the doors to the school were locked, and I could not get inside the building. I pounded on the door, and finally a young woman came to let me in. Such was her first impression that I remember everything she wore. She had on an eggshell blue, mock turtleneck, short-sleeved; medium gray pressed wool slacks; and penny loafers. She was white, with short stylish blonde hair, clear blue eyes, about five feet-five inches tall. She carried herself with an easy confidence. I took one look, one that is frozen in my life's memories of pure joy, and I fell impossibly in love. Her name was Susan. What followed was my total infatuation with Susan, three years of crushing, silent, unrequited love, before she became the first great love of my life. Susan and I ended up spending seven years of our adult lives together.

I was surprised when Susan answered the door because she was one of the best-known students in school. Everyone expected her to be class valedictorian. Susan was one year ahead of me, so during my freshman year I had little access to her and her classmates. Susan was extremely popular, known for her kindness and lack of arrogance about her academic accomplishments. She was at her essence a middle class girl with her own newly formed progressive values. Susan had no idea at the time that we were meant for each other.

On this first Saturday morning encounter, she welcomed me in a way that transfixed me with her attention and lack of prejudice. I was dazzled by her wide smile and welcoming eyes, and every sense of my body tingled. Susan had a natural curiosity about this young Chicano radical. We spent that Saturday together at the English Club where I met many of her classmates, most of whom I may have seen but some I had not talked to before. They were a mixture of students from affluent grower families as well as students whom I already knew from Morada. I was reassured that many of the students who I perceived as the sharpest came from working class backgrounds and shared my determination for high grades and a path to college.

Something at that Saturday meeting made me approachable to nearly all the students in attendance, with the exception of those from grower families. Susan invited me to become a member of her daily lunch group. I joined it that very next week and stayed with it during high school. We ate in the large outdoor quad when weather permitted, but we always managed to eat together. There was a collection of about six young women, generally two or three young men and me. It is hard to calculate the impact of going from my virtually silent first year to being thrust into an older set of students who couldn't seem to care less about where I lived, all through Susan's invitation.

My two best friends emerged from this group, two gifted young women from middle class backgrounds. They were each other's best friends and but for their immediate love and affection toward me, my life at Lodi would have been profoundly different, one where I might well have been lost. One was Mary Luisa Valtierra from a large devout Catholic family. She lived two miles from my El Rancho Motel, raised by a devoted mother and her father who worked as an electrician. They were proud that one of Mary's brothers was a priest. Mary was about five foot three inches tall and didn't realize she was beautiful. A long-haired Chicana with constant, wry humor, she was also a contender for valedictorian status. The other young woman was Cheri Coulter, who lived with her teacher parents two miles from the El Rancho. Cheri came from an exceedingly kind and understanding family. Both parents were proud of their lengthy careers as teachers. The Coulters produced this intellectually curious, tall, long-haired, striking young daughter who had ample experience under her belt dealing with her brothers. This gave her some perspective on how to approach me on my own terms in a very compassionate manner, given my academic strength and my poverty. Although I remained focused on my attraction to Susan, these two young women remained at the heart of my support and survival. Their friendship endures to the present day.

Through Susan's invitation, my entire social agenda was unknowingly set into place. I met the first approachable young men, all two to three years older than I, who apparently had no problem in treating me as an interesting rebel, as well as an equal. We were united by our intellectual inclinations but also by the recognition that we had to find a place in this new politicalized world. One new friend, Bill, came from the richest grower family in Lodi. Unlike his prominent anti-union grandfather who owned over five thousand acres of Tokay grapes, Bill, too, was looking for an alternative. But all I needed were the basics, just that Susan be there, and that Cheri and Mary would be at my side. I never gave up my fantasy during these years that Susan would somehow be able to read my mind and intuit that I was prepared to do anything to be with her. Instead, I accepted a core friendship, utterly nonsexual for the entire remaining two years she was at school. I did not consider Cheri and Mary remotely as girlfriends because I saw them as my long-lost sisters.

The sexual mores of the day were changing rapidly and even Lodi youth were feeling the era's newfound and controversial sexual freedoms. I do not recall any of us being able to describe exactly what these cultural changes were other than by referencing the anti-war movement, the hippie movement or just being all consumed by the intoxicating rhythms and lyrics of rock and roll. But through all of this societal confusion, normal for these new times and our ages, teen sex became not only possible but quite attainable.

I had the confidence to begin dating by the spring of my sophomore year when I was fourteen years old. The weather was warming, and my new friendships were solid and reassuring. By now I was a full member of our friendship group. With my friends' vehicles to ride in, I began to explore the local Mokelumne River and streams that coursed alongside the Lodi grape fields. The adjoining rivers were slow moving, maybe 200 feet wide, ten to twelve feet deep and graced every large grape field with ample irrigation. Bill, the one wealthy boy in our group, provided access to the private beaches of his grandfather's ranch for our use. On the weekends this gave us total privacy, allowing secluded space for riverside fires and campouts. We swam in the quiet cool waters, at first in our bathing suits. Then most of us chose to take off all our clothes to swim and bask in the weekend sun. This was electrifying in its sexuality. Seeing the bodies of completely naked young, vibrant women was a true "Oh, my God" experience.

I dated many young girls over these years as we taught each other the rites of youthful lovemaking. My first chosen sexual experiences conferred a grace that saved my life when it came to my own sexual identity and expression. Despite my history of abuse, it turned out that unlike so many children who suffered abuse, having physical and truly affectionate lovemaking was a pure escape into joy. I found that that there was no lingering connection between the horrors of the Hobsons' sexual abuse and what I brought to sex as I lay with a young woman. Instead, I found sleeping with young women an act of mutual kindness and tenderness. Lovemaking was my unexpected place of refuge as a young man, a true blessing that, had it not turned out that way, would have dwarfed my life permanently. My sexual experiences were such a resounding source of support for my ego and self-esteem and once started, never faltered. Although I regret that I eventually hurt a few of the young women's hearts by moving on, and they bruised mine, we still lived in a naïve world where your former lovers just might be kept among your friends. I was lucky enough for this to be generally, but not always true.

Now that I had been able to abandon my isolation, I naturally reached out to my own people, the other Mexican and Chicano students. I was regarded as a complete oddity, if not something worse by most of them. At first all they knew of me was a one-sided view based on my academic standing. Other than gym, I was not in the non-college track classes to which the Chicanos were relegated since I was one of only two permitted into the honors classes. This was a big deal to the other Chicanos, setting me apart as an Anglicized Chicano, who spoke a bizarre, ultra-formal and correct form of English that I had learned from the Hobsons. In their Chicanitos and Chicanitas eyes there was a cultural divide that made me unrecognizable to them.

The Chicanos did not know of my circumstances. They had no knowledge of the motel and knew me only by my artificial name, Tony S. Hobson. My real name of Antonio Salazar y Bailon, with my parents listed as Petra and Jesus Salazar, had been stripped from me for over a decade. I was an anomaly, and they were wary about meeting me. I was clearly someone not of their world, ostensibly not of their language and had no familiarity with poverty or farm work. To the other Chicano students during my freshman year, I must have appeared standoffish, remote, inaccessible, and uninterested in them.

Of course, they knew nothing of the Salazar family. How could they know that I came from a migrant farmworker family with thirty-plus years on the national picking circuit, that I was the eleventh of fourteen children, and that we, too, lived in the abject poverty common to Mexicans and Chicanos? Instead, I appeared to be a member of the elite. Not one of their own. They had no idea that although my kidnapping was a secret, I had only been able to survive my decade of kidnapped life by being taken under the wings of the Chicano families I met both at the Ranch and at the El Rancho Motel. The acceptance into these families along the way prevented my mind and spirit from shattering and reinforced the initial love shown by my mother Petra.

Once I broke free from silence in my sophomore year, I rushed toward my own people at school. There I found a surprised, but welcoming Chicano cohort. I spoke Spanish well and unlike my formal English with its remaining bouts of stuttering, I spoke with a rapid rhythm, devoid of stuttering and filled with some humor and confidence. More importantly, I immediately shared my real name, the names of my parents and siblings and the work my family did as farmworkers. I had just completed my first of four full summers picking fruit with the Ramirez family, and my experiences quickly merged into that of their own families.

Lodi was my first school with a strong Chicano presence. Lodi High had eight hundred Chicanos among the four grades, and I felt a strong desire to connect with my fellow Chicano students. Once kidnapped, I focused on remembering my thirteen brothers and sisters whom I had now not seen for ten years. I had never had Chicano children as playmates until I reached the El Rancho and was befriended by the Ramirez family and their children. Although I thrived in their company, none were at my grade level. I loved their son Wattie, but he was three years younger than me. I longed for Chicano friends from my high school.

Word quickly spread about me among the Chicano students that I was one of them. I soon joined a core group of fifteen or so Chicanos in which every one of us had similar backgrounds, particularly farm labor. We shared stories of our families' rituals, problems with parents and siblings, and money worries. Most came from large families with often many siblings attending the same high school but in different grades. We openly discussed the lack of money without embarrassment since we were all in the same position. We were in the safety of our people. But as Chicanos, our group was anything but somber. We teased each other, made jokes, spoke in both Spanish and English, particularly with our favorite curses, making fun of the teachers and the school.

I was now torn about how to spend time with my Chicano friends at every turn, particularly because my lunch period was taken up by my other new group that had become critical to my survival at school. I realized that I had to both break away at times for lunch as well as find other opportunities to balance my friendship groups. I used the thirty minutes when I arrived early to school each day and the thirty minutes waiting for the afternoon bus to arrive. During the morning arrivals and afternoon departures, the students broke up into large to small groups, standoffish, unwelcoming as only teenagers can create.

The Chicanos clustered into one of the largest groups. I stayed with this group every day until my bus came. This one act alone allowed me to begin to know the Chicanos from several grades. What could be perceived as our self-segregation was nothing but cultural affinity and survival in a school that systematically taught Chicanos in a segregated environment. We knew from the start that we were considered an inconvenient burden by the administration. I remember our attitude of casual indifference to the white students, making sure that we stayed entirely separate from them as we waited for our buses. Sharing many of the same cultural experiences as well as the poverty of our families provided us a sense of safety. Yet, at the same time we were teenagers and not a quiet group. Instead, we filled the air with rapid conversation, teasing, flirting between the boys and girls, and the expected competitiveness that sometimes arose. To me it was exhilarating. I felt replenished by the waves of laughter, the intermittent conversations in Spanish, students who looked just like me and of course the beautiful Chicanas in the group. Once my bus arrived, I boarded it buoyed by my own people and even more certain of the correctness of my political orientation.

My new Chicano friendships became the foundation of my political efforts at Lodi High. I went from my initial year of total isolation to becoming a central figure working with other Chicanos to make us a powerful force. We became so galvanized that we led the first demonstration against the school board based on its racist policies, something that had never happened before. I now had what I had been missing for a decade: scores of new Chicano friends. I held on for dear life to the strength they gave me.

CHAPTER XV

Meeting Cesar

MY CORE GROUP OF FIFTEEN CHICANOS was made up of sopho-
mores to seniors, all of whom came from farmworker backgrounds.
The other Chicano students looked at us as the emerging Chicano
leaders of our school. Our group began to quickly grow, all built on
the unity of our farm work experience and the understanding of
the exploitation our families suffered. We shared the experiences
of horrific working conditions, low wages, hot weather, and the
harsh authority of the contractors who brought our families into
the fields.

Cesar Chavez was legendary to all of us, but violent threats
against the UFW prevented their efforts from unionizing our
ultra-conservative region. We knew about the UFW battles to
unionize throughout the Central Valley and Salinas and the physical
beating of UFW supporters. Growers routinely brought in waves
of Mexicans, Chicanos, and other groups as strikebreakers. Cesar
was becoming so much more than a spokesman for the UFW. He
emerged as a savior for the farmworkers, unflinching in his
strength and sacrifice to unionize people just like our own families.
As young Chicanos we were transfixed by his reputation. Soon
we had a chance to become part of the UFW movement.

In April of 1970, during my sophomore year, we learned that
Cesar was coming to Stockton for another rally. It was at a union
hall in Stockton in the early evening. We heard that Cesar wanted
to meet local supporters prior to the rally, and the UFW needed
volunteers for this event. We were ready. About ten of us traveled

in two cars, arriving at the Stockton union hall by 4:00. None of us had ever been to a union hall. This one was enormous and could hold hundreds of workers. The hall was almost empty when we arrived, with just a few people working on setting up chairs and doing sound checks. A UFW member met us at the door. He instructed us to go down to the front to meet Cesar. Cesar was seated in front of the stage, with a few UFW members mingling around him. Cesar had created a large circle around him of maybe twenty chairs. We went down as instructed.

Cesar stood up when we arrived, and he asked each of us our names and shook our hands. The moment I looked into his eyes I felt such a rush of uncontrolled emotion that it took all my strength not to weep. My near lack of self-control caught me entirely off guard, but I did not embarrass myself in front of him or my friends. Cesar must have seen something in my eyes, though. After our introduction, Cesar took the time to hear each of our families' stories. He may have given us five minutes each, but the richness of our families' values and the experiences of our lives just burst from each one of us.

My story was simple. I introduced myself as Antonio Salazar and told him the story of the Salazar family (although I still used the fiction that I had been "adopted" at age four) and of my recently completed picking season. I was by then back in control as I shared seeing him in last summer's demonstration and that I wanted to work on behalf of Mexican and Chicano farmworker families when I finished school. This was the beginning of my twenty-year relationship with Cesar Chavez and the UFW. He soon took me under his wing, became intimate with my Salazar history and guided me from then on with every step I needed to be an effective advocate. I was only fifteen, but I knew I was somehow graced with an opportunity to work at his side, being my own true self, but never disclosing my kidnapped status.

Cesar was soft spoken on this occasion, so respectful of our group of Chicanitos and Chicanitas. We all felt enormous relief to have a leader so approachable, so willing to listen. The legend of Cesar had materialized in front of our eyes, and all of us were now eager to help Cesar in any way we could. Cesar gave us an immediate voluntary assignment for the rally. He asked that we share the stage as his youth brigade, a collection of young men and women who would be his "bodyguards" at the rally. We were stunned that he entrusted us with this honor, to protect Cesar from attackers, to keep him alive, maybe at the cost of our own. Our imaginations ran wild, but the task of being a chosen bodyguard for Cesar was all-consuming. We focused quickly, checking out the hall, exits and the back of the stage. We were assigned our positions around the podium where he would be speaking.

This was a labor unity event attended by many local unions members whose leaders introduced Cesar. These unions brought several hundred members to the rally. In addition, at least one hundred or more UFW farmworkers had arrived, children in tow, giving us a deep level of comfort now that our people were present. The rally began. We had no stage fright, just a thrill as Cesar walked out after we had taken our position on the stage. The applause of the audience was thunderous, and we had a brilliant glimpse at labor unity and support for Cesar.

The rally ended in great success, with financial donations. Cesar called us all back to meet with him before he left. He asked briefly what we thought of the rally, and he could sense our pride in the moment. Cesar then made an important offer that shaped many of our lives over the coming years. He asked us to become his body-guards at future rallies. We eagerly agreed. From that point on we attended Stockton and Central Valley demonstrations. Most of us teens looked up to the older Brown Berets, a militant Chicano rights group, and we closely followed their preferred garb of brown shirts, berets, and militant pins. We shared the stage with other youth; often there were twenty to forty of us in an impressive formation creating a solid barrier around Cesar. We took our responsibilities seriously, and they came to define us as newly branded militant Chicanos.

I had now built trust with my fellow Chicano students. My commitment to the UFW had no limits. I remained centered not only by my ever-growing militancy but also by two more full seasons of picking fruit in my sophomore and junior summers. The newfound militancy of our Chicano group turned its eyes to Lodi High. I worked with our group to galvanize the Chicanos into a potent political voice and voting bloc at the school. In two short years we transformed ourselves into quite a force at the high school, the likes of which the administration had never seen. We decided to challenge the school board itself. We had been silent for decades, and we had had enough. I remember we organized a group of sixty or more students to go to the school board of this ultra conservative, anti-Mexican town. We asked for fairer treatment and better access to courses. The school board was stunned at this rebellious display. They turned red-faced and shaking as they faced angry Mexican students. We carefully planned our school board demonstration with no yelling, but we were sure that we were perceived as a threat.

We decided to up our game and to run the first Chicano as a student body president candidate for the four-thousand-member school. I was selected and eagerly volunteered for this task. I ran against a white boy so affluent that on the day of the election, he used his father's Rolls Royce to lead a parade of fifty cars that surrounded both campuses, filled with jocks and their banners. If this were not enough, his father had a plane flying overhead with a banner urging election of his son.

With a student body of four thousand, we had our huge voting bloc of eight hundred Chicanos and a will to win. I approached every one of the numerous clubs, often with the help of other Chicano students. I skipped the sports teams, as they had their own chosen candidate. I spent fifty-six dollars on my campaign. The student body did not know I was only fifteen years old at the time. We won in a landslide, electing the first Chicano student body president in Lodi's history. This thrilled our community and further threatened the administration. I was already well known for my politics and an ability to unify students in this new anti-war pro farmworker environment.

The administration never lost its anger at our school board demonstration. They also didn't know how to interrupt our newfound power at the school. One image particularly shocked them. We were a rich school. The student body president and its officers were given a budget of fifty-four thousand dollars to cover our term and our graduation expenses. Of this, twenty-five thousand dollars had traditionally been set aside for completely new football uniforms each year. I controlled the money, and I refused to release the funds to the sports department. I said I would pay for individual uniforms that were needed, but I was not about to hand over money that was unnecessary and needed for other educational services. I refused to change my mind and many students supported me; from that moment on I was despised by the athletes and the administration for my position.

My high school experience was fulfilled by two other significant events. I did in fact join *The Pegasus*, the annual school literary publication and published my first poem, calling out for peace in the midst of war mongers. The other was much more emotional and remains my warmest memory of high school. It involved Mary and Cheri, my two best friends who were in honor classes and lived near the motel. I turned sixteen in August of 1971. Cheri and Mary unexpectedly showed up at the motel with a surprise. They baked an enormous sheet cake for my birthday, and it was shaped like a UFW flag. It was an act of true kindness and it showed they recognized who I was as a person. They both knew of my identity with the UFW movement, and they had the love and care to come to my decrepit motel and to do this for me. I will always remember eating my UFW cake with them in the large front yard of the motel.

John and Sara forced themselves into my life in April of 1972, six weeks before my high school graduation. John had recently disappeared for two months, reappearing at the motel without explanation. We later found out that he was institutionalized at Stockton's local county psychiatric ward where he denied that he had any family. The newly reunited Hobsons joined forces against me. They called the police and had me arrested as a completely out of control and incorrigible minor warranting sending me to juvenile hall. In addition to this classic basis for the arrest of a juvenile, they further emphasized to the authorities that I was a fraud and that I had earned none of the scholarships that I had won during my senior year for college. The oddest thing occurred when I was taken to juvenile hall. It was in the same Stockton County facility that John had been in, built around a brick quadrangle. I had my own window, and I discovered that I could see directly across into the very room that John had been in at the psychiatric ward. The irony was not lost on me. I waited for my evaluation and learned how to weave plastic strips into odd items. I had access to books, and I read.

I was evaluated after a week of interviews by a group of about six administrators. They called me into a conference room to hear their conclusions. All the time, I was quietly hysterical about my missed school, what explanation I would give if I were ever released and whether I would make it out in time to graduate and go to college. The department heads told me they had called my school, checked my transcripts, considered my age, and verified my scholarships and offers to many universities. In going around the room, they indicated they had never seen a child like me before in juvenile hall. Instead, they said something shocking to me. They announced that they had concluded that the Hobsons were insane. I was actually complimented on my survival and academic success. Each one of them passed out a business card to me. On the back of their cards were their home phone numbers. Without exception, each one offered to immediately take me into their home at the next crisis, until I could leave for college. I had never had the raw truth of the Hobsons' insanity confirmed to me by another adult. To hear these powerful people recognize my reality was overwhelming. But nothing compared to knowing that I now had a way out, that I could call these people if needed and they would get me to school. I was immediately released back to the Hobsons. I had just about a month left before graduation.

The Hobsons threw me out the day following graduation at 5:30 in the morning with one suitcase. I had spent my last night with them. I stood on the frontage road by myself. I called one of my dearest friends, Greg Dahl, and on behalf of his family he invited me to his home. I soon moved to Willie's home, another friend like Greg from our circle. Willie's father was an attorney, a kind man who seemed to know what I needed for protection. He successfully filed a petition on my behalf to become an emancipated minor. But for his legal intervention, I would have remained at the mercy of the Hobsons. This one enormous gift to me further secured the foundation of my new life without them.

It was the summer of 1972, and I was waiting to head to the University of California at Santa Cruz, a university I selected in large part because Susan was a student there. There was a large summer lunch program in Stockton that served the region. Acampo, a small poor migrant town of under 300 people, was located a few miles in the country outside of Lodi. Acampo was chosen as a recipient of the summer program in 1972, due to the increase of migrant workers during the season. The program taught *campesino* children eight to twelve years old basic skills and provided lunches and some day camp activities. All the Chicano students at our high school provided the staff, making this a fun summer for us. It solidified our already close relationships and gave us pride in our work.

The program carried out by my Chicano friends ended in a farewell dance for the students. The dance was a big deal for these Chicanitos and Chicanitas, but it was amazing how we all worked to transform a couple of modest school rooms into a fancy afternoon dance environment with a very tiny stage for a microphone. The dance music included classic contemporary favorites like the Jackson Family. The lights were dimmed, there was ample food and surprisingly enough these kids began on their own to dance. One moment still catches in my throat. One of my friends announced the one and only song that was dedicated to anyone that afternoon. It was a song that the kids asked to dedicate to me—Michael Jackson singing *Never Can Say Goodbye*. I was accustomed to complete control of my emotions, but I nearly lost it, simply because I loved these kids and this special recognition meant so much.

Two days later, John Hobson arrived at Acampo. The program had only a few days left. He announced that he had gotten me fired for lying about my age being eighteen but who knows everything John told them. He must have come down hard on the lead eighteen-year-old Chicano in charge of the lunch program, lying to him that I could not work there as a sixteen-year-old. I was immediately let go. I was left with no money or income three weeks before the start of college. California in fact allowed sixteen-year-olds to work, but I believed John's lie, which had a continuing restrictive impact on my efforts to earn money for college. Just one more of John's efforts to hurt me at every turn.

CHAPTER XVI

A Savior Emerges: Dr. Norman O' Brown

IT WAS LATE AUGUST OF 1972, and I had managed to survive the weeks following the loss of my summer job in Acampo, which was a result of John's intervention. I had almost no money when I arrived at University of California Santa Cruz, but I knew that when I registered for classes, my scholarships would be released. I was thrilled that so many of my high school friends were also going to UCSC. Susan was already a student at this university. She invited me to ride with her to college. I could not believe my luck that I was traveling with her alone and that my first college experiences might include this young woman with whom I was silently in love.

We arrived about a week early as she already had secured university apartment housing with an all-women household. Susan could not invite me to stay over in her apartment since it was for women only. Instead, out of nowhere, she offered to spend the nights with me on a nearby hill in a sleeping bag. The thought of her being with me at night in the outdoors, surrounded by miles of Santa Cruz Redwoods, was like a dream. I slept next to her, began the first intimate conversations, and carefully controlled my heart to remain silent as to what she really meant to me.

During our week on this grass-filled hill, Susan was warm toward me but gave clear signals that this was to be an entirely platonic week. I remained respectful toward her. Susan's gesture to not leave me alone on the hill reinforced my belief in her kindness. I felt that from the moment I had instantly fallen for her nearly three years earlier, that I had chosen the right young woman.

This soon turned out to be true, as she would be the first great love of my life.

The University of California at Santa Cruz was a new University of California campus, just established in 1965. It is located on two thousand acres of rolling forested hills overlooking the Pacific Ocean and Monterey Bay. In 1972, the focus of the administration was in large part on the need to build architecturally fresh, modern, and important buildings for what were to be eight individually contained colleges. I was set to attend Cowell College, the first campus built at the university with a mission to provide the academic rigor and training of Oxford University. Cowell was perched on one of the highest hills on Campus with an unobstructed view of the two miles of untouched hills between it and the Pacific Ocean. Cowell was a large site, surrounded by redwoods, situated in an elongated set of white buildings. The college featured a huge concrete quad where every angle highlighted unobstructed views of the ocean and the Monterey Bay. To the left was a large cafeteria with more ocean views. To the far right were the dorms with their own grass-filled quad. They housed a few hundred students. The setting among the redwoods was unlike any other UC campus.

To become familiar with the layout, I walked the Cowell campus many times before registration opened. I was one of the first in the registration line when it opened, anxious to get my state scholarships to pay my tuition and living expenses. I had earned these based on my high academic standing in high school. I arrived at the registration window, identified myself, quietly excited to finally be here at UCSC. The Registrar pulled my file and then took her time reading it. She looked up with a serious face and said that all my monies had been revoked, and that I was no longer entitled to any scholarships.

My mind froze, and my heart began a silent freefall in disbelief. The Registrar said that John and Sara had written to the Chancellor and informed the University that I was a fraud and not entitled to any scholarships. All of my college funding was gone. These were the identical meritless charges that the Hobsons had used to further support my spurious arrest in May of 1972. This was the same insanity that San Joaquin County officials in Stockton had identified to me only months earlier, qualifying me for immediate release from juvenile hall. I was incapable of asking the Registrar whether I was still admitted to the school. I knew that if I did so, I would likely be given the answer I feared most, that even my attendance at UCSC had been disallowed. I would be unable to control my emotions and my carefully built internal damn holding back my pain and abuse would burst and I would cry. I could not ask the question because I wasn't prepared for an answer. I was so stunned by the punitive action of the Hobsons that I felt the full defeat of my horrific life with them. I did not know if I could endure this moment.

I had just turned seventeen the week earlier. I had no experience with how to deal with such an insurmountable crisis. I was dead broke. I only had the hill with Susan to spend the nights. Now I had no campus housing available to me, no money for tuition or books. Even though I told Susan about the loss of my financial aid, I could not share with her my deepest fear that I had lost my place at university.

My world was crashing before me. I was reeling from John and Sara's last four months of brutal attacks. I had already become accustomed to their life of desperation, alcoholism, and mental illness that was present every moment I spent with them. Nothing, however, had prepared me for the insane level of viciousness they showed from May to September 1972. They had me arrested on meritless charges. The day after my high school graduation they threw me out at dawn on the frontage road of Highway 99. Of course, I was thrilled to be waiting for my friend Greg to pick me up that morning. At the same time, I was desperate about securing housing and employment for the entire summer. I found the perfect job with the Acampo summer program, but John had me fired in late August under false pretenses. Unknown to me then, John and Sara, during the summer, had written to the UCSC Chancellor. They asked that I be disqualified as a fraud to deny me funding and render me ineligible to attend the university. To make matters worse, I was deeply shaped and hemmed in by John's lies that no one could hire me before I turned eighteen, which I believed. Since I had already worked three summers in the fields with many minors my age working alongside me, I knew that working in the fields was an option. By September, though, the picking seasons was nearly over for the year, leaving in my mind no chance for regular work in Santa Cruz. I was totally lost and all I could think of was ways I could survive and still remain in school. Since I could not enter the dorms or participate in any of the activities at Cowell College, much less eat the cafeteria food without proper student identification, there was one place that I could be mostly alone, but still on the Cowell campus. Behind the Cowell dorms was a small wood cabin, with steps up to a small porch surrounding it. It was used for holding small meetings of fifteen or so students and an instructor. This little cabin became the center of my life.

I was grateful for the cabin's silence and privacy. As I sat alone on its steps, with no other place to be, an older man approached me. He introduced himself as Dr. Norman O' Brown and told me to call him "Nobby." I later learned that he was one of the most famous professors at our university, trained at Oxford, an internationally recognized Classics scholar and leading intellectual force in the international political discourse of the day.

Nobby first asked my name. I told him it was Antonio, and he asked me if I knew my name's origins. I told him that I thought it came from the Catholic saint, San Antonio de Padua. Nobby complimented me on my knowledge but then engaged in a most stunning history of my name from early Greek and Roman history. Nobby went to the very roots of my name, listing with quiet authority every iteration of my name to the present day. It was an authoritative display of knowledge. I was instantly attracted to this gentle man whose intellectuality seemed boundless.

Nobby then asked me who I was. I was deeply unsure about what to say about myself, but I was determined not to share with him the loss of my funds. I was profoundly embarrassed at the loss of my financial aid and had no strategy to solve my problems. I was also fearful that if he found out, he would completely lose interest in me. He carefully reassured me that he was truly interested in my background. But one fact transformed my initial hesitation about him. Nobby told me that he had been born in El Oro, Mexico. We began to speak in Spanish. I could not believe that I had found someone who I initially believed was so distant from my culture, but in reality, was a white "Mexicano."

I told him about the Salazars, my status as the eleventh child of fourteen migrant farmworker children and my academic success. But Nobby was not interested in a summary. He wanted to know about my life. We spent almost two hours talking. I told him about my farm work, my radical ideas and working with Cesar Chavez. I said nothing about the Hobsons other than the fiction that I had been "adopted." I made clear to Nobby that my goal was to get an education, help farmworkers, but most of all to find the Salazar family once I had finished school.

Nobby ended the conversation, apparently having made some judgment about me as we talked. He asked me to meet him the next day at the same place. I was taken aback by his interest in me. I did not understand the implications of our first conversation. I vowed to show up and arrived a full hour early to make sure that I did not miss him. As I waited, I was filled with conflicting thoughts. Why did he want to meet with me again? Who really was this distinguished professor from El Oro, Mexico, and why would he ask for a second meeting? I already knew that I was in awe of him. I realized I had to find some way to let him know that I was likely no longer a student at UCSC based on the Hobsons' vicious actions.

The second conversation began with Nobby asking me some more general questions about my background before he homed in on eliciting more details. He instinctively knew that my story was filled with enormous blanks and guessed that my life with the Hobsons had been much more difficult than I had dared describe. I answered his questions as honestly as I could, but I held back the true circumstances in which I was raised.

I knew that I could no longer delay sharing with him my status at the school. I told Nobby what happened to me from juvenile hall to the present. I let him know about John's and Sara's vindictiveness against me, including my recent firing from the Acampo summer school resulting from John's actions. I described the importance of my Chicano identity and my life goals. I had never shared these difficulties with any adult other than the counselors at juvenile hall. It was an almost unbearable leap of faith to tell Nobby the truth of my circumstances.

With this background, I came round to telling him about the loss of my scholarships based on the Hobsons' charges made directly in writing to the UCSC Chancellor. The implications were clear. I was unlikely to be a student at Cowell. Nobby expressed concern about what had happened to me but did not seem remotely discouraged. Instead, he astonished me by asking me to meet him at the cabin the next day. I had no idea what was left to talk about, but I took it as a good sign, the first and only one on the horizon that appeared to me.

I met him on the third day on the cabin steps. Nobby seemed a bit more formal than he had been with me before. He was very direct. Nobby said that he had walked into the Chancellor's office the previous day to talk about my circumstances. To me, talking to the Chancellor was like talking to God himself, someone unapproachable, with great power over thousands of students. I could not believe that Nobby would meet with the Chancellor with me as his focus.

Nobby had done something that altered my life. In his warm yet serious way, Nobby told me that he had explained my circumstances to the Chancellor. Based on Nobby's intervention, the Chancellor restored all my financial aid. My registration at Cowell College was now secure. I was overwhelmed with gratitude, disbelieving that someone could pluck me out of thin air and through one intervention restore my future.

Nobby watched as I absorbed this news, seeing my relief as well as my deep gratitude for this intervention. And then Nobby took a serious tone toward me. He said that he would oversee my education at UCSC. He told me explicitly of his expectations for my studies. Nobby asked that I never compare myself with other students. He directly stated that I should expect to work harder than any other student that I would ever meet and that I was never to complain of the level of work required to excel. Furthermore, I would work for other professors at the university via work study programs to learn the rigors of true scholarship and research.

Nobby was precise in his nonnegotiable expectations. I thrived under his direction for my five years as a student. I did not have any idea how important his influence would be on my academic career. Nobby became my first savior at the university. I had the honor in my first year of doing public readings of Latin American poetry with him, in Spanish, with a focus on Pablo Neruda. Through his guidance I attained many fellowships as an undergraduate. These provided me with nearly two years of study in Latin America and the Danforth fellowship for graduate school. I have held Nobby in my heart ever since, grateful for his faith in me. I know that but for him, my university life would have been stolen from me.

CHAPTER XVII

A Rough Start Turns Around, The 1973 Salinas Lettuce Strike and Cesar Chavez

JOHN SUDDENLY DIED IN 1974. I had known him for thirteen years as my kidnapper and sexual abuser. I felt little remorse at his death. I was occupied with being at last free from the Hobsons and facing the challenges of my sophomore year. I chose Latin American Studies as my major. I was privileged to work with two Latin Americanist professors, Dr. Ralph Guzman and Dr. David Sweet. Both of them had a major impact on my career in this academic field.

My freshman year was uneven. The dream of being with Susan materialized by October of 1972 into a full-fledged sexual relationship, and I could not have been happier. But my true focus was elsewhere. I had an internal drive to be a success in every course, to try to be the best student in the class, all the while being consumed with anxiety regarding my evaluations. I stumbled my first quarter, and it scared me to death. I wondered what I had done wrong to receive only mid-level evaluations. I deeply hoped that this first quarter was not to be representative of my time at UCSC.

During that first quarter, I was privately also having a hard time emotionally. I kept trying to leave in my mind the Hobsons in their decrepit motel, as well as hoping to heal from the trauma in my life. I had my best friend at UCSC, Greg, the same young man who had picked me up when the Hobsons kicked me out the day after graduation. Greg was quite handsome, maybe five feet and ten inches tall, a solid young man's body, and a captivating and seductive smile noticed by the girls. But what set Greg apart beyond his ready and quick mind was his innate kindness to people, and the warmest sense of humor. We saw each other with regularity, and I had loved him for his instinctive and unfaltering thoughtfulness toward me. Other than one other boy, Dana Jackson, who attended UC Berkeley, Greg was my closest friend on earth.

I remember the night well, on November 10th, 1972, when Greg came over around 10:00 pm. My roommate was absent for the night. I was consumed with worry about school and also surprisingly enough about the three-week winter break. No student was allowed to stay in the dorm during these weeks. I had no place to go, no roof over my head and no one with whom to spend the holidays, neither Thanksgiving nor Christmas. I refused to feel like an orphan, but I knew in reality that is what I had become. Greg sat on my dorm bed, and he asked me how I was doing. I tried small talk to avoid the mangled emotions and hurt that I was holding in.

I had not wept for eight years since my last rape and near successful suicide attempt at the Ranch, when a caring cowboy came to my rescue and had my abuse stopped. Greg had known me well for several years, and he understood my insistence that I not lose face over any of the challenges of my life with the Hobsons. But something inside me broke. I began to cry, and for an exceptionally long time. The grief just poured out of me; my sense of loneliness from the loss of the Salazars was insurmountable. In that moment I could no longer endure the sheer cruelty of the Hobsons. I wept silently, and Greg quietly absorbed the scene with grace, quiet reassurance, and love. I must have wept at least an hour with him, the longest period of my life thus far.

When I regained control, I did so without any of the profound embarrassment that I thought I would feel. Instead, I knew that Greg's support was one of true affection and I could tell he felt it was reciprocated. Greg must have also felt relief that I could finally express my feelings about things that he already knew caused me much suffering. This moment has crystallized in my life as a key time when I received the love and support of another young man, a friend I could trust with my heart. I never cried again at UCSC but knowing that Greg was there for me provided me much needed strength. Greg and I became roommates in downtown Santa Cruz, and it turned out to be an ideal match. I had managed to stay with friends and their families during the holidays that initial year,

grateful for their generosity and the chance to enjoy these traditional family times together.

I returned to Santa Cruz in January of 1973 reinvigorated. Upon
my return I was preoccupied with how to excel. I knew that I
needed to be better prepared for this next quarter. I used the only
strategy that I could think of. Before the Christmas break, I decided
to ask each professor for the coming quarter for their syllabus. I also
borrowed all the course books from their offices. I used my three
weeks off during the winter holidays to read every book at least
once. I studied outlines for each course prior to my return to
school. I accomplished this with an internal discipline that I wasn't
sure that I had until I actually accomplished my goal. I returned to
my second quarter prepared for each course. From that moment
on I excelled academically. I knew that I could not embarrass Nobby
with less than top work. Both Nobby's unflinching support, coupled
with my own determination, ensured my success at UCSC.

The remaining quarters of the 1972-1973 academic year went
well. I embraced my Latin American Studies major. I found that my
major addressed my needs for formal education in Chicano history
as well as introducing me to the world of Latin American history. I
developed a particularly close friendship with Dr. Guzman, who
was often kind enough to invite me to his home to dine with his
family. Dr. Guzman was a professor of Chicano Studies, and he
took great interest in my farm-working background, as well as my
commitment to the UFW movement.

I was only seventeen when I completed my freshman year. Dr.
Guzman came up with a brilliant idea, one that had a marked
impact on my future. Santa Cruz is about thirty-five miles from the
agriculturally rich Salinas Valley, known for its giant lettuce, arti-
choke, and strawberry fields. The 1973 UFW Lettuce Strike was in
full force in Salinas. There was not a single lettuce field that had
been unionized despite repeated efforts by the UFW to convince
workers to join them. However, there was one field of workers that
was unionized. It was a massive strawberry field owned by the
Driscoll Company, whose strawberries were highly profitable.

Dr. Guzman knew Mr. Driscoll personally. Based on this relationship, Dr. Guzman and I worked out an independent study
that could both advance my course work as well as provide me

employment. Dr. Guzman arranged for us to meet Mr. Driscoll at the Driscoll strawberry field. Mr. Driscoll drove up in a rare and ultra-luxurious car of the day, a Citroen Maserati. It was a vehicle so stunning in its foreign French design that I memorized every angle of this exceptional vehicle. I was unexpectedly nervous about the introduction. I shook Mr. Driscoll's hand and Dr. Guzman began to explain who I was and the plan for the summer. Mr. Driscoll would hire me as a strawberry picker at two dollars an hour and twenty-five cents for every completed twelve packet crate of strawberries. Dr. Guzman then described the academic ambitions behind this project. I would be receiving independent study for reviewing all migrant housing available in Salinas after I completed my daily work at the farm.

This became my fourth and last summer picking fruit. Our group of workers numbered a little over sixty members. First, I had to find a temporary home in Salinas. I joined a household just outside of the Salinas city limits. All conversations were exclusively in Spanish, something which I deeply relished. It was a relatively large home with three bedrooms and an eighteen-foot trailer in the back yard. There were about twenty adults, two-thirds men and the remaining number women. The men were assigned to only one bathroom in the house. I lived in the trailer with about eight other campesinos, all men. The remaining men were married and slept with their spouses. These bedrooms were also overflowing with other female relatives who shared the limited spaces with these couples. Any remaining male relatives slept in the living room. Nearly all the women worked in the fields, but every woman was expected to prepare full meals every day for the entire household. The food was wonderful, identical to the Salazars. I felt completely at home being there. We all waited to have our Sunday goat barbecues, an event so central to our lives that was both expected and looked forward to.

We left for work in our vehicles at 4:45 in the morning, never being late for our mandated 5:15 starting time. Strawberries were a delicate fruit and could only be picked until 2:00 pm in the afternoon before further picking would damage them. I was a good strawberry worker, and I was respected for not complaining while I worked all day on my knees. I soon knew so many people in the field that conversation was easy not only with my own group, but with their friends who worked with them.

Although we worked the normal six days a week, we were back at our home by 3:00, leaving me ample time for my independent study. My goal was to visit every site where Chicano and migrant workers lived in Salinas and to document their conditions. I walked through the open fields to cross to the bridge to Salinas proper. It was only a 2 ½ mile walk before you were in the heart of downtown. In 1973, Salinas was a predominantly Mexicano and Chicano community. This meant that large swaths of the downtown area were filled with Mexican bars and stores, almost feeling like a part of Mexico. It was also close to the Single Room Occupancy (SRO) hotels that were supposed to be limited to one occupant for each room. My work took me to every known SRO, flop house and cheap motel in Salinas where I interviewed any *campesino* who was willing to talk to me about their travels to the area and where they were housed.

I found out that the SRO hotels routinely put two to three or more men in one SRO. The hotel owners charged each man the same price that would normally be paid by one man paying for a private SRO room. Now, given these multiple groups of men each paying full price, this was extremely lucrative for the hotel owners. Salinas was a town dominated by growers' interests. The SROs ran no risk of being found in violation by the fully cooperative local housing authorities since this only involved the exploitation of seasonal Mexican workers. In addition, these SRO owners, through their Spanish-speaking henchmen who often lived on site, imposed harsh, inflexible rules that were meant to keep the workers silent about their true living conditions or risk being immediately ousted from the premises. It was a dark picture of desperate, single men, with no alternative but to accept these SRO living conditions. Often scores of men shared just one to two toilets per floor. Nevertheless, these men needed to leave just like everyone else by the 4:45 deadline to head out for field work, despite living in run-down, crowded, and costly conditions.

I managed to visit every cheap motel in the area, a known housing favorite for workers and their families. These were the cheapest motels imaginable, but every single one of them was in far better condition than my El Rancho Motel. I became a known entity throughout the community, and the farmworkers seemed to appreciate that I was even concerned about their conditions. I submitted a detailed compilation of my findings to Dr. Guzman at the end of the summer, and he seemed pleased with my ability to do independent research.

After I finished my work in Salinas, I finally turned eighteen in August of 1973, entering not only my sophomore year, but qualifying for cannery work I knew would be better-paying. It felt that I had waited for this moment an exceptionally long time. It provided a layer of financial security for which I had longed. The new school year also brought a major loss. I was truly blessed with the attention of Dr. Guzman who led my early studies until he unexpectedly died an early death during my sophomore year. I was crushed about this loss to his family as well as losing a compassionate mentor. I did not handle his death well, once again enduring the loss of a caring adult who had believed in me. My changed circumstances meant I needed a new full-time advisor for Latin American Studies. I spoke with Nobby for guidance and he recommended that I try Dr. David Sweet, a white, left-leaning Latin Americanist located in Merrill college. I may have already taken one course with him at the time, but now I needed him to be an additional advisor for my goals at UCSC. David was a large, dark-haired man, with extensive Latin American travel and research experience. He was gentle but strong in nature, with a ready sense of humor. Without hesitation he agreed to be my advisor. David and Nobby were at my side for the duration of college.

I finished my sophomore year. I then faced a complex dilemma. I had been trying to survive on work study during my sophomore year, unable to accumulate any savings. I was broke again. Lodi was the site of the enormous Pacific Coast Producers, which hired over two thousand employees every canning season. I had been ineligible to work there due to my age, but most of my older university friends from Lodi worked there exclusively in the summers during college. The cannery's hours were 24/7, 6 ½ days a week, twelve hours a day.

The money was huge in comparison to other available summer employment. Instead of a starving minimal wage, earnings per week averaged five hundred dollars. This was such a stunning amount of money that it created its own economic environment. Hundreds of Lodi residents relied on the four to five months of income for the rest of the year. They supplemented it with unemployment insurance until the next canning season.

I faced an enormous crisis of faith. The Pacific Coast Producers was an all-Teamster plant. The Teamsters at that time were the avowed enemies of the UFW, going up against them to represent farmworkers, and often in the pocket of the growers. I could neither work there nor find a job elsewhere with wages high enough to both sustain me for the summer and save for my educational expenses for the coming year. I was trapped by my UFW identity and activities with the union. I had just completed a stint on the sole UFW ranch in Salinas and was even more militant than before about Raza and the UFW movement.

By this time, I had known and worked with Cesar Chavez for three years. I served loyally as one of his bodyguards, often at large demonstrations, and he knew that I had years of experience in the fields. But more importantly, I had given him almost the complete truth about my Salazar family, and he knew that I was deeply identified with the UFW struggle.

I do not know exactly why Cesar insisted on so many details of the Salazars and also of my life with the Hobsons. He did know about my living circumstances, my poverty in high school as well as my success in college. I believe to this day that my work on his UFW ranch in 1973 had solidified his faith in me, along with my work on migrant housing. I had only one idea in my head about this crisis. I knew I had to speak with Cesar and tell him of my very real dilemma. It was simply that I could not earn enough money to continue my education without a high paying job; I had to have some savings to survive.

It was so hard to get up the nerve to ask him something that was repugnant to our UFW forces: to work at a Teamster factory. But I knew that without his permission, I could not take the job at the cannery. It was as simple as that. I hoped that I would not disgrace myself before him, that I would not lose his goodwill or faith in me by having the arrogance to even suggest I work with the Teamsters. I knew that I had to ask Cesar for permission. He would have the final word.

I sought Cesar in the Central Valley when I returned to Lodi in the summer of 1974. I waited until I had my first chance to meet up with him, all the time chilled with anxiety about how to approach him and what the implications of his answer might be. More than anything I did not want him to think less of me, no matter what might happen.

I met with Cesar in Stockton before another of his UFW rallies. Cesar was surrounded by a few of his members, maybe five to six farmworkers. Cesar seemed relaxed and happy to see me again. I was nervous. All I could think was that I needed to ask him as quickly as possible whether I could work at PCP. I began briefly with my recent successes and told him how important finishing college was. He seemed to quickly agree but then I informed him that I was without funds and had no way to make enough money to survive my junior year.

Cesar paused, as if he knew I had an important question to ask him. I was in front of his other workers, realizing that there was no opportunity to meet with him privately as I asked him about my core problem. I tried to calm down, to handle my question with dignity and to not fall apart in front of him. I reminded him that in Lodi was the huge PCP cannery plant. I told him that I was going into my junior year, completely broke and without any hope of savings to support myself for the coming year.

And then I asked him whether I could join the Teamsters so I could secure enough money to finish my education. I had no idea what he would say or what he would think of me once I made this request. I steeled myself for the full range of potential reactions. I knew that once he said no, I would fully comply, and I told him that immediately.

Cesar looked at me quizzically and with affection in his eyes. This was the last response I had ever imagined. He said in front of the other men gathered there, "Antonio, we know you." He was so quietly enthusiastic with me, completely unperturbed by my question. He seemed pleased at my deference and that I was willing to accept any decision that he might make. Cesar said that the UFW would continue to be my family and that he knew that I would continue to fight for La Causa. In that dramatic yet matter-of-fact moment, my future ability to financially survive to complete my education was in the balance. Cesar told me to go ahead and sign up for work at PCP and to use the money I earned to finish my schooling. I was astounded. I had never anticipated a positive answer. Cesar, after knowing me for three years, had in fact full confidence in my loyalty. I continued to work in numerous UFW activities as an undergraduate, all the while grateful for his acceptance of my circumstances.

Cesar's permission and his faith in me was one of the most affirming events of my life. I was a struggling young man who wanted to stay loyal to my people and to become an educated advocate on their behalf. I know with certainty that but for Cesar's kindness and belief in me, I would not have achieved my educational goals and career. This one moment defined my future and allowed me to continue my relationship with Cesar for the next twenty years.

CHAPTER XVIII

Latin America

IN THE FALL OF 1974, I competed for a University of California Fellowship based on my academic performance and a research proposal I submitted. Through the support of my professors, I was awarded a fellowship to represent UCSC at the Universidad de Los Andes in Bogota, Colombia, also known as Uniandes. Established in 1948, this was the first private university in Colombia with a modern mission to be independent of political and religious institutions. I remember my appointment with our Chancellor after being awarded this fellowship. It was our first meeting, and I was nervous about what he might say or ask of me. The Chancellor was friendly, yet direct. He told me I now represented UCSC and would attend a prestigious foreign university, with my credits accumulating directly to UCSC. Then came a most surprising directive. I had long, curly black hair I kept pulled back in a neat ponytail that reached the middle of my back. The Chancellor said, "You are representing UCSC, and you must cut your hair." I could not quite believe that this was a direct order from the Chancellor, but I could not challenge him.

I went to downtown Santa Cruz to get my first haircut in close to three years. Within moments my coveted ponytail was gone, leaving me with a classic short haircut. I went to San Francisco to purchase a modestly priced blue sports coat, gray slacks and a couple of shirts and ties. My standout purchase was my first suit, a brown three-piece corduroy suit for ninety-nine dollars. I was ready for my trip to Colombia. I hoped when I arrived, fully shorn and with more formal dress, that I was acceptably dressed for my studies in Colombia.

My proposal for the fellowship was to evaluate one of the key populist leaders in Latin America, Jorge Eliecier Gaitan, a Colombiano labor lawyer who emerged to save the nation. In the spring of 1948, he became the first indigenous President-Elect of Colombia, as well as the first indigenous elected president in all of Latin America. Gaitan was assassinated on April 9, 1948, in Bogota, at the instigation of Colombia's right-wing leaders. In the tumultuous week following the assassination, thousands of people died in Bogota alone in clashes between Gaitan's supporters and the military, known as the "Bogotazo." During the next three years, Colombia was thrown into a new era called "La Violencia." During La Violencia, an estimated 300,000 people, mostly poor Colombiano campesinos, were killed by the historically oppressive Colombian government.

I was first drawn to Gaitan's career through my earlier research, which was the basis for my fellowship proposal. I discovered that in 1928, Gaitan served as a militant labor attorney following the notorious Matanza de la Bananeras in Cienega, Colombia near Santa Marta. Santa Marta is on the Atlantic coast south of Cartagena, relatively close to Venezuela. Its massive banana plantations, owned by the United Fruit Company, required hundreds to thousands of workers. In addition, the United Fruit Company was protected by Colombian troops, who fired on crowds of strikers. When the workers went on strike, it affected the entire Colombian banana industry and became central to Colombian politics of the day. Newspapers covered this violent strike because the growers slaughtered as high as two thousand banana strikers. Gabriel Garcia-Marquez wrote about the 1928 strike in *Cien Años de Soledad.*"

Gaitan represented to me the best of what a militant labor lawyer could be. He helped to lead a populist movement that highlighted his own indigenous background and encompassed a full-fledged, inclusive, and populist agenda. Gaitan was known for his captivating oratorical skills that drew tens of thousands of Colombianos to his rallies. Gaitan's favorite rallying cry as he ended every speech became a national theme. It was "*A La Carga,*"

(Charge!), and he sent off his supporters, workers and campesinos alike, to fight for their rights.

Gaitan's leadership carried him and his movement to the presidency. I deeply appreciated finding an inspirational labor lawyer like Gaitan. Gaitan reflected my values: defending field hands, suffering beatings, witnessing many deaths, yet having the courage to advocate for workers all his life. I wanted to absorb every aspect of his life as a guide for my own aspirations.

I spent almost two years in Bogota, extending my undergraduate education to five years. The first year I lived with Susan in downtown Bogota in a modern second-floor one-bedroom apartment, with a wall of enormous windows overlooking the ornate Palacio de Bellas Artes. Within the first two weeks in Colombia, a window of access to the American and Colombian ruling class opened to us by sheer happenstance. We were in the line at the American Embassy, and an American white woman in her forties overheard our conversation. She really took to us as a young couple, introduced herself and invited us to her home. It was in El Norte, a ruling class neighborhood, eighty to a hundred blocks from where we lived. Her family occupied a near mansion- sized, white, single-story home with a dozen servants. Her husband was the President of a large American pharmaceutical company for Colombia.

The family welcomed us, and we started upon a social calendar that, but for this chance meeting, would not have been open to us. We met other wealthy Americans, presidents of large international corporations. We were introduced to their social clubs and invited to house parties that seemed to never stop. The wealthy Colombian guests owned *fincas* so large that they incorporated vast valleys located just outside of Bogota. The young adult children liked us as well and took us to view land. Often, dozens of workers tilled the fields and tended to the livestock. We and our hosts meanwhile attended elaborate picnics and barbecues featuring famous Colombian beef and excellent local wines. To me the contrast was nearly unbearable given my roots and the focus of my research.

I began my audit of classes at Universidad de Los Andes, and immediately discovered that this was a ruling class university for the nation. I could walk to the university from my neighborhood apartment, which was located in the old colonial downtown area, a world away from where the new Colombian elite now chose to live. I attended courses without difficulty. I was not surprised that despite its progressive mission statement, the university taught from a reactionary point of view based on ruling class historical perspectives. I cast aside my hope that it was the anticipated progressive school as I realized the true conservative nature of the university.

I noticed one remarkable feature of Uniandes that distinguished me from other students. I noticed that every student arrived at the university driven by their chauffeur. This made little difference to me, and I considered it relatively inconsequential given the ruling class status of Uniandes. I happened to mention this in passing to the kind American couple. To my chagrin, they refused to let me be the only one to arrive, particularly given my UC fellowship status, without a chauffeur. This family had three chauffeurs available. There was no opportunity to reject their solution. That day they provided me with a chauffeur for the remainder of my time in Bogota.

My chauffeur's name was Julio, and he had worked for the household for several years. Julio was in his late thirties, with dark hair, a relatively small build, and kind eyes that were often filled with visible exhaustion as he struggled with his long hours to support his large family. Julio's salary was sixty dollars a month. He lived in the distant southern regions of Bogota and traveled by bus three hours a day each way to and from his employers' El Norte home. His daily hours often extended into the evening without warning. But no matter what, he met me at my downtown apartment to drive me a dozen blocks to school.

Julio's sixty-dollar monthly salary was slightly above the minimum wage, but I had savings as well as a scholarship. I could not bear his horrific commuting schedule, six hours a day. I paid him an extra one hundred dollars a month for the full time I was there. This not only made him grateful and very much helped his family, but it also opened up our relationship. We spent our time in a 1973 light blue four door Plymouth Valiant, then costing over twenty thousand dollars due to import taxes for a middle class American vehicle. I absorbed many lessons from Julio about the Colombian working class, and these contributed to my thesis research.

My nearly two-year stint was interrupted by a brief return to the United States when I used the time to earn the high wages at the cannery. By the Fall of 1975, through the help of additional university monies and my own savings, I was able to return to Bogota for almost a full year. During this second year Susan was also in Colombia, but our status as a couple was sporadic, and our attempts to again live together in Colombia went through many challenges.

I used both years for my research, exclusively working with Spanish resources and conducting numerous taped interviews. Gaitan's legacy was still extraordinarily strong as he was considered the long-lost hope of the majority of Colombianos living under considerable oppression in 1974-1976. This oppression was visible everywhere in Bogota. Each corner was guarded around the clock by two soldiers with semi-automatic weapons prepared to mow down dissenters. Checkpoints were at every turn. An arrest could occur without proper identification.

I remember my anxiousness, as I spent days of my time in the poorer sections of southern Bogota. This was the oldest colonial area of the capitol with cobblestone steps, churches from the early sixteenth century and narrow alleyways opening up to Bogota plazas that could hold thirty thousand people. I decided to attend every labor demonstration that I could that was advertised through both El Tiempo, then led by Gabriel Garcia-Marquez, as well as covered in the leftist press. The demonstrations drew at least a few hundred if not several thousand workers and campesinos. The demonstrations took place both in the numerous large plazas in Bogota as well as in the streets. Military forces surrounded and monitored the demonstrations. The military was there to intimidate us with a show of force far larger than needed for a pacifist rally calling for justice for workers as well as human rights. The military police provoked us with their shields and clubs, particularly those protesters at the front of the demonstration. I took precautions to protect myself since I looked Colombiano and could easily be swept up into their arrests. I kept attending these labor and campesino demonstrations, not out of courage, but knowing my involvement was essential to reinforce my identity and solidarity with the labor movement.

My interviews with workers and campesinos whose families had survived both the Bogotazo as well as La Violencia formed the backdrop of my thesis. I was fortunate enough to access the resources of all of the major libraries in Bogota. I came well prepared to my interviews with leading Colombian scholars. Most importantly, I gained access to Gaitan's family. I was able to interview at length his radical daughter, Gloria Gaitan, a leading figure in Colombian politics. This successful interview and her approval of me opened the door to the Colombian leftist intellectual elite that normally would not have been accessible to me.

I returned to my last year at UCSC as a militant anti-imperialist, with a focus on the horrific history of US coups that had overthrown elected Latin American governments. I needed to finish my Latin American Studies major and graduate. I completed a well-received thesis based on my two years of original Colombian research on Gaitan. I was asked by my professors to compete internally with other UCSC students to see If I could be selected as their sole candidate for the Danforth Fellowship.

The Danforth Fellowship was limited to about twenty annual national recipients. It provided tuition and support covering four years of graduate studies. Each of the more than three thousand national universities could only choose one undergraduate student to compete for the Fellowship. After an interview with a large University committee where I defended my academic record, I was selected to be UCSC's candidate for the Danforth.

I do recall one unexpected comment: The committee said I had done well yet noted I was "impenetrable" in presenting my record. Their use of this word shocked me, but I instantly recognized its truth. I had been forced to defend myself since childhood and to do so required building impenetrable walls around me to survive. I did not realize that these defenses would be so visible to the committee. Their one word critique hit me so hard, that I carried it with me for the rest of my life. Through the help of my Latin American advisor, Dr. David Sweet, and Nobby's support for my application, I was fortunate to receive the Danforth. Although I was focused on becoming a union labor lawyer, I accepted the award to further research Gaitan's life through graduate studies at Stanford University.

CHAPTER XIX

Just One Look and a New Forty-Year Love Begins

IN DECEMBER OF 1979, in my first year of law school, I broke up with Susan after nearly eight years of our intense relationship. I blame myself for the breakup for many reasons, but by December I knew that the situation was untenable. Our breakup was miserable in all aspects, creating a deep sense of loss in both of us as we tried to sustain some kind of friendship. But the fundamental truth remained. I left Susan for another woman who had overtaken and captured my heart and my romantic imagination. I was not going to lose the opportunity to be with this new woman. I saw my future with her.

I first saw Katherine Poss as she crossed through the archways of Stanford's Spanish colonial quadrangle. I glimpsed her from behind as she walked fifty feet ahead of me. I noticed the sway of her gold paisley print mid-calf skirt and her white blouse, but most of all I noticed her rhythmic and confident stride, one that struck me as the essence of femininity. I could not see her face, but from behind I noticed her curly hair, her porcelain skin as well as her delicate arms and legs. It was not usual for me to gawk at women, but seeing Katherine stripped me of my normal inhibitions; I was caught off guard by a strong and unbidden physical attraction to her. Katherine was unknown to me, yet just that glimpse was enough. I needed to find out who she was and to meet her. I knew she was not in my Latin American History field at Stanford.

Many Stanford grad students and faculty chose to carpool back and forth from San Francisco to Stanford. I had a four door tiny

Fiat 128, and I decided to join a carpool of history grad students. Luck was with me. In my new carpool route Katherine was the last passenger we picked up in the morning.

When Katherine left her top floor Victorian flat at Day and Church Street in the Outer Mission, it was the first time I saw her up close. I could not believe my good fortune when I watched her walk toward the car. She had a heart-shaped face, sparkling brown eyes, an enchanting smile, and carefully but lightly applied makeup. She was physically the most appealing woman I had ever seen. Katherine also wore perfume, something that I appreciated and was not so typical in the feminist circles with which I was familiar. When I wasn't driving the carpool, I finagled to have Katherine and me end up in the cramped back seat, where I could slide an arm along her shoulders in response to the car's jostling. Katherine told me later that she just thought I was a friendly guy, a good confidant, but she had no idea of my romantic interest in her.

Katherine and I hit it off quickly, but there were clear limitations. Katherine was dating a Puerto Rican man in the Mission, and I was living in the Haight Ashbury with Susan. Katherine and I became close friends but not for a second did we ever cross the line. We never exchanged a single kiss or a hug, in deference to our respective circumstances. Even so, it became increasingly clear to me that I was not prepared to lose Katherine.

In early April of 1979, nearly two years had passed with Katherine unaware of my unrequited love. I realized that I would soon be heading off to law school, and I had yet to have even one truly private moment with her. I knew that she had broken up with her boyfriend, but I had no idea if we might become closer. In addition to my physical attraction to her, I was impressed by the scope of her considerable knowledge of progressive and feminist politics and her deep commitment to social change.

Katherine had worked all four years of college (except for a year at the London School of Economics) at Project Upward Bound, a federal program that helped prepare inner city minority youth for college. She was typically the only white staff member. This work grew from her high school activism when she worked on Martin Luther King's Poor Peoples' Campaign. Katherine had a fierce devotion to her students and a sophisticated analysis about the racial, class and gender stratification of the public school system. She brought this background to Stanford, and it informed her dissertation research and her alliances and activities. She was the first Assistant to the Dean for Student Affairs in the School of Education, an early member of the Center for Research on Women and a founder of the Graduate Women's Research Network. She was the only non-Puerto Rican member of the Stanford Puerto Rican Students Association. Her involvement with these students merged into years of participation in the Puerto Rican Solidarity Committee, which supported the movement for Puerto Rican independence and did ground-breaking work on the environmental exploitation of the island. I later joined Katherine in this work.

Katherine's beauty, intellect, kindness, and political convictions were an irresistible combination. I had to act. I decided to invite her to a "good-bye" lunch at San Francisco's historic Mario's Bohemian Cigar Store Café in North Beach, located in Little Italy. Katherine accepted, and I nervously anticipated our lunch. The Bohemian Cafe was located on a corner of Saint Marks square, across from Saints Peter and Paul church, one of the largest and most ornate Catholic churches in San Francisco. It was a quirky, charming little place for wine and small plates. The old Italian restaurant held about ten small tables and the bar served another ten guests.

Katherine and I sat at the third table along the wall, ordered our red wine, and began what would be a two-hour lunch. I listened to her very carefully. I chose questions that reassured me that she had left her current boyfriend and was moving on with her life. I could not take my eyes off her animated face. I knew that beginning a relationship with Katherine would end my relationship with Susan. I had to assess if this was the road I should go down if Katherine was interested. Even then I was wondering whether I could see a lifetime with her. Katherine had no idea of the decision that I made on the spot during that lunch.

At that lunch, I made the decision to marry Katherine if she would have me. She had no idea, and she did not know this for some time. I turned my entire life upside down. I cared about Susan, and I know I caused her pain as I began to extricate myself from a first love relationship that was no longer working. I wanted to stay in

San Francisco for law school, but Susan had just secured a job in Dixon, California, a tiny rural town outside of Davis. Because both of us were on automatic during this transition; we did not face the true, unresolvable crisis of our relationship. I chose the University of California at Davis, which was located twenty miles from Susan's first job as a teacher. I had held on to the faint possibility of reconciliation, but by December I knew that my breakup with her could no longer be delayed.

I left Susan, and I headed to Katherine's home in San Francisco to begin the next chapter of my life. Katherine turned out to be a very caring, nurturing woman, and a loving romantic partner. I arrived at her flat and was welcomed by her two remarkable women housemates and the small daughter of the house. Katherine took great pains with my weekend arrival. She greeted me with fresh flowers along with an unopened bottle of Johnny Walker scotch. I felt the light-hearted spirit of a new love grow and take root as a new plant inside me.

I finished my first year and received a summer internship at a leading Democratic law firm in San Francisco. My housing unexpectedly fell through, but Katherine's flat mates approved my spending the summer there with Katherine. The household women became lifelong close friends, and one woman in particular, Marty Williams, remains one of our closest friends in Katherine's and my shared life. I remember Katherine's classic statement about living together when I was starting my third year of law school. Her response was amusing, yet firm. Katherine said she would never consider going to all the work of packing up her considerable library unless it was permanent. This sounded reasonable to me, consistent with Katherine's independent spirit.

Katherine made the move after we became engaged in May 1981. We found our first home together in the older downtown section of Sacramento, located on a wooded street of large oak trees in a home that had been constructed by a master plasterer. Although the home was modest, we had a plaster cupola in our living room ceiling. Katherine and I moved in with a yellow Formica kitchen table from the late fifties and a cinder block and plywood bed. Katherine was still working on her dissertation and set up a home office.

We got married in the middle of the winter in Buffalo, New York, where Katherine grew up. Katherine was raised in a Jewish family that included generations of well-known Muscovite rabbis. Her father had been raised orthodox but rejected orthodoxy when he went to college. Katherine's mother, raised in a Conservative Jewish family, was also not a believer. Katherine's father served in Guadalcanal in World War II. Like so many Jews in the post Shoah period, Katherine's parents had no belief in God, but raised their four children in the reform Jewish religion in honor of those who had perished. Katherine's parents, Gilbert and Bernice, made it very clear to me that they considered religion to be an individual choice. They had no expectation or desire that I convert to Judaism. Katherine's family rabbi kindly performed the ceremony for us in the family's synagogue .

Through my marriage I gained a new family. I was able to meet Katherine's parents along with her three siblings before the wedding. Katherine's family accepted me from the moment of our engagement. Her parents provided us with encouragement and assistance at every turn. They became the best model of a mother and father in my life.

Katherine's father was an optometrist who was one of the area's only eye doctors willing to see elderly Medicare patients in Buffalo's nursing homes. Ms. Poss was an administrator at SUNY Buffalo and taught the first course there on women's history. Modest, non-materialistic, they saved all their money to put their four children through college. They were progressive without being ideologues, active in residential desegregation efforts, voter education, and numerous human rights and volunteer activities. Her parents transmitted to their children their deep appreciation for the arts and their eye for the Avant-garde. They furnished their suburban home with Eames, Noguchi and Herman Miller pieces that were quite affordable at the time and that baffled Bernice Poss's more conservative sisters.

An enduring love of the natural world was central to their lives. They were avid bird watchers and gardeners and grew enough produce from their backyard garden for the entire summer. Their most important shared quality, however, was their moral righteousness, a fundamental belief in the equal worth and dignity of all human beings that informed their actions. These parents could not have been more different from John and Sara. I was blessed to know them.

CHAPTER XX

Coming Home to Petra and the Salazars

MY REUNIFICATION WITH THE SALAZARS, one that I had fervently sought since my kidnapping at age four in February of 1961, had consumed every waking moment, every ambition of my life. It was now late May of 1982 and I had not seen them for almost twenty-three years.

I prepared carefully for my reunification. I had just graduated from U.C. Davis Law School two days earlier. I now had reached my dream of acquiring the skills and degrees to help my family and my people. We could finally afford to hire a private investigator to search for my family. I did not know if he would be able to find the Salazars with almost no facts to begin his search. Although I knew the names of each one of my thirteen siblings, having lived with them in my mind as I struggled to survive, I knew nothing of their exact birth dates, their occupations, their addresses or whether all of them were still alive.

An unanticipated and unnerving worry dominated me as the investigator's search began. If I were lucky enough to find the Salazars, would I even have a chance to be accepted by them? I realized that I felt extremely vulnerable, preoccupied with night-mares of rejections, uncertain how to introduce myself back into their lives. But I refused to believe that if my mother were still alive, that she would have forgotten me, that she no longer loved me and that I would be too far away from her world to be recognizable. Petra's teachings of early, enduring love and her kindness as a mother had enabled me to survive to 1983. I just wrapped myself in her images and quietly calmed myself to end the journey I had started twenty-four years earlier.

I had one document upon which the entire search was based. I had ordered a copy of my original birth certificate. It listed my parents as Petra and Jesus Salazar. Apparently, this was all I needed to achieve my overriding goal, which was to return to my mother, Petra. Soon the detective was faxing Katherine and me copies of my siblings' phone numbers and addresses. This included my eldest brother Roman, some twenty-two years my senior, and his wife Cecilia. We started with him.

I had been supported in my search by my closest San Franciscan friend, Tony Colon. Tony's role was to make the first contact with Roman to see if he had a missing brother called Antonio. Tony approached this assignment with great care. He knew how important my family was to me, and he feared that I would be rejected outright. Tony wanted to be the one to absorb the blows should they come out against me so that I would receive their response through him. Tony said that he spent less than two minutes on the phone with Roman, prepared to jump off as quickly as possible if there was either denial, lack of any interest or sense of hatred against me for my innocent kidnapping. But Roman responded with great affection and confirmed that I was the long-lost kidnapped brother. He was stunned at the news. Most importantly, he was welcoming to Tony, eager for every bit of information. Tony thanked him without going into any detail of my life other than to say I had just finished law school. He told Roman I would call him right away.

I called Roman with my heart filled with love but also trepidation. I had armed myself with the basic truths of my life. I had been kidnapped, raped, and abused. I knew there was no easy way to share this terrible story with the Salazars, and there was a real possibility that I would choose to forever keep silent about what I had endured. The prospect of returning with my story brought back unbidden, painful images of shame regarding the rapes. I worried that if the Salazars ever found out all that John and Sara had done to me, I would be blamed and easily disposed. At the outset, I knew my true story might be a step too far, too much to absorb with too many risks.

But the other truth that had shaped me from my earliest fury at the Hobsons was I did not want to be made "white." As I became educated, I refused to become an assimilated Chicano who rejected his roots. It was because of this defining principle in my life that I ran to every Chicano or Mexicano experience that I could find. This began with the neighboring Mexican chicken workers in Hemet, who gave me my first return to Spanish when I was six. It was followed up by Jaime and Maria Elena, the Mexican cowboy family at the Ranch who enabled me to survive the first two summers of assaults. During my three years at the El Rancho Motel, I had been adopted by the Ramirez family and picked three full seasons of fruit with them as I returned to the identical farm work upon which the Salazars had built their lives. By the age of fourteen I had become radicalized by the UFW and joined Cesar Chavez's movement, deciding I would become an advocate for farmworkers. When I went to UCSC, not only did I focus on Chicano and Latin American History, but I worked my fourth full season of picking fruit. I picked strawberries on my knees for three months as I conducted my migrant housing surveys in Salinas. And I had just completed my dream of becoming a labor lawyer so I could represent unions and my own people.

These were the worries and defenses I brought to this moment of reunification. It never occurred to me that my return all by itself was enough or that any of the underlying elaborate justifications that I had created were likely unnecessary. Instead, I waited years while gathering my "creds" so that I had at least have some justification for returning to their lives. Did I think that Petra would only love me as an attorney? Would she only love me if I fully loved my father Jesus, a misogynist drunk accustomed to the nightly beatings of Petra and his children? I had so over-complicated my return to her that I lost sight of the sole requirement that she in fact had. Petra wanted to see her lost son before she died, and she likely hoped that we could speak together in Spanish. That was all she needed.

Although these were the thoughts that burdened me, I refused to let them slow down my return call to Roman. I had not spoken with Roman since the age of four. The first thing he said was, "Tony, we miss you, where have you been?"

I replied, "California, is my mother alive?"

Roman replied, "Mama is still alive, but our father died two years earlier." The fact that Petra was still alive was all I needed at that moment. I had met my crucial deadline. I would be able to return in time to show her what her son had accomplished with her strength and in her honor.

Word of my return traveled like wildfire throughout my family and within a day, my extensive, tribe-size family knew that "Tony" was coming home. I planned with Roman that I would be there in Phoenix a few days after my law school graduation, with Katherine at my side. In the interim I received from Roman and Cecilia an overview of my family, including the deaths of some brothers, so that I had a working idea of the basic relationships of my siblings prior to my arrival.

Everything was set for a carefully planned and quiet personal reunification. Our plans were shattered when we were contacted by a television reporter. He said that a family member had contacted three news stations, including his, to cover my exit from the plane as I met my family, and I should prepare for an interview. I knew with disgust how this would be spun. Poor barrio Chicano family meets long lost attorney brother. Nurture over nature. It would be unbearable. I stopped him dead in his tracks. I told him that I was immediately cancelling the flight since my privacy of an intensely personal moment was going to be violated. I further told him with cold conviction that I had waited twenty years for this moment, and I could wait another twenty years if need be to avoid the media. Katherine and I changed our flights.

I calmly called Roman and let him know how I wanted my return to be. I said that Petra had the right to see me first, alone, without anyone else present. I arranged for a nice second floor suite in a hotel and had my family drop her off at the room at a specific time. Katherine and I had our own separate room away from the suite to ensure that I had total privacy when I met Petra alone.

The moment came as I knocked at the door and it opened. In front of me was Petra. I said, "Hola, Madre," and I could get no further. I embraced this small woman and we both wept. I had cried only a half dozen times since my kidnapping as the rawness of my loss had forced this upon me as a way to survive. But now she was before me, familiar in every way. It was like only a millisecond had passed since I last saw her, yet it had been a lifetime. We finally broke our long embrace, looked into each other's eyes, and I could tell she saw her son.

Petra's soft, oval face, framed now by white wavy collar-length hair, was instantly recognizable. Petra had the warmest of dark brown eyes, although her weariness was reflected in them. Even so her presence still conveyed her quiet strength to survive as she had from her illegal marriage at the age of thirteen in El Paso, Texas. Her body and face reflected the harshness of her life. Petra was now in her late sixties and with worn lines in her face and gnarled hands from over forty years of backbreaking work in the fields. She had a short, womanly body from giving birth to fourteen children. She radiated the natural warmth of a mother. But most of all Petra had the same rare smile of my memories, one that became irrepressible with her happiness at my return.

We made our way to a table overlooking the patio, and we began to speak. I could see the pride in her eyes as soon as she realized I was fluent in Spanish. I postponed any talk of my accomplishments because I urgently needed to tell her what she had meant to me and how, but for her, I would have not had the strength to survive the Hobsons. I became emotional again. I was at first worried about my own tears, but when she began to cry as well, the moment became perfect.

It was Petra's turn to share. The family had broken up within ten days of my kidnapping, never to be brought together again under one roof. She said that Jesus had blamed her, thrown her out, but for years he still required her to come by each day to leave three meals on the porch for the remaining children. I was overcome that my kidnapping caused an irreparable breach. I reeled from the news that Jesus, being the completely vicious man that he was, destroyed our entire family permanently over the excuse of my kidnapping, while still keeping my dominated mother as an indentured servant. The one bright spot was that Petra found another man, Rogelio, who was kind to her and with whom she spent the rest of her life. They lived within a few blocks of our home in the projects, allowing her to stay close to our family. Petra informed me that Jesus had died two years earlier from pesticide-related disease from his decades of farm labor.

Petra talked about the family's two years of fruitless efforts to find me. My father reported my kidnapping to the Phoenix police, but our family's status as mere Mexicans with a lost Mexican child prompted little effort into the official search. Apparently, the case lingered for two years before there was an outright refusal from downtown to do anything further to find me. I believe that if we had been a white family, with a white kidnapped child, the authorities would have made a genuine effort to find that child, rather than essentially writing off the crime from the beginning. In addition, my kidnappers were white kidnappers, whose actions were allowed to go unchallenged.

Petra then updated me on my siblings, their marriages, children, successes as well as the incarceration over many years of three of my brothers. The room's atmosphere was not only intimate but became increasingly relaxed. I was so grateful for every scrap of news. But the fact that my family had looked for me finally answered a key question in my life. I had not been abandoned. I had not been forgotten and they had done everything in their limited power to find their lost son and sibling. This alone almost made my long journey worth it.

I then began to tell her about the February 1959 kidnapping and its aftermath, sharing with her the ways I daily held onto my family's memories. I told her about my adobe burial grounds, the Mexican families who helped me and my farm work. I slowly began to tell her about the Hobsons, everything except the sexual abuse. This included the forced isolation, the weeks of silence, the denigrations, and the motels where we lived. I went into as much detail as I thought she could absorb on that first meeting.

I took great care in recounting my educational opportunities. I needed it to be brief and to keep in mind that most of my siblings would have had extremely limited educational opportunities. I was not a person who was full of himself but instead wanted to be as much as I could be like my family, despite all the differences. I told Petra about Cesar Chavez, and she immediately recognized his name. I told her he had taken me on as a student to train along with many others, to advocate for farmworkers. I mentioned very briefly my undergraduate education, just citing my majors and a brief description of my life in Latin America. I remember listing Stanford in just a sentence on my way to law school. I described my law school years through the lens of becoming an attorney for unions and farmworkers. I told her a bit about Katherine, whom she would meet tomorrow.

The moment had arrived to say good night. We would see each other the following day at her home with all my siblings present. I had no idea what to expect in terms of their acceptance, but once I met Petra, I knew that no matter what, I had accomplished my dream. Would my siblings resent me? Would they see me in their own minds as unapproachable, an alien among those who shared the same blood? Or would they take Petra's lead and accept me for who I was?

Katherine and I arrived at my mother's home, a modest two-bedroom home with a parched front yard. Petra's house was located in the heart of one of the oldest and poorest barrios twenty blocks from downtown Phoenix. We entered and Petra was dressed in her familiar house dress, sweeping the floors. Then I noticed something unexpected, particularly in the middle of a major city. Except for her kitchen and the bathroom, which were covered in linoleum and tile, all the floors including the living room in this urban home were made of hard Arizona dirt. It shamed me to think that I had complained of the $3.50 a night El Rancho Motel that did have real floors. I knew that if I had lived in the Southwest this would have been a common sight, particularly in rural campesino settings, but this was in the heart of Phoenix. In my California fruit-picking experience, even my visits to campesino housing in Salinas, I was used to rough, unfinished broken-down wood floors, but these dirt floors caught me off guard. It was an image that I needed to see to understand my mother's living conditions

My sisters started to arrive with their families, and they came inside to meet me and to start cooking. They included my favorite sister Stella who had bathed me as a child every night. I was introduced to Helen and Licha, two of my oldest siblings, of whom I had little memory but was eager to get to know. All of my sisters were stunned when they saw me. I found out that I had most of the same facial characteristics of both Jesus and my brothers. I also shared our dark skin, along with a similar slender frame of many of my brothers. From the moment they saw me there was no question as to who I was. It was undeniable that I was the missing Tony.

My sisters then heard me speak Spanish to our mother without any hesitation. They were warmed by my Spanish, particularly my older sisters who were fluent and used predominantly Spanish in their lives. We all jumped into the extraordinary moment, flew into our native Spanish and the joy among us seemed boundless. Katherine, with her generous heart and her ready soft smile, turned out to be an essential presence, assuring the day continued to go smoothly. My sisters and my brothers' wives took to her instantly, welcoming her into their world, and making sure she felt included as a new Salazar family member.

But I had yet to meet any of my brothers, my sources of true worry in this reunion. I met my first one as he walked out of my mother's second bedroom. It was Roy, my youngest brother. Neither of us could believe what we saw. Although Roy was at least five inches shorter than I, we were fairly close to identical twins. We embraced briefly yet warmly, eager to get another prolonged look at each other to confirm if what we were seeing was an illusion. But it was true; we looked remarkably similar, except for the fact that he was slightly sturdier than me. He told me that he had been a professional boxer for about a decade, so that easily explained our different body types.

The next brother to arrive was Roman with his spouse Cecilia. At that time Roman and his wife had been the only ones to achieve middle class status through Roman's job with the City of Phoenix as a gardener and Cecilia's as a bank teller. Roman looked much like me as well. Everything about us, from our faces to our hands and skin color were so similar that yet again there was no doubt that he was my brother, just an older version of me. He carried himself with a quiet dignity, unpretentious, very bright and married now for almost thirty years. Both Cecilia and Roman, while fluent in English, lived their lives at home in Spanish, and were surprised that I spoke Spanish well. With our shared looks and language, Roman became the one to introduce me to my arriving brothers.

The rest of my brothers arrived as expected with their suspicions and resentments in tow. I was determined to face them and had planned countless strategies for taking on every contingency short of a physical brawl. Roman took me outside to meet them:

Rudy, Robert, Daniel, and Henry, who were clustered by a fence under the shade of a forlorn tree, waiting to find out who the hell I was, undoubtedly someone they could easily dismiss from their lives. But I didn't realize that I was unexpectedly playing with a full set of aces that could not be beat. I walked out directly and as they watched my approach, a sea change instantly occurred for all of us. I shared their facial features from both our parents and there was no mistaking that I was the brother they had lost. Equally disconcerting to them was not only my striking similarity to all of them, shared some our father's facial features, but most important, I had his identical gait.

This was a good start, but it had its limitations. Rudy had just left nearly fourteen years in Florence Prison located in Florence Arizona, the same one where my missing brother Ralph was still imprisoned. Rudy was a serious shot caller with a reputation for brutality. He was almost six feet tall, pure muscle from years in the prison gym and breathtakingly handsome with his bigote, perfectly ironed khaki pants and shirt, and spotlessly shined black shoes. He was the most handsome *vato* I had ever seen, conveying enormous strength and unquestioned authority. Rudy had that unique hardened, prison stare that went for a thousand miles as he looked at you as if you were an inconvenient piece of lint. It intimidated me to my very core because I knew I had little room to break through to him. Although my other brothers were warmer, following Roman's and Roy's example, Rudy was having none of it.

Some of their wives were present, and this helped calm things down, forcing everyone to accept brief hugs before I introduced myself. I had one more concern as I started. I spoke the most formal English that you have ever heard. I was also blessed with a unique deep-sounding voice, often commented upon as something exceptional, and it became a distinctive trait that has helped define me. I never told people the true price I had paid to be oppressively taught formal English by the Hobsons in this rarified form, but I knew of no other way to speak. I had always been able to help diminish the overwhelming formality of my English by returning to my Spanish-speaking environments whenever I could. But then I had the problem of speaking an educated Spanish, given my years of research in the language. I knew that both these factors could alienate my brothers once they heard the first words come out of my mouth. I had no choice; I was who I was. I could not change my voice, but I could try to tone it down to make it bearable. I just began by telling them about the previous night with Petra and how much it meant to finally come home to them. I broke into Spanish carefully, knowing that my youngest brothers' Spanish would likely be limited to just a few words of our commonly used Pocho language. The last thing that I needed to do was to show off my academic Spanish skills.

I knew there were two leaders in the group of brothers I faced. They were Roman and Rudy. I spoke to Roman, but I willed myself to look directly at Rudy at all times. I knew that it could not be a blinking contest because I would lose straight out; I was so far out of my league. Instead, I focused on his mouth, his overall countenance and demeanor, looking for any signs that Rudy might begin to accept me. There were none. My information about him was so limited, so adverse, that I knew that I had to avoid an outright loss because he might take many of my younger siblings with him.

I asked myself what they really needed to know, right now, no bullshit about their long-lost brother. It was quite clear. They had to assure themselves at that moment that I wasn't some privileged, anglicized brown boy who had already left his people way behind for the white man's world. I had a desperate story, and I just had to tell them what it was, regardless of my accents, regardless of my educational status.

It was crucial to me as I began to tell them my story that I risked zero vulnerability, preferring to become impenetrable if needed. I started to tell them of the night of my kidnapping and that I had never forgotten a single sibling, a single name but instead had thousands of images of them when we were together as a family. I told them the truth that but for these images which filled my heart, I would not have had the strength to survive the cruelty of the Hobsons. My statements were straightforward. They understood that I had never forgotten them for a minute and that returning to them meant everything to me.

They asked many questions, and I answered each one, from where I had I lived to what my work background was. Once they found out my years of total isolation by the Hobsons, the long weeks of silence, and their vicious treatment of me, the mood changed again. I told them the Hobsons had been the worst of monsters. As they heard about the El Rancho Motel, my stint at juvenile hall, and my escape from the Hobsons at sixteen, I could feel the first glimmers of acceptance. I then followed this up with picking fruit for four seasons, one on a UFW ranch in Salinas and the dam started to erode. Rudy hadn't taken his eyes off me, but somehow he signaled that I might barely be OK. I could see the relief in my younger brothers' faces who had looked to Rudy to make the decision, and I noticed Roman's approval of how our conversation had unfolded. Rudy said, "Let's go eat with Tony," and I knew that I had passed his first of many tests for acceptance. I was also grateful to Rudy's wife Frances, who made an instant connection with Katherine and worked to smooth out the day for the two of us. It turned out that Rudy would become one of my closest siblings. We have called each other every day for decades as our young families grew up together.

The traditional meal was a feast of all things Mexican, from the hottest of fresh salsas and endless tamales to perfectly barbecued meats. The meal was set out in the front yard with at least twenty-five or more family members present with their spouses and children. Balloons decorated the yard, tied to the fold-out chairs, the nearby chain link fence and the one struggling Arizona shade tree. My sisters insisted on serving me my meal, a reminder of long-lost care. Everyone started to relax, and laughter surrounded the table as the children got up and down throughout the meal to play with their cousins. At the head of the table was an enormous sheet cake that Petra had baked in my honor. I was overtaken by the joys of having for the first time my own mother's cake to celebrate with my family. I was asked to cut the first slice, and then I basked in happiness as my sisters took the rest of the cake into their own hands, serving eager children cake as the adults waited.

The image of my family on this day of reunification was all I had imagined and dared hope for in my long-delayed dream. I had received the rarest of miracles with my return to the Salazars. I felt myself fall into a state of grace, profoundly grateful that my hopes had been answered. But the most important thing for me was to see the quiet joy on Petra's face as she absorbed how we interacted as siblings, so pleased that her longed-for day was turning out the way we had both wanted.

I did not expect to learn most of the essential details of my siblings' lives that first day. But it was only May of 1983, and I have had almost forty years to interact with the Salazars, to be loved and to love my family as the core to my being. I would learn many good things about my family, and see great economic progress finally take shape with some of our family members to my great admiration and relief. At the same time the story of unbearable racism dominated every aspect of the Salazars' lives. I made it my life's mission to serve them not only as a loving brother but as a legal representative for the family for all these decades. Now that I had the Salazars I could be a more complete human being, a better spouse, a kinder father, possibly a more skilled attorney, all because the reunion had given me back my full identity.

CHAPTER XXI

Marriage, Work, Family and Faith

I RECALL STARTING TO UNPACK my suitcase after returning to Sacramento in 1980 where I was living during law school. I had just made the grinding weekend bus ride to visit Katherine in San Francisco. Nestled among my clothes I found she had hidden small soaps, cologne samples, and a love note. No one had ever done something like that for me before. This was just the beginning of a life together in which Katherine allowed no birthday of mine to pass without a birthday cake, multiple cards, and gifts, things I never experienced in childhood. This was my Katherine, the woman I met when we were both graduate students in PhD programs at Stanford and for whom I had changed my entire life to reach my dream of marrying her, for what I hoped would be a lifetime of love. Katherine was intellectually gifted, devoted to anti-racist and women's struggles, as well as politically active in solidarity movements. But what captivated me most was her unfailing kindness to me and her inherent humility. Katherine has all of these qualities, along with physical beauty. This is the woman I have been blessed to be with for over forty years.

After Katherine and I finished law school and passed our state bar exams, we were eager to return to San Francisco, which both of us considered to be our true home. Driving up and down its hills, as each new view appears revealing the soft fog or blue bay, the pastel stuccoed houses, the pink blossomed plum trees, or Glen Park's eucalyptus gulches, we feel its magic to this day. With the help of Katherine's family, we were able to acquire an 1886 Victorian worker's cottage on a small street in the Castro District. I recall the fervor with which we pursued our first remodeling efforts, choosing Mexican paver tiles and blotching the walls with ten shades of off-white paint samples. Katherine and I found legal jobs, and she started her training as an intellectual property litigator at a major law firm. She would come home at ten at night carrying take-out burritos. My sisters often called her and asked, "What did you fix Antonio tonight for dinner?" and Katherine just laughed. "I guess they think I'm not doing a very good job of taking wifely care of you."

I had the privilege of using my law degree in the way I dreamed I would. My first job was working as an organizer for the California State Employees Association as I awaited my Bar exam results. I next had the great fortune to become the first in-house counsel for the Service Employees International Union, Local 790, the largest public sector union in San Francisco. With SEIU I was in charge of handling all termination appeals before the Civil Service Commission. I represented the union in numerous arbitrations. I negotiated the renewal of the union contract for the San Francisco Unified School District workers. The SEIU was a very progressive union nationally, and Local 790 was at the forefront. I was able to take on the first city workers' union case successfully defending a transgender worker in 1988, changing city-wide policy.

My SEIU experience led to a position with the Communications Workers of America. CWA was a million member plus national union representing telecommunication workers such as operators and line installers, as well as workers in the publishing industry for all major newspapers. I was hired as District 9 Counsel assigned to California, Nevada, and Hawaii cases. I represented CWA in arbitrations, cases before the National Labor Relations Board, the state Public Utilities Commission and in multiyear Federal Court litigation.

One of the CWA cases for which I am most grateful to have represented striking workers is La Conexion Familiar. The all-women workforce of nearly two hundred telemarketers working for Sprint in San Francisco were fired one hour before a CWA election where pro-union support was overwhelming. In one year of litigation with the NLRB I was the sole attorney against a squadron of employer counsel during a six month trial. In this case of importance to the national labor movement, the union won 53 unfair labor practices against Sprint.

I also secured a federal consent decree against Contel, then the third largest national telecommunications company. Exploited Latina telecom employees were forced to speak Spanish on the job without extra compensation for their language skills. They faced termination if they failed to comply. In contrast, white employees who were fully bilingual were exempted from this requirement and faced no risk of disciplinary action, much less being fired. We won a three year consent decree reversing the discriminatory practices. Another memorable CWA victory occurred in my representation of the union through two six-month trials before the CPUC. In two separate attempts, nonunion employers tried to strip away CWA 10,000 union jobs. In these proceedings I was pitted against over thirty attorneys as the sole counsel for the union. The union prevailed at the first trial, for a value of 6.2 billion dollars in regulatory fees. In the second attempt a year later, I again achieved an identical victory for the union.

My burgeoning legal career coincided with my rise in the California Democratic Party. I was elected statewide for two terms as Controller of the CDP. I had the privilege of working with CDP Chair Senator Art Torres on political campaigns and fundraising. I was honored to work side by side with renowned UFW leader Dolores Huerta in many political campaigns, supporting candidates and labor issues. Coming from a farmworker family, my work with her was particularly significant to me.

By 2000, I came to represent California Indian tribes seeking protection of their sovereignty and gaming on tribal lands via state legislation known as Tribal Compact I and II. The tribes realized that they needed organized labor as an ally. Representing the Morongo Band of Mission Indians, I helped guide them and other tribes through their labor strategy. This work led to a state regulatory scheme that protected the tribes and unions, bringing together my most valued clients. I also assisted tribes with economic diversification by coordinating non-gaming development, such as a huge spring water plant on tribal lands.

During these early years we were both trial attorneys, learning the tools of our trade and keeping exhausting work schedules. Weekends had little meaning, as the work rolled into Saturday and Sunday. One Sunday we managed to get away to Golden Gate Park and went to our favorite spot, the succulent garden in the Arboretum. We found a bench in the sun and dozed there in a rare moment of relaxation. We did try to keep up with the many friends we had made through our involvement with political and social movements, meeting up with them to see a play or a museum exhibit or at a house party fund-raiser. The performances in Dolores Park of the San Francisco Mime, Troupe, where I served as a board member, marked the beginning of our summer, even if a rare fog covered the park. Readers at our core, we also went to public author readings. To this day, the ability to attend these readings and talks fuels our love affair with San Francisco. Katherine sometimes convinced me to go see modern dance with her, and we never missed a Bill T. Jones/Arnie Zane performance when that company was in town. She had known Bill since they were working at Project Upward Bound in Rochester, New York. Katherine described her meeting the Jones family as encountering a comet that showered her with sparks. She is still a board member of Rhodessa Jones' and her collaborative partner Idris Ackamoor's performance company *Cultural Odyssey*.

We spent our vacations in those days going either to Buffalo to visit Katherine's parents or to New York City to visit her brother Robert, with occasional trips to Boston to see Katherine's sister Ellen. Katherine is nineteen months younger than Ellen, the oldest child who left high school early to go to the University of Chicago and eventually into medicine. Ellen and Katherine are extremely close, and Ellen has been an incomparable supportive sister to both of us. Katherine's brother Stephen became a large firm litigator, and Robert fulfilled his parents' cultural dreams by pursuing a life-long career as a musician, making his mark on the New York City post-punk scene. He continues to compose, perform, and record. Staying so often with Robert and his wife Debra on the Lower East Side made that neighborhood our Manhattan home. We ate with them under the many-colored lights of an Indian restaurant and explored the odd little stores, all prior to the gentrification that has so blanched this neighborhood. When we went to Buffalo,

Bernice and Gilbert took us to their country cabin south of the city, where Gilbert excitedly showed me a new tree specimen he had discovered. We ate vegetables they had grown in their backyard suburban garden; the garden produced in such quantity that their neighbors had to refuse the overflow of zucchinis and yellow squash. Around their dinner table, the Poss family never ran out of things to say about politics, the arts, or just how other family members were doing, and Katherine's face always shone while being in the company of her parents.

I had already ingested the strength of the reunification with the Salazars and their loving example towards me. Her parents' striking message of acceptance into their family was getting through to me. When I spoke with her parents on the phone, I somehow instinctively summarized my accomplishments as a way to justify my marriage to their daughter. Her father finally said to me, "Antonio, all we care about is that you love our daughter and treat her well, and we know you do that." Gilbert and Bernice had become new parental-like figures for me, and just accepting this simple message was freeing. It finally reached me that I had nothing else to prove to Katherine's family. Gilbert's sudden death in 1985 was a deep loss of the kindest father-like figure I had ever known. I had to go to Katherine's law firm and tell her he had suffered a stroke. I waited until we arrived home to tell her he had died. Then we made the sad trip back to Buffalo.

Katherine and I decided that we wanted to begin our own family, and Katherine conceived in late summer of 1987. By November of that year our lives were altered by two shattering events that came almost at the same moment. Katherine was pregnant with twins, and we looked forward to having our own babies to care for and love. Then Katherine miscarried. This loss would be magnified by everything that came after it.

Katherine knew that she would be trying to conceive again, and she decided to have an early mammogram so that she would not expose any future pregnancy to radiation. It was late November of 1987 when she received her test results. Katherine had breast cancer. I remember the phone call I made to Katherine to see how she was faring. I was in Manhattan on business, and I called her on a public street phone. I nearly collapsed in the phone booth when she told me of her cancer diagnosis, but I showed no desperation. I told her we would survive this.

Katherine's mother and sister came out for her surgery. Today I happened to look at the hooks on the back of our bedroom door. Hanging there was the beautiful Dior robe that Ellen brought Katherine when she came on that trip. Katherine has kept it all these years. Her cancer occurred at a time when surgical options were limited, and she was told that a total mastectomy was the safest choice. We lived through this cancer without any of the breast cancer awareness that exists today. This was before pink ribbons, breast cancer websites, advocacy for research funds, or outreach to young women of child-bearing age. I recall Katherine's anger at how little money went into breast cancer research when so many women died each year from the disease. Today her treatment would be entirely different. Today she would be offered a multitude of approaches with a panoply of new drugs as well as less intrusive surgeries short of a full mastectomy. Then the prognosis for pre-menopausal women with breast cancer was not good. You had the mastectomy, and then you were sent away to hope for the best.

The difficulty with hope is that it can be artificial as it was with me. Although I never expressed any doubt to Katherine on her recovery, in truth I felt almost no hope for Katherine's survival. I had found the woman that the universe had been kind enough to bring into my life, and now I was losing her. I had a complete sense of private helplessness while I expressed rock solid faith in her future. I was drowning in both the miscarriage loss and the prospects of Katherine dying. Katherine worked mightily with a gifted therapist to summon her internal resources as she vowed to keep going. She returned to work, knowing that it was both a necessity and a modest escape from her diagnosis and surgery.

During December of 1987 and January of 1988, each night I held her until she slept. I almost never slept during these initial months. I lay there in complete silence and soundlessly wept for hours about Katherine's possible death. Nothing in my life history said to me that the love I found would not be ripped away from me. Each morning, I woke up early to make Katherine's coffee and breakfast and begin another day of my false hope.

Katherine's operation took place in early December. My worries consumed me but within two months of my nightly silent grief, a solution took shape in my mind. I realized I could not make it without a child to care for. We needed to move on with our plans to start our family. By late January of 1988 we both independently came to the same decision and engaged an adoption agency. I knew immediately that this was the only answer for us, but I approached the adoption with care. My silent goal was to have Katherine live for a least one year with her child before she died of cancer. If nothing else, there would at least be a family picture that my child and I could always treasure. Katherine and I discussed that her future was uncertain. I remember Katherine telling me that she accepted that I could end up being a single parent. I never spoke with Katherine about the depths of my real doubts. I refused to tell her I was already preparing for her passing. I negotiated with God and went to find our family.

When we hired the adoption agency, we assumed it would take many months to find a baby, but we found our child within a month or so. A jolt of sheer life poured into me at this news. Our child was conceived on the Mexican side of Nogales, Arizona and would be born in July on the United States side. About a month after we had located this baby, we were approached with the offer of another child, who would be born sooner. Katherine told me that while she was thinking about this, a voice came to her and said, "What about me? What about me?" She said she knew it was the voice of our unborn Nogales child, and so we told the other family we already had a child waiting for us. A compassionate American nurse on the United States side of Nogales monitored the prenatal care and arranged for a safe and healthy birth. On July 1, 1988, we received a phone call that we had a healthy son. We flew to Arizona and had him in our arms the next evening, our tiny, perfect, brown-skinned baby with a mop of black hair. Our son was the miracle of life we needed. We called him Gilberto in honor of his deceased grandfather Gilbert, following the Jewish tradition of naming children after lost relatives. From the moment we met our son, he became our Beto, now in his early thirties.

Just before Beto was born we had a great loss followed by an enormous tragedy. Katherine's grandmother, Adeline Lippman, with whom we were especially close, died in mid-May. This was a sorrowful event as she was the family's beloved matriarch. She was always deeply kind to me, inviting me on my own to visit her apartment to enjoy a lunch at her favorite restaurant. She was tall, elegant, funny, full of life and accepted me at face value. She died only two days after we had visited her in Buffalo.

Two weeks later came the other event that scarred our lives and created an unfillable void. Katherine's mother Bernice was killed on June 1, 1988, by an intoxicated driver going eighty miles an hour in a twenty-five mile per hour zone. Katherine's mother died immediately along with a top academic from China who was there on a newly launched university cultural exchange. Bernice's other two Chinese passengers survived the crash but were severely injured. Not only Katherine's family but the SUNY Buffalo community were bereft by Bernice's loss. Katherine later testified at this man's sentencing hearing, bravely pointing out to the judge testimony in the civil depositions that contradicted the criminal record and getting the judge to correct the record. She argued her heart out until the tears came and then sat down next to me where I held Beto in my arms. Ultimately this killer received only a light sentence for these multiple homicides because the record of his earlier probation for a drinking-related assault had been lost by the DA's office.

During our visits to Bernice in Buffalo, I fell asleep to the murmur of voices as mother and daughter talked far into the night. Our lives had been planned around Bernice eventually spending six months or more a year with us. She had been thrilled about the upcoming adoption, and she was coming just after the baby's birth to help out. I knew that having Bernice around would be the extra support Katherine needed to sustain her fight against cancer. Katherine was inconsolable from the moment she heard of her mother's death. It would permanently define the contours of our family and Katherine's siblings' lives. I now lived with a spouse who was hollowed out with sorrow and who dwelt in a land of grief for many years. I understood the depth of her loss given my own history of kidnapping and loss of family. With Bernice's death I had lost another mother figure, one who had taken me to her heart.

I was also buffeted by the deaths of three additional brothers during the first decade of my marriage. They were the deaths of Ralph Salazar, followed by the deaths of Robert, "Spaceman" and

Henry, "Cuckoo." Before my reunification with my family, my brother Jesse Salazar had died at age thirty-three. In addition, my mother Petra died during this same time frame. I am so grateful that I had several coveted years as an adult son before Petra passed, during which I learned her lessons of life and enjoyed her pride in me.

Katherine summoned every bit of love that her mother Bernice had given to her to transfer that love to Beto as she became a new mother a month after her own mother's homicide. I watched her hold Beto and sing to him or prop an alphabet picture book before his infant face and read him a story. Seeing this provided me joy amidst my fears and made me the father I am today. Katherine met her grief with courage and carries it in her heart wherever she goes, but it never stopped her from taking care of her family as a mother or provider.

Katherine thankfully survived the first two years (it has now been 33 years), and we were ready to find a sibling for Beto. Our second child, Adela Bernice, was named in honor of her great-grandmother and grandmother. Adela was born in San Antonio, Texas on June 19, 1991, to a young mother in her twenties who already had two children who required her full attention. Under Texas adoption law we had to move to San Antonio for several months during the adoption process. We rented an apartment with the all-important pool for Beto who was soon to turn three years of age.

Adela was born into Katherine's arms. We were subsequently approached a few hours after her birth by the hospital staff. They informed us that Adela had been choking and turning blue periodically and was in the NICU. Specialists were coming in the next day to rule out major birth defects. Perhaps because we were adopting, the nurses were incredibly cold to us. One said, "Just leave. She will either make it through the night or she won't." They told us we had the right to reject our child then and there based on her medical viability. We were outraged at the suggestion that we might return our daughter over this issue. I remember our saying to them she was already our daughter and that we loved her. Adela became Adelita, a sparkling child full of energy with an extraordinary athletic ability that won her a college basketball scholarship. At thirty she has a long-held interest in helping youth from the foster care system and has completed double master's degrees in clinical and forensic psychology.

As parents, we provided our family with a Mexican-Jewish home. We raised our children in the Reform Jewish tradition, and they attended first a Spanish-English bilingual public school and then a Jewish day school. At Buena Vista Elementary, all the children danced with their classmates at San Francisco's Carnival, and I recall our delight as we watched them step by in their little costumes in the carnival line. Both speak Spanish and can read Hebrew. Beto became a *bar mitzvah* and Adelita became a *bat mitzvah*. These were moments of great pride and terrific family celebrations. For each one Katherine's extended family came from all over and many of my Phoenix siblings attended. These moments, when we stood on the *bimah* before our family and friends to bless each child, are two of the highest moments of happiness I hold in my heart. When I look back on these rites of passage for Beto and Adela, I see their accomplishments, but I also see my own emergence into the light, surrounded by my Salazar family, Katherine's family, and the family we have made together.

My children's connection with our congregation brought me closer to Judaism. By this time, I had already been attending temples since college, drawn to the faith's understanding of morality and social responsibility. I was already a deep believer in the role of faith in my life. At age ten, I had survived my last rape and suicide attempt, only to be saved by Roy, the gay cowboy from San Francisco who halted my sexual abuse. I had witnessed many Catholic prayers before meals with the Mexican families who looked out for me in my childhood. I followed their rituals, but God was elusive to me. As I returned home from the last year of the ranch, I needed a protector. My belief in a God was formed in seconds, undefined, without a name or ritual. I kept this belief hidden from the Hobsons, but it reassured me that I would somehow survive.

I had been openly loved by Katherine's family spectrum of Judaism, including devout followers to non-believers. I had been told early on by Katherine's family that there was no expectation that I would convert to Judaism but instead I should follow my own spiritual instincts. As I lived with Judaism in my family's life, I saw a faith that I believed in. Although I had spent years both observing Jewish traditions and education, but I made no decision to convert.

As a labor lawyer, I encountered Bay Area Rabbi Allen Bennett, one of the first openly gay rabbis in the US. He needed help with the renewal of his rabbinical employment contract. He has fought for decades for the inclusion of LGBTQ+ rabbis throughout the nation, a challenging and on-going struggle for acceptance. Due to his early courage, there are now scores of LGBTQ+ rabbis leading congregations and teaching. Handling his case unexpectedly uncovered a need by other rabbis for assistance with their employment contracts and status. I have now been representing rabbis for over thirty years.

I had the good fortune to be invited for two weeks with other community leaders to visit Israel, Jordan, and Palestine. The trip was balanced to provide contact with Israeli and Palestinians on issues of education and respective resources for governance. I traveled with about two dozen others, many from the non-Jewish clergy. My coterie of travelers included Rabbi Bennett and Christine Pelosi, the politically active daughter of Congresswoman Nancy Pelosi. I was there representing the San Francisco Latino Democratic club. We were joined by my friend Mitchell Salazar, the head of the Real Alternatives Program (RAP), which devoted itself to halting gang killings in San Francisco's Latino Mission District.

But by far the trip's most moving gift was the permission to visit the Wailing Wall in Jerusalem. In the heat of the day, I slowly approached the wall with weighted steps and inserted a prayer to God in the ancient stones. I only prayed for one thing, and I have never shared it with anyone. I can say only now that God granted me my prayer, which drove my evolution to Judaism.

After that trip, I realized that I was now ready to identify with the Jewish faith and I wanted to begin the process of converting to Judaism. I spent three years with Rabbi Bennett in the conversion process studying in the Reform Jewish tradition. My spiritual life finally had definition. Rabbis from my congregation joined Rabbi Bennett in the conversion rituals, marking a joyous occasion. Katherine and I have continued to take courses together on the development of Jewish philosophy. These years of studying and reflecting on the origins of Jewish intellectual thought and the meaning of the Torah continue to be some of the most rewarding experiences Katherine and I have shared. Our faith is a family strength. We take pride in the fact that Beto spent ten years working in Jewish summer camps and teen organizations, becoming an Assistant Director and winning the respect of colleagues and his campers' love. Beto's reputation in the Jewish community, where he also taught Sunday school in Bay Area temples, qualified him as a regional leader for the Western states youth organizations for the largest reform Jewish organization in the country

I have been blessed with Katherine's survival and fortified with the courage she showed with her cancer. I relied on this same courage as I encountered a crushing health issue of my own. I was fifty-four years old when I began a long slide into unidentified poor health. At the Cleveland Clinic I was finally diagnosed with vasculitis, an exceptionally rare, chronic autoimmune disease which involves inflammation of the veins. My body suffered greatly, but I was so pleased that after five years of not knowing what plagued me, I at least had the name and the parameters of my disease. I have been fortunate with the outstanding medical care that I receive and am grateful to have stabilized. My illness and its profound impact on me and my family is just one more lesson in life to take nothing for granted.

This journey of mine from the date of my kidnapping at age four to the present has been about holding onto the early love I was given by my mother Petra. In the absence of her unconditional love and kindness to me, I would not have survived on my way home. As an adult, I was the most fortunate of men as I found a woman who I felt was placed on this earth for me to discover and love. As I've written, Katherine has been the center of my life for four decades. Despite all my challenges from family to health, Katherine has never blinked when it came to helping me face a crisis. I now look back and see how our relationship was forged and how we both became good parents in spite of the obstacles we faced. Our children unknowingly saved us both. But it was Katherine's unwavering support that added to the steel in my spine to find my family, as well as to finally write this book. How do you thank someone who has done that freely all her life on your behalf? One cannot. No se puede.

CHAPTER XXII

Familia

Familia, siempre ha sido la unica cosa esencial donde podemos disfrutar lo bueno y sobrevivir los daños que hemos encontrado.

ON JULY 10, 2020, my beloved sister Stella died from COVID-19 in a Phoenix hospital. Stella fought the disease courageously, as she has faced every obstacle in her life, but she succumbed after four weeks. How I longed to be by her side, to hold her hand with its small, rounded fingers, to tell her how much she meant to me. But in the new stony terrain of COVID land, there could be no good-bye. Her husband was on the same COVID ward, and he was allowed to see her in her last days. But her adult children, including two recovering from COVID outside the hospital, did not have this chance.

COVID-19 has stalked the streets of Arizona's Mexican and Chicano communities like a rabid coyote. At the border, and in the barrios of Maryvale and south and west Phoenix, where so many of my family live, it has ripped back the screen doors, and entered the homes of the "essential" workers, those not allowed or able to stay at home as they clean hospitals, care for elderly, deliver packages and work in construction, factories, or fields. There is no equity in death for my people, just as there is none in life.

The loss of Stella is incalculable for me, but I prop myself up with my many memories of her. She was the young girl who tickled me in the tub as she bathed me as a toddler, making soap crowns in my hair as she washed away the dust from the day's crop picking. Stella accompanied me to my family's spirited nightly basketball games, helping to provide our snacks as we watched or played. During the long years of my abduction and isolation, I pictured her pretty face, and told her, "Sister, I am coming home to you." When we reunited we had an instant, mutual sensation that our hearts would remain joined together from that moment on. Stella's was the first family home where Katherine and I stayed in Phoenix, a modest house her husband was slowly expanding, cooled by a swamp pump.

Since that first visit, Stella welcomed me to her home scores of times. When I arrived in the morning there was always fresh coffee waiting, and a breakfast of *papas, carne con jalapeños, cebolla, ajo, frijoles y nopales al lado*. Stella brought the food to the table as I was forbidden from helping her, and she placed a half dozen of her freshly made tortillas in front of me, with more *jalapeños* and home-made *salsas*. I drank multiple cups of my favorite *café con leche*, and she always had a full selection of *dulces* as we began to talk for hours at her kitchen table about the family. Stella mothered not just her own children but took in her nieces and nephews when called upon. She radiated a mother's grace and warmth. On my Phoenix family visits I often saw Stella three times in a week. I relished each hour we had together, as she filled in the outlines of the family life I had missed, bequeathing a gift of background stories as I learned about every Salazar strength and tragedy.

Stella, you have been one of my life's greatest loves. I chose now to focus on the dear times we had as the way to heal my torn heart and to learn from the model of strength you showed throughout your life.

Stella is not the only sister I have lost to COVID-19. Three weeks before Stella's death, my oldest sister Helen died from coronavirus. Helen had been living in a nursing home for about a decade following a severe stroke. The nursing home had a COVID-19 outbreak throughout the facility. Through the nursing home's negligence, many patients perished from the pandemic outbreak, and my sister was not evacuated in time to survive. Helen's loving children, who regularly visited her at the home and monitored her care, were allowed to see her once from the courtyard window before the home closed down all access. Helen's loss has been difficult for the family to accept, given their anger at the nursing home's failure to move her and other patients before they came in contact with the virus.

Helen faced many challenges in her life. She had two sets of children, the second of which was a bi-racial Chicano/African-American family whom she raised largely as a single parent with few luxuries. She did so with the dignity and perseverance that is a hallmark of all my sisters, none of whom have had an easy lot. Without exception they escaped my father's home or reform school for marriages at age sixteen. Helen forged her own path, living a life where she daily confronted poverty and later the bigotry against Mexicano/African-American inter-racial families. These pressures often whirled her away from the extended family.

We always included Helen and her accomplished children in our family reunions. Helen liked to sweep in as if she owned the place, accompanied by her retinue of children and grandkids, ready for a good time. Helen was famous for her dancing. At the first of these gatherings following my family reunification, Helen took me aside. With a steady gaze and frankness, she told me, "Tony, I remember you. I remember when you were taken. I know you were dressed in your favorite jeans, red T-shirt, and black sneakers. That's what we told the police. But I do not believe they tried hard to find you. We never knew where you had gone, and we had so much sadness." Helen's words gave me tremendous relief. The abduction had really happened, and I had been loved and missed. Of course, I knew this, but when one lives a nightmare, hearing that it was reality is like a healing embrace. It was many years before my other siblings could describe those events so directly.

With the loss of Stella and Helen, I have leaned even more on my sister Alicia "Licha," the loving matriarch of the family. Licha was born in 1938 in lower Minnesota, where the family was picking crops. She has unmatched insights into our enormous family. When Licha was an adolescent, my father Jesus placed her in a reform school because he deemed her "incorrigible." She spent several years in an oppressive convent school managed by the nuns and priests of the Catholic Church. Her escape was to marry at sixteen, which alone allowed her to leave before the usual release age of eighteen. She became Alicia Rivera and enjoyed a marriage of over twenty years before her husband's early death in his forties. She carried on raising her children on her own. Her beloved offspring include first born, Henry, Rosemary "Reina," Jesse, Michael John

Rivera, Briana and Edward. Licha labored at the Chambers Belt Factory for many years to support them.

Licha is feisty, speaks Spanish at an unbelievably fast rate, English at the same rate, and wields her own *dichos*. Licha's cherished expression is "If you don't have *frijoles*, you have nothing," a comment reflecting her bottom-line life and sixty years of cooking for her own and extended family. In times past she was a sought-after singer in the local clubs, known for her moving renditions of *rancheras*. Licha performed with great fanfare for many years, introducing herself as "Paris Champagne In the House" singing in both languages. Just now she sang to me on the phone in Spanish, her eighty-year-old voice still strong and sonorous.

Licha has steered our entire family for over half a century through smooth passages and turbulent waters. She tried to keep the family partially unified after my kidnapping, and she pulled me back up into the Salazar family tree on my return. When I saw her for the first time, I was overwhelmed by her physical beauty. Licha is about 5 feet-3 inches tall, slender in build, and always appears in fashionable clothes and styled hair piled high on her head. Licha is fair-skinned, which she builds on to bring off her quintessential "Chicana Look."

This style starts with perfectly applied ivory foundation, to create a canvas for her vibrant colors. It is a style born in the late 1950s, modernized today by young Chicanas who choose this traditional look often associated with low-riders. Licha's look emphasizes her arched, penciled eyebrows that enhance her striking eyes. After choosing an intense red or pink color for her main lipstick, she lines her lips in elegant shades of black or deep brown. The family much admires Licha's pride in her appearance and dress.

As our unfailing matriarch, Licha brings familial and cultural strength to us. She has experienced the heights and depths of motherhood through her son Michael Rivera, who rose to be one of the only Chicano lieutenants in the Phoenix police department. A ten-year air force veteran before he joined the police, my nephew Michael was an extraordinary person, who succeeded in creating lines of communication between the Latino community and the police department. He was a deeply religious Christian who volunteered at youth ministries and taught at two local colleges. I saw another side of him as we spent precious time on the phone chatting about his latest romance, one where he always gave away his heart too soon.

When Michael died suddenly of a heart attack at fifty-three, Licha, his children and siblings were inconsolable. His funeral procession stretched for miles, and it showed me as nothing else could, what he meant to his community. After the family came a motorcycle phalanx of the eighty police officers who served under him, followed by scores of police cars carrying law enforcement representatives from throughout the Phoenix department and from as far away as the border. And then came over fifty lowrider cars. One after another, they moved together, the driver's left arms out, cars gleaming with their multiple coats of paint, their images of the Virgen de Guadalupe, the bulbous shapes, big fenders, or sharp fins. They danced in a coordinated rhythm, low and slow, then undulating up and down, wending their way to the cemetery in a show of loss and respect.

Licha endures despite hardship and grief, as all my sisters have done. These women, the heart of the Salazar family, are shaped not just by limitations and pain but much more by love, which I see expressed in the children they have raised.

The sister closest to me in age, is Virginia who has six children. I recall one visit to her Phoenix home on New Year's Eve. This is when my own children, Beto and Adela, learned that her neighborhood celebrations meant lying on the floor while many rounds of gunfire shot into the air.

In my own Salazar photo album, started when I reunited with my family nearly forty years ago, I return often to the first picture of me with my Salazar brothers, lined up in front of my mother's house. Our high cheekbones, wide foreheads and thick black hair connect us down the line, our brown skin subtly ranging from *café con leche* to chestnut brown. We share a heavy bone structure and range in height from 5'4" to 6'2".

My brothers. By the time of this photo in 1983, one of us, Jesse, was already gone, dead of cirrhosis at age 33. I have lost other brothers in the intervening years, deaths that reflect the culmination of their decisions in some small part, but in larger part the racism written into their stories in lack of access to education, poverty, job discrimination, and bodies weakened by pesticide exposure in the fields. While death punctuates a life, though, it does not define it.

Each of my brothers had a reservoir of wisdom. I believe that this is accurate even for those of my brothers who were lost to substance abuse. The family tales about them are extensive and have helped me fill in the gaps of my absence. I think of my older brother Robert, a heroin addict for forty years, who could talk about his life with perception and dignity. I recall a conversation he had around a kitchen table in a sibling's home. Katherine recognized that Robert was a singularly expressive man. She had a heart-to-heart talk with Robert, in which he explained his life to her in direct and unflinching terms. Robert told Katherine, "I am a heroin addict, that is who I am." Yet we knew our handsome brother Robert was a man who married a beautiful, college-educated woman who bore his children and stuck by him as long as she could. Robert ultimately succumbed to his addiction. It was painful to see the path he traveled, but I saw it as a steep gorge he cut through the harsh Arizona landscape of field work, limited educational opportunities, and the residential redlining and economic segregation of Chicano barrio life.

Henry is also dead, although he was born after my brother Daniel and me. I recall his broad, pale face flushed with excitement, cheering on our favorite boxers at one of our ritual brothers pay-per-view fight nights that were a highlight of my Phoenix visits. Henry and his son "Little Henry," whom he always looked after, lived on and off with my sister Virginia, in her many-roomed ranch-style home. In contrast to most of the other brothers, Henry was not a raconteur or philosopher. He was an alcoholic. I believe that he, like my brother Jesse, suffered from the genetic metabolic condition found in so many Latinos and others with indigenous blood that leaves them unable to process alcohol. Henry's body was found lying in a public park. At first the workers thought he was sleeping. It was only after the sprinklers went on and he failed to move that they realized he was dead. It is a sad image, but I like to think of the drops of water washing away all of his earthly cares.

I was just starting my legal career at the time I reunited with my family. I harbored the hope that I could use my education and accumulating legal skills to help the Salazars in whatever small ways I could find. I have assisted over the years, providing legal advice, attorney referrals and preparing wills and related documents. Never, however, has the yearning of my intentions clashed so harshly with the reality of Arizona's penal system as in the events leading up to the death of my older brother Ralph in 1991.

At our first family reunion, my brother Ralph was absent. Ralph was housed at the notorious, decrepit maximum security Florence State Prison in Florence, Arizona that had been built in 1908 by prison labor. Katherine and I first met Ralph in the Florence visiting yard after passing through the multiple petty security checks. We were allowed to take nothing in for Ralph but bags of quarters for the prison vending machines that spewed artificially-flavored snacks and soft drinks. Ralph came towards us, a giant of a man, my tallest brother at maybe six feet two, two hundred and twenty pounds. Ralph had large expressive eyes, along with an inherent gentleness that was such an unexpected contrast to his hostile environment.

I wanted to hear first-hand about the parole violation that returned Ralph to prison. I knew the story from family who had witnessed the arrest, but I could not comprehend the ruthless racism in the chain of events that resulted in his return to prison for eight years. As we sat at a shabby picnic table, surrounded by inmates with their families, Ralph affirmed the injustice of his story. At the time of his reincarceration, Ralph was on parole based on his model prisoner record. On this day he was visiting a hospitalized family member along with most of the extended family. Ralph took a break outside to sit at the secluded back of the hospital lawn. As he quietly took a few sips from a beer in a paper bag, he was rousted by the police and taken into custody on a minor misdemeanor open-container violation. Instead of contacting his parole officer, the DA sent Ralph back to prison to serve the remaining eight years of his sentence.

I was stunned as Ralph verified the ineptitude and racism that had put him back in prison. I have always asked myself, how would they have treated a white man with the identical record, particularly if he had his own attorney? Would that white prisoner on parole have been sent back without any contact with his parole officer? And would a white man be forced to serve eight years for a mere open container violation without any remedy, or would have he been given so more rational treatment?

Ralph was reincarcerated when he was already in poor health. He was denied a return to a half-way house where he had been living while on parole, because, as he was told, only a maximum-security prison such as Florence had adequate medical facilities to deal with his declining health. Yet Florence provided little if any care. Inevitably, we received notice that Ralph had gone downhill and was fighting for his life. He was desperately ill with hepatitis and needed advanced hospital care that could not be provided at the prison. I immediately flew to the hospital in Phoenix and found his body transformed. Before, Ralph had a regular sized stomach but now his stomach was grotesquely distended into a protruding, hard ball. I immediately began the paperwork for compassionate release.

When I greeted Ralph in bed, his face lit up. He struggled to respond, and in his exhaustion, he was content to listen to my responses to his questions. He wanted to know more about what had happened after my kidnapping and my family life now. I focused not on the Hobsons but on my search to come back home. This information seemed to calm him, and he listened intently to every word, only occasionally drifting off.

A round-the-clock rotation of two sheriffs was at his bedside. I was appalled to see that they had shackled every one of this critically ill man's four limbs to the bed. As Ralph's death approached, he could not even touch his haggard face or rub his eyes. Removing the handcuffs would have been the minimum required to provide him a humane death, yet the State was indifferent. I was filled with frustration and horror seeing Ralph die in this fashion. I vowed that he would not die shackled to his bed if there were anything in my power I could do to remove his chains.

I filed a motion on a Friday to have Ralph's shackles removed. Given his complete lack of mobility and his strong record as a low security level prisoner, there was no legitimate reason for him to remain cuffed to his deathbed. Couldn't Ralph die with some basic dignity? The matter was set for this motion on Monday on the

9:00 AM calendar. I spent the weekend at Ralph's side, straining to hear an occasional snippet of his life.

Monday morning finally arrived, and I was at the administrative office early to hear whether the judge had granted relief. My matter was heard by 9:30 AM. The judge granted my motion for compassionate release and ordered all the shackles immediately removed. I rushed from the hearing to the hospital and arrived at 10:20, pushing my way through the wards. Ralph had just died fifteen minutes earlier, every limb tightly shackled.

The two sheriffs remained by his bed. I presented the order, and they removed the shackles from Ralph's dead body. My family had not arrived yet, so I was completely alone as I absorbed the news. I wanted the chance to grieve with him alone, to say goodbye to a kind brother whom I had just begun to know. But I refused to show any signs of grief in front of the officers. The sheriffs were the face of an oppressive authority and racist criminal system. It took all my will to not express my rage at them. I focused only on preserving Ralph's dignity and mentally keeping my family as the protective shield I needed in this vulnerable and lonely moment.

I was despondent because an irrational and biased criminal system had allowed this to occur. The defeat was permanent and profoundly personal. My heart contracted with this first sibling's death since my return. I knew that I would never hear more from Ralph about his life or his dreams. I had only my family's anecdotes about our giant, philosophical brother. Ralph had long ago put aside his youthful criminal past when the hand of Arizona's "criminal justice" system, that so hates my people, reached out and pulled him back into its maw. And I could not extricate him.

Roman, our oldest sibling and brother, has endured Ralph's death and the deaths of a total of six other siblings. He is now the ninety-year-old family patriarch. Our closeness has been further solidified through my handling legal matters for him and his wife Cecilia, who died after sixty-four years of marriage. But the essential and defining connection between us is unique among my sibling relationships. We have both searched for and been reunited with our original mothers. Born in Groveton, Texas, Roman was three years old when Jesus forced his first wife, Roman's mother, back to Mexico. He refused to let her take little Roman. My father needed a girl to take care of his toddler son while he worked in the fields. He married my mother, Petra, when she was thirteen, an illegal marriage for which Jesus was arrested and briefly jailed. Roman loved Petra but never forgot his biological mother Sebastiana. He looked for her for over twenty years until they found each other when Roman was in his late fifties. They shared an intense love for each other, which they were able to enjoy for many years. Roman's and my searches for our mothers give us a unique bond.

Roman is a slender, dapper man, still cutting a handsome figure in his ninth decade. At any family gathering he is up gallantly escorting a lady onto the dance floor. Roman worked on the national picking circuit from the age of eight with both our parents. When he joined the army, the application filled out by the army listed him as only "field hand." Despite these harsh beginnings, he had the sheer will power and energy to move ahead and work for Maricopa County for over thirty years, buying the home in which he and Cecilia raised their fine family. Over years of Cecilia's Mexican meals, long and frequent phone conversations with shared confidences, we sons of two different mothers have nourished an unshakable brotherly love, deep mutual respect, and friendship.

We are all so different, my brothers. Armando, a few years older than I, struggled with advanced diabetes and other health issues. Armando was a handsome dark-skinned man, nearly six feet tall, naturally slender with the sharp angular features of my father Jesus. He was a devout Christian who spent thirty years, seven days a week, proselytizing in favorite spots near his home, but his medical problems threw him out of his routine.

Mando's character is best captured in his lifelong devotion to writing poetry. He memorized his lengthy poems, old and new, and shared them with me on each visit. What I treasure most is the poetry that he wrote specifically for me. He would approach me at a barbecue or a pay-for-view fight at Rudy's home and quickly take me aside. "Tony," he begins in an excited voice, "I have a new poem for you." He then recited his poem from memory, regardless of length. When he stopped, he always asked, "So, Tony, what do you think?" as I was overwhelmed by his deep love, bordering on reverence, for me that he has shown from the moment of my return. Although I discouraged his adulatory treatment as much as I could, having his love, so tender in its expression, is priceless. Once I finished complimenting and thanking him over and over again for his poem, he used our favorite word between us: "checkmate." "Did I checkmate you Tony?" and I would respond, "Yes brother, it's checkmate time for me." Armando then burst into laughter down to his belly, filled with such satisfaction and contentment, that it brought tears to my eyes. Mando would die too soon of strokes, and COVID-related causes.

Roy is my youngest brother and sibling. He leads the family's complete devotion to boxing. Daniel, slightly older than Roy, also reached professional status, but, unlike Roy, he managed to leave the sport before serious injury. Roy has the heart of a lion. At five feet five inches in height, and a heavy build, Roy was ferocious in the ring. Roy had a great future, and his boxing career is a source of pride to our family. I had spoken with him many times about being accepted for the U.S. Olympic Boxing Team Trials based on his outstanding amateur record. Three weeks before departure he was riding a bike and fell, cutting his hands on some glass. His hands were injured severely enough to prevent him from participating in the Trials. This loss was life-altering. Roy's hands healed, and he went into professional boxing. His combined amateur and professional career is approximately 105 knockouts or wins. The physical costs to achieve his record, however, have been great. Roy was unable to leave the professional circuit before he suffered some damage to his brain. Despite the lingering effects of his injuries, Roy continues to embrace life with the cheeriest attitude imaginable, one that is contagious in company. He has worked for decades in brother Daniel's "Daniel Wall Design DWD" business. He has a devoted relationship with his girlfriend of twenty years. Roy provides the color commentary as Rudy, Daniel and I gather at Rudy's home where he hosts the pay-for-view for major fights. As we yell at the screen and punch our fists, I am suffused with the warmth of my brothers around me.

My brother Daniel is only a year and a half younger than I, and he has a place deep in my heart. We have been close since I returned to my family, but I still learn things he has never been able to discuss with anyone else. When you have a defining event in your life, like my abduction, you come to see and understand it over time, through the lenses of age and experience, the reactions of others to your story, the links you become able to make to your own emotions and behavior. Only gradually have I been able to see how the kidnapping rent apart my whole family and affected my siblings as individuals.

My father Jesus blamed both nine-year-old Rudy and my mother Petra for what happened. He banned Petra from entering our home within ten days of my kidnapping. It was only decades later that Daniel could tell me what my abduction meant to him. "I lost my mother," he told me, as his eyes welled with tears. He was barely three years old, sharing a room with our mother when he witnessed the cruelty that defined his life. He was there when my father walked into their room, furious with our mother and gave her only an hour to pack her belongings. He has lived with this memory and loss, unable to express it until our conversation. To hear from my baby brother his searing experience of the abduction creates another dimension of sadness.

Daniel remained with our father, along with our younger siblings, Henry, and Roy. Daniel was simply too young to recognize the malignancy in our family that the older siblings knew all too well. Daniel, in contrast to his older siblings, states with pride that after the permanent breakup of our family, Jesus became a changed man. He stopped getting drunk, lost his violent temper and started cooking the family meals. For Daniel, our father became a kinder man.

He was the only parent Daniel was allowed to keep in his early life. Daniel has told me many times of the intense love and admiration that he has for our father Jesus, who cared for him and my younger brothers, Henry and Roy. Jesus' remarkable transformation in his older age apparently allow him to finally show the affection to his children that he always harbored but was incapable of expressing before he forced the breakup of our entire family within ten days of my kidnapping.

Along with my own precise memories of what we endured as children, and which our mother Petra suffered daily, my complete images are fully supported by all of my older siblings without exception. Even so, my older siblings can recount positive images of our father with moments of great happiness with him, often revealed in detail and pride. I treasure all these memories that they hold and have provided me with a more complete understanding of our shared father.

Daniel became a fine young man based on the strength and love that our father showed him and my younger brothers. In speaking with my younger brothers over the years, they confirmed the change in Jesus. Although they all took physical care of him as he grew older, it was Danny who lovingly bathed Jesus each day when he was seriously ill. I hold this image of Daniel as an example of his great love for his father, one that is unblemished and precious to me as well. I have come to cherish that Daniel found this enormous comfort with our father enabling him to be the gentle, kind and perceptive man that he is today.

I am exceptionally close to Daniel, and we speak by phone many times a week. For some reason, maybe because we are nearest in age, we share our private emotions and grief easily with each other. I admire my baby brother's examples of devotion and integrity and take direction from his moral compass. Over the years Daniel has become a devout follower of Jesus Christ, embraced by Rudy and Frances' family and their ministry. Daniel is the hardest worker that I have witnessed. He is a master plasterer whose work is much sought after by his affluent clients who want custom finishes for their fifty-thousand-square-foot homes in Paradise Valley and Scottsdale. Daniel often works, without a day off, three to four months at a time to support his family. When I check the temperature in Phoenix, as I often do, and see it has reached 116 degrees for another day in a row, I worry about my brother Daniel toiling in the sun, hour after hour.

Of course, as a true Salazar, Daniel has a whole other side to him. He has for decades been a gifted poet, working for months on lengthy pieces on the hardships of Chicano life, each of which he presents in drafts and in final form to me. He also juggles his evenings to include his devotion to painting. Daniel sends me photos via email as each painting evolves. Through his gifts of his art, I have the daily pleasure of seeing his paintings in our home. But what brings out Daniel's true creative spark is his fabulous voice that he devotes to "Old School" soul and Mexican songs that define our identity across the board as a family. Just listen to him sing one of Katherine's all-time favorites, The Persuaders' "It's a Thin Line Between Love and Hate." On an occasional free night, Daniel goes to karaoke bars to show off his considerable skills. He posts his recordings on Facebook under the heading "Like it or Not." My favorite memory of him is at Adela's *Bat Mitzvah*. We have a treasured family photo of the Salazars in attendance. During the festivities Daniel grabbed the microphone to sing in his rich voice to Adelita. He created the perfect moment.

My brother Rudy is six years older than I and his life reflects unbounded strength. He is the brother of my soul. Rudy is the young cholo who had just emerged from spending fourteen years at Florence Prison when I met him in 1983. As I described early in this account, I had reunited the evening before with our mother Petra, when we had realized our dreams of my returning in time to see each other. On the following day, when I met all my siblings at my mother's home, Rudy was the one who was most cautious to welcome me. Although he had many questions for me, in the end it was his simple invitation to eat that allowed our family relationships to begin.

My relationship with Rudy is a unique connection of brotherly love and friendship. We just "get" each other: our corny senses of humor, our romantic tendencies, our dedication to family and our ability to be deadly serious. He is the rare gem I unearthed as I grew to know my siblings. I covet the daily morning calls we have had for over a dozen years, as I absorb the depths of his mind and compassion in his heart. Following my abduction in 1959, Rudy experienced immense adversity. Although he was only nine years old, he was "in charge" that day of me and the other younger children. Our father irrationally blamed him for the Hobson's actions. Within ten days of my kidnapping, Jesus sent Rudy to a brutal Phoenix reform school run by the Catholic church. He was released at eighteen, a product of an abusive institution, witnessing and enduring harsh daily discipline and the violation of children and adolescents. He was hardened by his ejection from his family and nine long years of institutionalization. Rudy soon encountered trouble on the streets and was imprisoned off and on for well over a decade.

Rudy could have continued down that road of self-destruction, but he had an inner resolve that enabled him to take back his life.

Perhaps the spark of love that Petra had planted in me burned in Rudy as well. When he finished his final lengthy sentence, his long-time girlfriend Frances, who had waited years for Rudy, was at the gates of the prison when they opened to release him. She gave him a straightforward and stark choice. She told Rudy that despite her years of waiting for him, he could walk in the opposite direction away from her. He could continue on his road of crime and addiction, and she would never contact him again. Or he could take her hand, walk with her, and become a follower of Jesus Christ.

Rudy chose Frances, and he walked with her by his side, accepting Christ and becoming an evangelical minister for the past thirty years. Rudy is that rare example of a former addict who turns his life around completely and extends a hand to others still struggling. He has never looked back since he found Christ and has a record of total sobriety since the date he left prison. My admiration for his achievements is boundless. He is a part of me as much as our shared dark skin.

He and Frances created their own family with two successful daughters, Alicia and Esperanza, "Espi," who adore their father. When I visit, I am embraced by the family's hospitality. Frances, on every day of my lengthy visits, always cooks from scratch any Mexican meal that I want. Each morning she makes my favorite breakfast of *beef chorizo, papas,* and *tortillas.* Rudy generally takes care of lunch. He took me to every favorite tiny Mexican restaurant in Phoenix. He often coordinates bringing my siblings to these lunches, and we eat, and swap stories, and I am at home. After lunch Rudy took me to the homeless shelters for addicts where he is a well-known example of success, and he does a little preaching.

Alicia and Espi help Frances prepare nightly Mexican feasts for me. As part of their religious convictions, the family refuses to eat pork, similar to my Jewish faith. At the dinner table we joke and laugh in Spanish and English, and then share evening prayer circles, which have enriched my life. Rudy prays for me every morning as he rises at 4:00 AM to study his Bible and prepare his sermons. The two of us discuss our prayers for our families, always including our hopes for our siblings.

Frances, after her retirement from twenty years working at a bank, began a new chapter in her life. She chose to work for a large nonprofit agency for the food insecure that provided hundreds of food-filled grocery bags every day. Independent of this work, both Rudy and Frances pursue a full ministry, which includes donating hundreds of dollars a month, a self-tithing for the distribution of food for the homeless they encounter in the poorest sections of Phoenix. On a bi-weekly basis, armed with enormous commercial pots and pans, they deliver quantities of traditional Mexican meals such as hundreds of tamales and little burritos. If I need examples of courage and moral goodness, I need only to look to Rudy and Frances. And yet Rudy will remind me that his life was carved from pain, addiction, crime, and despair. He will allow no pedestal.

I picture us now at Rudy and Frances' home all sitting around the dinner table. Alicia and her husband Lalo have brought their two young children, for whom Grandpa Rudy always has the perfect toys. Katherine and my daughter Adela are visiting also. Although there are many nephews and nieces in my large family, my daughter Adela, he states over and over again, is his favorite niece. He has taken her under his wing and now calls her every other day to advise on issues from love life to career. My brother Daniel arrives and after dinner we put on our music. Now is one of my favorite moments. Rudy and I get up and dance together in a line, stepping to the sounds of the Temptation's "My Girl." Daniel rises to sing along. I could not ask for more.

Rudy, brother, as I was writing about how much you mean to me, you were in a Phoenix hospital, struggling to stay alive. Because of COVID-19, I could not be by your side, nor could Frances, Alicia or Espi. I called the hospital many times a day, trying to reach through the phone to make contact with you, to learn how you were doing, to conference with Frances and Espi as the doctors or nurses wanted permission for more tests. For six weeks you fought your toughest battle. We had moments of hope. Sometimes when I called you I could tell you were listening, even responding with soft sounds as I described our adventures. "Rudy, remember when we went on those long rides in your truck? And we sang along to oldies CDs? We visited our favorite second-hand stores, and I tried to find a gift for Katherine? Those were fun times, weren't they Rudy?" And I continued to talk as the phone rested against your ear, big brother, hoping for your low chuckle or a sigh.

Yet you declined, felled by a non-COVID infection that had caused numerous strokes. And on August 6, 2020, at 6:06 AM, you left me. Rudy, you are now free from pain, gone to the heavenly rest you knew awaited you. But brother, the music is playing. It's "I'll Be Around" by the Spinners. I hear you, Rudy, singing along:

> *Whenever you call me, I'll be there*
> *Whenever you want me, I'll be there*
> *Whenever you need me, I'll be there, I'll be around.*

Take my hand, Rudy, and come step with me to the music one last time.

CHAPTER XXIII

Knowing

Faith

FROM JUNE TO THE FIRST WEEK IN AUGUST 2020, I lost three of my siblings, Helen, Stella, and Rudy. Mando died in April 2021. These recent deaths mean that I have lost Petra, two sisters and six brothers from the family I tried so hard to find. I could look at their deaths as just more tragedies in a life filled with great pain. Let me explain why this is not my choice. This is a personal explanation, although I am well aware of our world's terrible suffering, through famine, flood, and war, that provides perspective to any single individual's life.

I am often asked whether I believe in God, a divine presence by whatever name you choose, that is greater than all of us. Do not confuse me with someone who believes he was placed on this earth to serve a particular god and is guided at every turn by faith. That is the most distant of images and does not apply to me. I had no name for the faith that came to me at age ten, in the months after my attempted suicide. At nine, I had tried to take my life by hanging myself in the shower after my last rape at the Ranch where I had been sent for a third summer to live with my predators.

As I wondered over and over why I survived, in seconds, inexplicably, a belief in a divine presence came to me. In that instant I knew there was a sacred power, and I accepted this gift with its unknown potential. I believed then as I do now that this divine presence broke the shower pipe, thus saving my life. This divine presence provided that my life should not be over at age nine and that there was a more promising fate for me. I reached my faith despite John's and Sara's continuous themes of aggressive atheism. I had little knowledge of "god" beyond the grace Jaime and Maria Elena said before the meals they shared with me at the Ranch. But I knew that god was good. I never raised my faith with the Hobsons, knowing they would disparage and soil it. It was essential to keep it private, without ritual or a building in which to gather and worship.

I have traveled my life with a great deal of hardship but also with great good fortune and a sustaining faith in a power beyond my own understanding. As I struggled to survive, my faith helped me find the way up the heavily occluded steps towards a full and loving life. I have recognized this divine presence very strongly in moments of great joy, such as my marriage to Katherine, the return to my family, and the birth of my children. In my lowest troubled moments, a hand of destiny seemed to guide me through and allow me to survive. When I accepted Judaism into my life, my faith found a home. This is now the source and expression of my belief.

Reaching Out

Crucial to my life is that rarest of gifts, the unflinching love of my wife Katherine for these forty years. I also have been enriched by long-held friendships and the intervention of many saviors whom I met along my way, who cleared the path for me to succeed. Other than with Katherine, I shared little of the true underlying torments of my eleven years of isolated existence with the Hobsons.

I finally found an outlet to help me confront the trauma of my childhood and adolescence, as well as assist me in navigating my life. After much resistance as an adult, I sought out therapy to understand my life, to reach a balance with my existence and to recover from what I had suffered. My counseling with different therapists, over two decades, has been an essential outlet and allowed me to become the more complete human being that I am today. Why do I bring this into my story? I use my own therapy as an example because so many Chicanos do not or cannot in their circumstances ask for help in any form.

Our resistance to therapy is both cultural and economic, given the real-life costs of therapy. Rarely covered even for those with health insurance, therapy is inaccessible to the majority of Chicanos. Amplifying this is that many of us have historically been unable to seek help. We often consider doing so as an act of cowardice, a humiliation that brings shame and the risk that if our search for help is discovered, it will bring embarrassment and even danger. We continue our silence, often not being able to speak openly to a devoted family member or trusted friend who could keep our confidences as we share our true worries. Reaching beyond our own small circle might be considered a betrayal.

Too frequently Chicanas who have been threatened or brutalized are provided zero opportunity to consider the sharing of intimacies or join support groups that specialize in women's issues. I have no illusions about the pride and the hard work that my sisters did to raise their families in a world dominated by racism and sexism. I know that my mother and my sisters represent what Chicanas truly face every day, and that even though it was out of the question as a poor family, support groups or therapy would have been a great blessing to their lives.

I resisted therapy for years because it threatened my sense of machismo. I see our men at their best as proud and loving men. But I know from the lives of my brothers that they face racist obstacles at every turn. Sometimes this will express itself in explosive and abusive anger that can dominate the daily lives of all their family members. Just like our women who face the same life, sharing similar but distinct obstacles, our men need to have courage to find a way to reach out for help.

It is time to break from this pattern of isolation for ourselves if we can. It will not be done without reworking our cultural biases, but we need to learn that we need not go through life alone, that we can try through many outlets to share the painful challenges and interruptions to our lives. I was one of the rare ones who was fortunate to find support groups. Ultimately, I gained the means to pay for therapy. Although it took me years to break through my cultural resistance, I found the value in the support groups I attended, as well as therapy, to be the keys I needed to understand my life, my past and present.

Getting Help

When I was a tiny, abused boy, I did not know where to turn to for help. This is the truth of all those who have been abused or victims of sex trafficking. I see now how repeatedly the Hobsons threatened me with acts of intimidation so severe that I was forced into absolute silence. I was so scared for my life that I was not even able to tell my sympathetic teachers and principals, who could sense something was deeply wrong and wanted to know the truth of my existence.

From the age of six on, beginning right before I was about to go to school and had access to the public for the first time since my kidnapping, the Hobsons warned me of the consequences if I spoke to anyone of my abuse. They said that on the very day I informed on them, they would be arrested and go to prison. It would be my fault, and I would be "institutionalized" or lost forever in the state's foster care system, never to see my family again. This threat was repeated to me hundreds of times throughout my life with them. I was frozen in silent terror until the day I left them to escape to college.

Silence is the shield that all abusers use to hide their heinous acts, never telling you that they are running scared about discovery, knowing as soon as you speak up your school will notify the child protective services and that an investigation will start. They know that they risk likely arrest for child abuse with their lives permanently ruined by the authorities. You may not learn of their own fears, but their weakness can become your strength to break the silence, speak out and tell someone, anyone of what your abuser is doing to you.

As a survivor, I want all the children and young people to know not to believe the chilling and soul-tearing threats of their abusers, whoever they may be: parents, grandparents, uncles, neighbors, visitors, or captors. We know that abusers will tell you that at such a young age you will not be believed and that you cannot fight back. You must realize that your school, the police, or some adult will believe you, and that you need not fight alone anymore.

There is another feeling we as abused children share. It is the feeling of utter shame that we must have done some unknown thing to cause the heinous molestations against us, that terrorize us both night and day. The shame is not yours but belongs to your abusers. You can break free from your abuse with a simple hotline phone call or by telling someone in authority what you are suffering. This is all you have to do to begin to be protected.

See the Appendix for resources including hotlines for abused or sexually trafficked children, adolescents and young adults. These resources provide you free, 24 hours a day, seven days a week protective and suicide prevention services for you to use at any time, night or day.

Begin by telling your trusted family members who believe you. If you do not get a response from the first person you tell, you need to tell someone else, especially your school teachers or counselors who will begin to instantly fight on your behalf as grown adults. Teachers are trained to listen for abuse. You must tell them your situation because they will come to your defense. And yes, you can trust a social worker or counselor to take your pain seriously, because they are required to report it to the authorities. It is a simple gesture but I recognize how hard it is to reach this point. Pick up your phone. Call 911 and tell them what your abuser is doing to you and most likely your siblings as well.

For trafficked children, you boys or girls who are forced to work in the streets or in hidden locations for prostitution, there are abolitionist organizations, to help you. Abolitionist organizations are special groups whose main purpose is to rescue you and take you away from the horrors and emotional damage you are suffering at the hands of your pimps.

Tell your teachers, tell your counselors, call police at 911 or use the organizations listed in the Appendix. You will be immediately helped. Never forget that these resources are at your fingertips, just tell anyone in authority, any of these listed organizations or simply call 911 to start your rescue from how you are being exploited and treated.

Know that it is has never been your fault. It is not your fault, whatever you have done in your young life, that these horrific crimes are now committed against your body. You have had the violence of rape forced permanently into your soul, but today you are still alive. If the story of my life shows anything, it is that not only is there hope, but also the possibility of love and joy waiting for you. Remember that as you reach out, you are also helping other children in similar pain, as you recover by speaking your truth.

The most important thing is that our society acknowledge the pain that we abused and trafficked children experience and to provide all the funding, services and therapies for prevention and recovery. Society has historically failed to make the considerable investment to prevent sexual abuse and sex trafficking. We cannot permit this criminal neglect to continue.

And finally, the national media has begun to make child abuse and sexual trafficking an acknowledged full-fledged daily national crisis. Our community of abused children and young adults has now come to the forefront with new national trials ruling against sexual traffickers. At last the actual clients who have used the services of traffickers, be they in the United State or around the world, have been sued and their alleged activities been heavily covered by the international and national media. During the last few years, universities settlements on behalf of class actions law suits brought by hundreds of abused students and athletes have now exceeded over a billions dollars and climbing.

The legal cases against our religious organizations have now come before the public eye, yielding billions of dollars of recovery from these institutions for tolerating pedophilia in their communities, and they are now starting to seriously address and halt these abuses. Our community is grateful for this new attention by religious organizations to our core issues, as well as the remedial legal actions via lawsuits and welcomed reformed internal practices that are now providing recognition, hope, and at best a protective refuge to address our recovery and healing.

Antonio, We Know You

When Cesar Chavez placed his trust in me so many years ago, saying "Antonio, we know you," he became the first of a series of people in my life who opened doors that could have remained closed to me. Their trust allowed me to complete college, go to graduate school and then become an attorney. My labor union clients, individuals with difficult employment cases, my Indian tribal clients, came to know me and give me the gift of their trust. Katherine showed the greatest trust by marrying me and being by my side through every up and down. But I could not know myself without the love and trust of my family, which has grown steadily over the years since we reunited.

I am a Salazar, born at mid-twentieth century into a Chicano family that can only be understood if placed in the larger history of Mexican-Americans born in this country. The 2020 Census shows there are now over sixty million Latinos in the United States, with thirty million of Mexican origin. A significant percent live below the poverty line, and we have outsized rates of incarceration, high blood pressure and diabetes. Name as many prominent "Latinos" as you like, this country has not been kind to us collectively, particularly if you consider most of us live in states that were once part of our own Mexican homeland. Our culture is shabbily co-opted in "Taco Tuesdays" and Anglo bar-hopping "Cinco de Mayo" parties, while not one in 500 white rowdies is able to tell you the origins of the holiday. The native and Mexican-born field workers still lose their breath and lives to pesticide exposure, one explanation for my own auto-immune disorder.

We have not yet coalesced as a people to claim our American inheritance. We have not clearly educated this nation about where their produce comes from, who cleans after dark in lonely office buildings, who is that indispensable nanny who teaches their kids Spanish, and now, more frequently, who is writing the next break-through software or who is the young doctor or nurse saving their life. Just as my Salazar family has carried deep within them the seeds of endurance, the will to work hard, to see their children rise, our people will become known, recognize their power, and rise. To know me, Antonio, is to know the Salazars and to know my people.

CHAPTER XXIV
Photo Collection

This is the Hobson's front door at our projects in Phoenix where my family lived. The photo depicts both the Hobson's residence, as well as the proximity of our own home from their apartment. The Hobson's residence was at Apartment 92, 607 N. 19th Street. As the photo shows, the Hobson's apartment is located about one hundred feet from the Salazar's apartment, located within the same quadrangle in Apartment 95, 607, N. 19 Street.

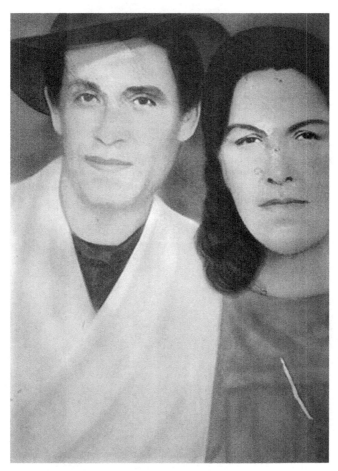

My parents, Jesus and Petra Salazar y Bailon.

John and Sara Hobsons, 1961

I was seven years old in June of 1962, the day after my 4th grade graduation. The prior night I had been told by the Hobsons that I would be leaving for the summer to learn to ride horses at a ranch. This photo depicts Sara and John separately posing with me the next morning with my new cowboy outfit. Two hours later I was flown unaccompanied to Reno to meet Mrs. R. who was the spouse of the owner of the Ranch The summer of 1962 was the first of out three summers at the Ranch where I was left abandoned, left to fare and defend myself on my own for three months.

Sara and John posing with me prior to my flight to the ranch.

This is the picture of the plane which I flew on two hours after the posed cowboy-clothed picture of me and John and Sara in early June 1962. I flew unaccompanied to Reno, Nevada to meet the spouse of the owner/manager of the ranch. Mr. R. led the assaults, shared me with his colleagues invited to the Ranch who violated me with impunity for the three summers I was sent there by the Hobsons.

A picture of me as an unpaid stable boy from 1962 at the Ranch. These are the daily chores I carried out under the loving supervision of Jaime, the Mexican resident cowboy.

John and Sara on the front steps of the Ranch's dining room during my first summer in 1962 when I was seven years old. This was the sole visit, lasting barely an hour, during the three summers of abuse as a sexually trafficked young boy. The Hobsons came to pick up cash for my continued services.

A picture of me in 1962 during the first three weeks of my initial stay at the Ranch.
I had been taught to ride a horse by Jaime, the kindly resident Mexican cowboy.
The assaults quickly followed three weeks later at the Ranch during my first
summer.

My sixth grade graduation, June 1965 at age nine. My photo appears in the front row, the first boy on the left, wearing blue trousers and no tie.

Sara with my dog Squire III that was purchased by her in late summer of 1964 while I was I was away at the Ranch. My dog "Squire", was taken away from me without notice in June 1967, the day after my ninth grade graduation. age 11.

Sophomore year at Lodi High School, Lodi, California.

Junior year at Lodi High School. 1971.

Lodi High School High, 1971 when I was elected at age fifteen as the first Chicano student body president of the 4,000 students.

Graduate school, Stanford University 1976, Palo Alto, California.

Playing classical guitar in front of the El Rancho Motel.

This is the $3.50 a night motel where I lived in high school for four years in Room 204, which was less than 200 square feet, with John and Sara Hobson. The hotel's clientelle was limited to white truckers and prostitutes.

Playing classical guitar at the University of Santa Cruz, Santa Cruz, California.

Brother Rudy and his wife Frances on the day I returned in early June of 1983 to my Salazar family to meet my siblings. This was the first time seeing him since February 1960 when I was kidnapped in from of my siblings at age four and a half years old.

My brothers from front to left, Rudy, Henry, Roy, Roman, Daniel and family friend at my reunion in early June of 1983.

Some of my brothers left to right, 2018, Roy, Daniel, Armando (deceased) with Rudy (deceased).

A classic family barbecue, hosted by Rudy in late 2019. These are my brothers from left to right, Daniel, Roy, Rudy and me.

At son's Bar Mitzvah with Poss and Salazar families. Salazar family members from left to right, back row, my sister Virginia, my spouse Katherine, our son Beto, my brother Roman and his spouse Cecilia, ending with Jesse, spouse of Stella. First row is my daughter Adela, myself, my sister Stella and my brother Daniel.

Katherine's relatives, second back row with pictures of my spouse sitting down next to Beto, with Adela in the front row, second to the right.

A picture of me in front of the Mexican Calendar, Distrito Federal, Mexico City.

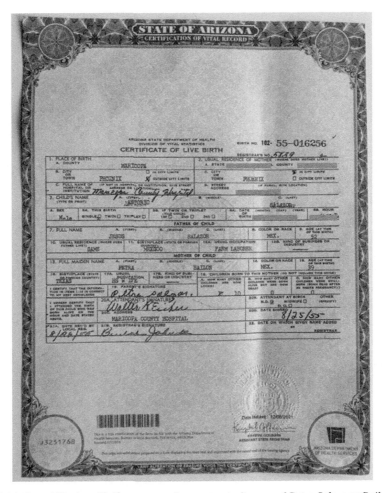

My birth certificate with the names of my parents, Jesus and Petra Salazar y Bailon.

Katherine and Antonio

A picture of my children, Beto and Adela Salazar-Poss.

APPENDIX

Tell your teachers, tell your counselors, call police at 911 or use the organizations listed below. You will be immediately helped. Never forget that these resources are at your fingertips. Just tell anyone in authority such as your teachers or counselors.

You can also call any of these listed organizations, most of which are bilingual or multilingual, so that they can often help you in any language you speak 24 hours a day. And no matter what, call 911 to start your immediate rescue from how you are being exploited and treated. The authorities will begin right away to assist you and your school, as well as help your trusted family members who have not abused you but are willing to help you be saved from your abusers or traffickers.

https://www.rainn.org/

RAINN (Rape, Abuse & Incest National Network) is the nation's largest anti-sexual violence organization. RAINN created and operates the National Sexual Assault Hotline (800.656.HOPE, online.rainn.org y rainn.org/es) in partnership with more than 1,000 local sexual assault service providers across the country and operates the DoD Safe Helpline for the Department of Defense. RAINN also carries out programs to prevent sexual violence, help survivors, and ensure that perpetrators are brought to justice.

National Human Trafficking Hotline

If you or someone you know needs help, call the **National Human Trafficking Hotline** toll-free hotline, 24 hours a day, 7 days a week at   1-888-373-7888 to speak with a specially trained Anti-Trafficking Hotline Advocate. Text hotline: **233733**
https://humantraffickinghotline.org

Safe and Sound
https://safeandsound.org/about-us/

Administration for Children and Families *Spanish available*
https://www.acf.hhs.gov/acf-hotlines-helplines

Government Site
https://www.state.gov/domestic-trafficking-hotlines/

Woman's Center Youth and Families
https://www.womenscenteryfs.org/index.php/get-help

Love Never Fails
https://www.loveneverfailsus.com/

Child Welfare Information Gateway *Spanish available*
https://www.childwelfare.gov/organizations/?CWIGFunctionsaction=rols:main.dspList&rolType=Custom&RS_ID=57

How to Report
https://www.childwelfare.gov/topics/responding/reporting/how/

Victim Connect Resource Center- national hotline consortium partners
https://victimconnect.org/about-us/national-hotline-consortium/national-consortium-partners/

The National Hotline Consortium- Letter to Pelosi
https://www.rainn.org/sites/default/files/Hotline%20Consortium%20HOUSE%20CC%20.pdf
Notes the increase in the National Child Abuse hotline related to covid-19, where abused children and youth are trapped with abusing caregivers with little or no outside support and contact. Rainn has seen increase in a number of minors accessing the National online hotline. The National Runaway Safe Line (NRS) has experienced significant increases across all its platforms (hotline, live chat services, emails and on-line forum).

Save the Children
https://www.savethechildren.org/us/charity-stories/child-trafficking-awareness

FBI
https://www.fbi.gov/investigate/violent-crime/human-trafficking

The United States Department of Justice
https://www.justice.gov/humantrafficking

Do Something Org
https://www.dosomething.org/us/facts/11-facts-about-human-trafficking

Crossroads
https://www.crossroadscares.org/helphumantrafficking

National Suicide Prevention Lifeline

988 has been designated as the new three-digit dialing code that will route callers to the National Suicide Prevention Lifeline. *While some areas may be currently able to connect to the Lifeline by dialing 988, this dialing code will be available to everyone across the United States starting on July 16, 2022.*

When people call, text, or chat 988, they will be connected to trained counselors that are part of the existing National Suicide Prevention Lifeline network. These trained counselors will listen, understand how their problems are affecting them, provide support, and connect them to resources if necessary.

The current Lifeline phone number (1-800-273-8255) will always remain available to people in emotional distress or suicidal crisis, even after 988 is launched nationally.

San Francisco and the Bay Area Resources

MISSSEY - Motivating, Inspiring, Supporting & Serving Sexually Exploited Youth

Mission: To provide services to commercially sexually exploited youth, and to work for systemic change with the youth we serve.
https://misssey.org/
MISSSEY, Inc.
424 Jefferson Street, Oakland, CA 94607
Email: info@misssey.org
Phone: (510) 251-2070

Shade Movement

Founder: Sarai T. Smith Mazariegos
Their Vision: To empower survivors of sexual exploitation, human trafficking, and domestic violence. Survivor Leadership is paramount to creating positive change and empowerment within and outside the movement.
https://www.shademovement.org/
S.H.A.D.E., P.O Box 99583, Emeryville, Ca 94662
Email: info@shademovement.org
Phone: (510) 437-0192

Ruby's Place

Mission: Ruby's Place is an innovative nonprofit committed to ending domestic violence, human trafficking, and violent crime through hope, advocacy, and connection.

https://www.rubysplace.org/

20880 Baker Rd., Castro Valley, CA 94546-5729

Email: info@rubysplace.org

Phone: (510) 581-5626

Alameda County Family Justice Center

Mission: To ensure the safety, healing, and self-empowerment of victims of domestic violence and their children, of victims of sexual assault and exploitation, human trafficking, child abuse, stalking, and elder and dependent adult abuse through easily accessible, coordinated, comprehensive and culturally sensitive services.

http://www.acfjc.org/

470 27th Street, Oakland, CA 94612

Email: info@acfjc.org

Phone: (510) 267-8800

Covenant House California- Homeless Shelter in Oakland

Mission: Covenant House California (CHC) provides sanctuary and support for youth ages 18-24 facing homelessness and human trafficking.

https://www.covenanthouse.org/homeless-shelters/oakland-california

200 Harrison Street Oakland, CA 94607

Email:info@covenanthouse.org

Phone: 510-379-1010

Oakland Elizabeth House

Mission: transitional residential program for women with children who have experienced homelessness, domestic violence, addiction, or poverty. Our mission is to support these women and children in their transition to independence.

https://www.oakehouse.org/

PO Box 1175 Berkeley, CA 94701

Email: oakehouse@oakehouse.org

Phone: (510) 658-1380

ACKNOWLEDGMENTS

Maestro Jimmy Santiago Baca, the award-winning Chicano poet and novelist, was referred to me by my friend and client Indian film maker Chris Eyre. Jimmy took me under his wing and supported this book at every turn. My wife Katherine Salazar-Poss was my first and most tireless editor and gave me unwavering emotional strength. My adult children Adela and Beto Salazar-Poss showed patience and encouragement throughout the process. My Salazar family inspired me and sustained me with their love.

A special acknowledgment goes to my dearest friend and law office manager of nearly 40 years, Phyllis Nelson, who has been with me every step of the way with my law practice and this memoir. Other friends and family did meticulous, critical editing. Thank you, Cheri Coulter, Marjorie Stone, Laurie Schuller, Janet Stone, Debora Simcovich, and Robert Poss. My friends Marty Williams, Julie Benbow, Berkeley Poet Laureate Rafael Gonzalez, and members of the "TiMex Gang," my men's group of twenty-five years, Tony Colon, Reza Azarmi, Enrique Ramirez and John Gunnararson, kept my spirits lifted. Tony was the friend who many years ago facilitated my reunion with my Salazar family.

Thanks go to Rabbi Allen Bennett, Rabbi Sydney Mintz, my intellectual property counsel, Ben Allision of Bardacke Allison, LLP, and Gail Caufield for imbuing me with faith and providing invaluable counsel. Regina Evans, a warrior in the fight against sex-trafficking, generously shared her resources. I had saviors and mentors along the way who never allowed me to give up hope. Norman O. Brown made my undergraduate studies possible, and my mentors Cesar Chavez and Delores Huerta (UFW), and other union leaders including Gladys Perry (CSEA), Joel Schaffer (SEIU) and Michael Hartigan (CWA) led me on my path as a union-side labor attorney. My sister-in-law, Ellen Poss MD, believed mine was a story that must be told, and she helped me to have a great professional team to advance the book: Smith Publicity, Black Chateau Enterprises, AuthorPop, translator Lucia Ortega, and my incomparable agent Leticia Gomez of Savvy Literary Services, who found me the ideal publisher in Nancy Cleary of Wyatt-MacKenzie Publishing, whose constant attention and kindness helped bring this book into the world.